LEE BUCKINGHAM

War Stories
of the
GREEN
BERETS
The Viet Nam Experience

Hans Halberstadt

Motorbooks International
Publishers & Wholesalers

*To: Martha ("Colonel Maggie") Raye—
Special Forces' own, well-loved, hard-core, hard-drinking Maggie!
A woman with more of the kind of character and integrity that men call "balls"
than just about anybody of any rank in Southeast Asia.*

*To: The late, great Walt Shumate,
who went off to join the "advance party" on March 1, 1993,
and left a lot of loving friends behind.*

*To: My numerous friends and co-conspirators at 3d Battalion,
12th Special Forces Group (Airborne), for their trust,
generosity, and tolerance.*

First published in 1994 by Motorbooks International Publishers & Wholesalers,
PO Box 2, 729 Prospect Avenue, Osceola, WI 54020 USA

Motorbooks International is a certified trademark, registered with the United States
Patent Office

The information in this book is true and complete to the best of our knowledge. All
recommendations are made without any guarantee on the part of the author or Publisher,
who also disclaim any liability incurred in connection with the use of this data or specific
details

We recognize that some words, model names and designations, for example, mentioned
herein are the property of the trademark holder. We use them for identification purposes
only. This is not an official publication

The story that appears on page 170 was reprinted, with permission, from Volume III of
the Green Beret Magazine, © 1989, RADIX Associates. The 2314 Cheshire Lane, Houston,
TX 77018. *See note on page 220.*

Motorbooks International books are also available at discounts in bulk quantity for
industrial or sales-promotional use. For details write to Special Sales Manager at the
Publisher's address

Library of Congress Publication Data
Halberstadt, Hans.
    War stories of the Green Berets / Hans Halberstadt.
      p. cm.
    Includes index.
    ISBN 0-87938-955-9
    1. Vietnamese Conflict, 1961–1975—Regimental histories—United States. 2.
    United States. Army. Special Forces—History. I. Title.
DS558.4.H34   1994
959.704'3373—dc20   94-28804

On the front cover: Green Beret Ben Baker designed the tiger stripe camouflage pattern
that serves as a background here for Special Forces memorabilia. Among the items are
MAC V (left) and Special Forces patches; photos from Don Green's collection; Ben Baker's
Montagnard tribal bracelets; and an anti-personnel grenade. *Hans Halberstadt*

On the back cover: A captured and now-inert enemy grenade sits amid a safe-conduct pass
and combat zone patches from the collections of Ben Baker and Clay Scott.

Printed and bound in the United States of America

Table of Contents

Acknowledgments

The idea for this book is entirely the fault of several members of the late, great 3d Battalion, 12th Special Forces Group (Airborne), who tolerated having me underfoot for a year and a half, back during the middle 1980s. I suppose the most guilty of these is Col. Gerry Schumacher, then commander of the battalion, who—in the grand tradition of Special Forces—met me at a saloon to negotiate the terms and conditions whereby I would be authorized to report on the antics of his unit. This may have been the bravest thing Gerry ever did, because another tradition in Special Forces is to escape and evade people in my line of work. A lot of his contemporaries—superiors and subordinates both—thought this idea was just a few French fries short of a Happy Meal. Thanks, Gerry.

Special thanks to Steve Sherman and Radix Publishing for linking me up with some of the folks here. Steve is making a terrific contribution to the maintenance of Special Forces history by developing a database of who was where, when, in Southeast Asia.

I'd also like to salute Greg Field and the whole rat pack at Motorbooks for having the vision to authorize this book and to encourage its randy, rowdy style. This is an unusual book for all of us.

Thanks to all of the following interrogation subjects and other sources, to all the guys I told, "Your secrets are safe with me!"

Col. Jack Abraham (Ret.)
Lt. Col. Otis Hedges Ashley III (Ret.)
Sgt. Maj. John Caviani (Ret.)
Fred Fuller
Harold Jacobson
Roy Jacobson
Lt. Col. Kenn Kubasik (Ret.)
S/Sgt. Dennis Mack
M/Sgt. Russell Mann (Ret.)
Sgt. Maj. Doy McPhail (Ret.)
Jimmy Monaghan
Capt. Jim Morris (Ret.)
Cliff Newman
Capt. John Padgett (Ret.)
Col. Gerry Schumacher
Clay Scott (Ret.)
Steve Sherman
Clyde Sincere
Howard Sochurek
Col. Larry Trapp (Ret.)
Mike Witcosky

Preface

This book began the way many books do, over lunch. The menu was vegetable soup and canned GI bread, and it was served in a remote, dusty little compound at a place called Gia Vuc, at the edge of the spine of mountains that run up through Vietnam. That was in November of 1962. I was 18, a helicopter door gunner, and impressionable. What impressed me at the time was that the Special Forces (SF) team who lived and worked in this distant and dangerous place had found a cook who could actually make GI bread edible; at my unit we considered it fit only for building material or perhaps projectiles to fire at the Viet Cong (VC). But here, it had been sliced and fried lightly in some sort of oil; it was spicy, exotic, intense, and delicious. That got my attention. And what I noticed was that the whole SF program was like that, full of unusual flavor and intensity, and I've been interested in it ever since.

It was obvious even in 1962 that the Army's odd, eclectic little band of brothers called "Special Forces" was very special indeed. These guys—sometimes called "Green Berets"—awed, inspired and occasionally infuriated the conventional part of the US Army. They were like Jesuits—independent thinkers, with their own program and a skeptical, irreverent attitude toward the word coming down from the "staff weenies" and "headquarters pukes."

While working on my first book about Special Forces (*Green Berets: Unconventional Warriors*, Presidio Press, 1988), friends in the 3d Battalion, 12th Special Forces Group, kept pushing me to get S/Sgt. Dennis Mack to tell me some of his legendary war stories. Dennis agreed to share them with me, and I recorded those amazing tales. But they didn't really fit into that first book, so I saved them and looked for more. There was, it turned out, an almost endless supply of these traditional, oral, first-person stories that are supposed to begin, "Now, this ain't no shit . . ."

These Green Beret war stories were funny, scary, and heartwarming, sometimes all in the same tale. And to make them even more interesting, they all had SECRET stamped on them, because nearly all came from people who had been ordered to never reveal the details of what they did in Vietnam, Laos, Cambodia, or Thailand. But, as I told you, these guys are independent thinkers and don't take guidance from the "leg" Army unless they happen to agree with it, and that is not very often.

Besides the official admonishment against telling these stories, there is an old, honorable tradition in "the community" that discourages communication with the rest of the Army unless absolutely necessary, and with the rest of the world almost always. So these stories have been, until now, for internal consumption, told over a beer with friends at the Special Forces Association annual convention, or on Thursday mornings when the Over the Hill Gang gathers at Fort Bragg for its weekly breakfast. These stories (with very few exceptions) haven't been told to wives, or children, or anybody else outside the SF community, until now. That's been true because these guys didn't think you'd be interested, or could understand, their adventures of twenty and thirty years ago. Also, they'd been ordered not to talk about them. But time does the same things to people that it does to good whiskey—it smoothes us and mellows us all, if we're distilled from good mash. These stories have aged well; it is finally time for them to be consumed.

Collecting these stories has been a little like seducing virgins: It isn't that they didn't want to do it, or weren't ready to do it, but it was a new experience for all of them, and all the moves and reassurances had to be carefully and properly made before they would provide consent. Some people with notoriously funny stories refused to even speak to me; others were polite, but kept their secrets. But for most, it seems that the time has come to share those times, people, places, and events.

Although these stories describe important historical events, this isn't a history book. Historians, for some reason, take important events and suck all the life right out of them, leaving you with a mass of desiccated data and no real sense of what actually happened. History normally leaves out all the fun and foolishness, the sex, the adventure, the heroism, and the cowardice . . . the things that, if you have ever seen them, can stay in your vision, clear and undiminished, until the day you die. It is hard to tell from most history books that anything ever actually happened to anybody—the things that individual human beings saw, smelled, heard, and did to make, for example, World War II or the crusades, happen. You would never guess, from reading a history book, that anybody in these grand events puked from fear, caught venereal diseases (VD), or stood up in front of a machine gun to throw a grenade with the full knowledge he would die in the process.

I wasn't a hero myself, but I saw some heroes in action; I didn't get shot, but I heard the bullets that missed me; I didn't have to bleed, but I remember cockpits awash in fresh blood. And I am profoundly grateful for the experience. What is odd, after all these years, is that these events that seem so ghastly to people who have never experienced combat can sometimes turn out to be a kind of blessing and a gift. These experiences taught me more about life than death, more about goodness than evil, more about love than hate, more about courage than cowardice. These are not lessons that can be learned easily or comfortably or without great personal risk. If you read between the lines, that's what these stories are about—a trial by fire that has strengthened and tempered the men who felt the heat.

That's what this book is really about: the lessons learned in the pressure cooker of war, of how people adapt to extreme stress, of how some specific people dealt with life in a combat zone. Stephen Leopold, for example, has nice things to say about some of his guards while he was a prisoner of war in the Hanoi Hilton. Gerry Schumacher and others tell funny stories about what pet monkeys do during mortar attacks. John Padgett tells about how his girlfriend (and later, wife) helped him crew a machine gun during an attack. Dennis Mack tells about the North Vietnamese Army (NVA) soldier he met, face to face, and should have killed. Instead, Dennis smiled at the man—who smiled back—and Dennis let him go. And nearly everybody has affectionate things to say about the tribal hill people of the highlands of Vietnam and the love affair that developed between (and only between) the big Green Berets and the tough, tiny tribesmen.

These are not stories about mayhem, death, or destruction, the silly, stupid fictions you see in *Rambo* movies, but about life, friendship, integrity, honor, and stress-management—all tried and tested in an extreme way. This book is a collection of those kinds of lessons, the secret stories of Vietnam, and the special warriors called "Green Berets." Nearly all of these stories happened in Vietnam, although I've included a few, such as "Sergeant Psycho and the Alien Life Form," that happened during training, because good war stories don't always happen during wartime.

Are they all true? That depends on what you mean by true. Some of the details might be confused here and there; in one I have suppressed the identity of a particular nation where some of these things happened because it involved US forces in combat in a nation where such combat was never supposed to happen. We changed a name here and there to protect the guilty. But the essence of these stories, collectively, includes more truth about what the men we call Special Forces actually did in Vietnam than all the formal histories I've read (and tried to read) on the subject.

There is one major military secret revealed in these stories, and it is a dark and deep one, the one that, twenty years and more after the event, still has a profound influence on the conduct of American military special operations. The secret is an informal one, and it is the key to understanding the Special Forces experience in Vietnam, Special Forces today, and what Special Forces will do in the future. That secret is the story of how the American people betrayed the American Army twenty years ago, and how the Army ordered this community of deeply honorable men to do a very dishonorable thing—to abandon their brothers in arms, the tiny little tribesmen of the highlands to the wrath of the Vietnamese of both north and south. It is the wound that will not heal. But that betrayal is only one part of the whole epic adventure, and perhaps it was inevitable, and perhaps it has been understood and forgiven.

So, put on your jammies, say your prayers, and snuggle into bed. Yes, the stories will be scary sometimes. Do the good guys get the fair maidens? You bet, lots of them! And do the good guys win in the end? Yes, in fact they do. And in spite of everything, they live happily ever after.

All set? Okay, here goes.

Once upon a time, in a strange and exotic land, far, far away . . .

DENNIS MACK

Dennis Mack was—and still is—a sergeant in Special Forces. He was part of the Command and Control (C&C) program run by the Central Intelligence Agency (CIA; often referred to by Special Forces operators as "The Agency"). It was a sometimes odd arrangement where things didn't always happen by the book. Dennis emerged from his adventures without much damage, mental or physical. He works for a utility company, lives in the country, and still serves in Special Forces as a member of 3d Battalion, 12th Special Forces Group.

Snake Tales

When I first got to C&C, I didn't really know what to think. I'd heard a lot of stories about guys going on missions and nobody coming back. Well, about forty of us rookies showed up at FOB-2 at Kontum, and nobody knew anything about what was going on. They sat us in a briefing room, showed us the targets, and explained what everybody was doing: mining the Ho Chi Minh Trail, snatching prisoners, and so forth. I started getting nervous. It was what we had trained for, but I don't think any of us ever really thought we would actually have to do it.

I was assigned to a guy who was supposed to train me. I can't remember his name now, but he had a big red nose and bright red hair, and he worked for the CIA. He started talking to me, and I had to get up and walk around. I was sick to my stomach. I thought, *I'm not John Wayne.* I started to leave, and he walked up behind me and said, "We're going on an operation in two days."

He took me to his hooch and started showing me what to take on the operation, how to load my rucksack, how to set up my web gear. Then he got some of the Yards together, and we went into the bush to practice patrolling. We practiced hand and arm signals, immediate action drills—it all went so fast that I really couldn't keep up. Before I knew it, I was on the helicopter; it landed, and we were out in the jungle on the operation.

Nobody said a word. Communication was with hand and arm signals. It went like that for three or four days, nobody saying anything. Then, while we were patrolling along, he suddenly stopped. He said to me, "I smell a snake!"

With that nose of his, I figured he could probably smell anything, but that this was all bullshit. So I sat down and took a break in place. All the Yards were looking around, and then he pointed at a log and said, "There it is!"

I looked, and sure enough, there was a huge snake's head poking out from under the log. I thought, *Now, that is a snake!* It was the biggest snake I had ever seen.

Well, he dumped everything out of his rucksack, and the Yards took it all and spread it out among their own. He ran over to the snake and started pulling it out from under the log, by the head! All the Yards jumped on it, and they managed to get it out. The jaws seemed to dislocate and opened incredibly wide; it was hissing loudly. I wanted nothing to do with this! The team leader put a stick in the snake's mouth and tied it shut with his cravat [the neck scarf normally worn to absorb perspiration]. Then he stuffed this big snake into his little canvas rucksack and tied it shut. I asked him, "What are you going to do with that thing?"

"Take it back to the FOB," he said. "It is worth big money."

I'll bet this thing weighed thirty or forty pounds, and he carried that snake for another two or three days. Well, it was a recon mission, and we never saw anybody or anything associated with the enemy at all. Finally, we got to the pickup area, and he said, "Tomorrow they'll come and get us."

We set up security, and it started to get dark. He took off his rucksack and put it beside a tree and lay down beside it. I was five or six feet away. I woke up in the middle of the night and was thinking, I can't wait to get out of here. I couldn't sleep, waiting for that helicopter to show up. Then I heard that *hisssssss* again, and thought, Oh, no! I could hear the snake moving through the bamboo, but I couldn't see a thing; it was black out! I got out my K-bar knife and was waiting for that damn snake to attack me. I sat there for the rest of the night, that knife in my hand, waiting for that snake to get me. But I was ready for it; if it did grab me, we were going to have it out, right now.

The next morning, when the team leader woke up, I poked him and whispered, "Your snake's loose. I heard him moving around last night."

He didn't believe me at first; but he checked, and I was right. Then he whispered, "That's okay—they don't go far. We'll find him."

So he and the Yards took off, with me minding the radio. Sure enough, they were back in about an hour, and they had that damn snake. Well, the helicopters came and got us, and pretty soon we were back at Kontum. The team leader got about fifty bucks for the snake—a lot of money back then. They kept it in a cage at the club for a long time. It was a big snake!

Laying on a Recon Mission

The team sergeant was God. If a captain or lieutenant went along, he was just along for the ride. The Yards were serious about it, and if someone tried to give me any crap, they'd have to deal with the team. They knew that one guy could talk on the radio—one guy could get them out. I carried the code book and the radio—nobody else.

I trained the team. It was essential to have a well-trained team. The sad part was that I was always getting a different American to accompany the team on each mission. They were always quitting, or, if they were good, they would get a team of their own.

When it was time for a mission, I got called into the S-2 shop, and they'd show me on a map exactly what they were going to have me do. After the briefing, I went into the files and pulled all the information on the area and studied it. I got out my map and marked all the areas where there had been mines planted, read about any contact with the enemy that had been reported in the area, and essentially memorized the whole operation and every detail within those five grid squares. Then the team and I would practice whatever we were supposed to do on the mission—a prisoner snatch, for example—for a day or two.

On the day of the insertion we assembled early in the morning at the air head. I inspected everybody to make sure they all had everything they were supposed to have. Then I had them walk around the pad while I watched them. Sure enough, once in a while I'd find somebody limping. One time I found that my tail gunner had shot himself in the leg with his .45 pistol and was afraid to say anything about it. When we took a look at his leg, I found that the bullet had gone into his thigh and had come out by the knee—and he was going to go on the operation. He was upset when I didn't let him go! The Yards were tough like that!

Everybody test-fired their weapons, and then we climbed on the helicopters. The ride to the insertion point often took all day, from early in the morning until just about dark. We'd refuel a couple of times before crossing over into Cambodia and then into where we were supposed to go.

Insertion was a critical time. The helicopters only had enough fuel for a few minutes on station. If we started taking fire in the LZ [landing zone], they would usually come back and get us out of there.

As soon as we hit the LZ, the team set up security—a perimeter defense—and we were all perfectly silent. We waited and listened. If there were any NVA in the area moving toward us, we would be able to hear them crashing through the brush.

While we were listening, I had to check the map to make sure that we'd been inserted in the right place (once we got dropped off miles from where we were supposed to be, and the helicopters were already on their way home). It was very hard to verify the location from the air; it really had to be done on the ground. When I realized what had happened, I called them on the radio and said, "You get back in here *now!*" When the time came for us to get extracted, the slicks would have gone to the intended landing zone—and we wouldn't be there. They'd figure we got wiped out. I think that's what happened to some of the teams that disappeared during the war. They weren't wiped out, they just were put in the wrong place and nobody ever heard from them again. So I made sure that the recon plane didn't get out of radio range until I was absolutely sure we were in the right place.

Once I was sure we were in the right place and hadn't been noticed, I gave the hand and arm signal for the route I wanted us to travel. It would always be the worst, most unlikely way—up a steep hill, through heavy brush, anything to make it difficult to be followed—and we'd take off. We moved until we reached a RON site and set up for the night, just as it got to the point where you could barely see.

My technique for occupying the RON was to find the site, indicate it to the team, and then move past it for a ways. We stopped again, pretended to occupy this site, then go back to the original site by a different route. Other than the one time I got lazy, this worked perfectly.

And that time, which I thought was my last time in the field, I did two things I never did before: occupied the RON too early, and didn't RON on the side of a hill. We got hit really bad. It was embarrassing.

Live and Let Live

I went on eight or ten operations into Cambodia to mine the Ho Chi Minh Trail. The way we did these missions was that the intel shop would tell us where they wanted the thing placed, then they'd fly us in on the helicopters, drop us off a few klicks from the trail, and we would move up to the location.

Once we got close, the team spread out, on line, and then moved up to the trail itself. We set up on the trail like an ambush—point man on one end, tail gunner on the other. My job, as the team sergeant and engineer, was to set up the mine.

On one of these missions, we set up in the usual way, and I started digging with my K-bar knife. The dirt on the trail was extremely hard packed from the passage of all the trucks, and digging was quite difficult and slow. I had just gotten a pretty good-sized hole dug and was just about to put in the mine, when one of the guys on the team signaled that someone was coming. I moved back into the brush, out of sight, with my CAR-15 at the ready.

The sentry ambled up the trail, with his AK-47 slung over his shoulder, behind his back. He got to the hole, looked down at the dirt, and kept looking at the hole and the fresh dirt. Then he started exploring and walked off the trail, into the brush—right toward me. I was fifteen or twenty feet off the trail, and he just walked right up to me! He never unslung his rifle, which was still behind his back, but I had my CAR-15 pointed right at him, right at his face. He looked at the rifle—and he looked at me—and he didn't know *what* to do!

Well, I smiled at him, thinking, *You are in* big *trouble now, buddy.* He smiled back. Then he backed up, got back on the road, and kept on walking! I let him go. I really didn't want to shoot him; I really couldn't shoot him! If I had shot him, his buddies would have known where we were, so I thought, the heck with it. He never went for his weapon. I watched him back up to the road, and I figured that he would try for his weapon when he got to the road—but he didn't! He started walking, and I just let him go.

I went back out, finished putting the mine in, put the dirt back over it, wet it down with water from my canteen, and we pulled back to a RON site not too far away.

That night, about dusk, we heard the trucks fire up, and a little while later you could hear them pull out. I thought, I don't believe it! Then, a little while later we heard the mine go off! He didn't tell anybody; live and let live!

Russians

There was a black guy who was cooperating with the NVA from somewhere in Cambodia. He was calling in American artillery on American ground units. He sounded like he knew what he was talking about, scared and excited on the radio. Although he didn't have the right code words for authentication, a lot of batteries would execute the fire mission anyway.

We were sent in to get this guy. They figured out his location with radio direction finders and thought they knew where he was. It was a really stupid mission. The chance of actually seeing this guy was maybe one in a million. And the only way to actually take him out, if we did find him, was with a sniper. So I got elected to be the sniper, and the only sniper rifle we had was an M1 with a sniper scope. I spent a whole day trying to zero that weapon, and then that's what I carried on the operation.

We got on the ground and moved for two or three days and didn't see the enemy at all. Then, on the third or fourth day, I saw tracks. They were fairly old, but I figured that there was somebody in here. We were within five hundred meters of the coordinates where the guy was transmitting from, according to the briefing.

It was getting dark and time to pick a RON [remain overnight] position. Ordinarily I always picked a site on the slope of a hill because the enemy is just like anybody else—lazy. He'll go up the hill, down the hill, or around the hill; but he won't go crashing along a slope when there's an easier way to travel.

The op had been going perfectly, but I screwed up and decided that we'd sleep on level ground. I picked a site on a little finger of land above a river.

The slope was far too steep for anyone to come up, so the only way we'd bump into NVA would be if they came up this narrow finger of the hill. We put the Claymores out, and I started writing my message for the recon plane.

While I was preparing the message, I got the feeling that something was wrong. The team was kind of scurrying around, uneasy about something, not talking. I looked up, and there were two Europeans in green uniforms, with caps and AK-47s, just standing there, maybe fifty meters away—really close! I thought, what the hell is this? I could see the point man wanted to kill them, right now, but the interpreter was holding him back. I found out later the interpreter thought we were supposed to meet these guys here. The interpreter had to make a decision, and fast, so he said, in English, "Halt! Who are you?"

One of the two guys held his AK over his head and said, in Vietnamese, "Company, ASSAULT!" When he said that, I set off the Claymores! The Claymores just shredded these guys—boots and everything flying through the air. The jungle just erupted.

Their first assault went right through us. They outnumbered us maybe twenty to one. But they got to the edge of the slope, and they hesitated. That's when we got a lot of them. I shot two or three in the back, right there. They assaulted through us again, then pulled back. I thought, Oh, no—what are we gonna do now? I was scared!

I told the interpreter to get the team out of the position and down the hill; they jumped up and ran. I watched them go over the crest of the hill, then stood up to follow. But the NVA had moved up some sort of automatic weapon, and when I got up it opened up on me. One bullet went through my pant leg; then it went through my rifle magazine, hit the bolt, and froze the weapon. Another went into the radio. I got off one round and the rifle jammed. I threw it down and got out a grenade.

The only thing that saved me was that when they jumped up, their officer said, in Vietnamese, "Whoever kills that American, I will kill! I want him!" When he said that, I threw the grenade and went over the hill—with two of them right on my ass. We were all rolling down the hill, and when we got to the bottom, the interpreter and point man were there. They shot both of the NVA. I grabbed the AK and spare magazine from one of them, and we took off down the trail.

They had a lot of captured American M79 grenade launchers, and once we got to the river those rounds were just raining on us. We were running as fast as we could, and the grenades were keeping up with us. They were firing at us from above and could see us pretty clearly. But we got away and kept going, all night.

I gathered the team together and told each of them, one at a time, "You will not fire your weapon! If you fire at them and they see us, they will surround us immediately. If they fire at us, do not fire back." They came within ten or fifteen meters of us that night. They were searching everywhere, with flashlights, and they were serious!

The recon plane came by, but the radio was out and I couldn't contact him. I thought, Boy, we are in big trouble now! So we were headed toward Thailand, away from Vietnam, because there were so many NVA along the border that there was no way we were going to walk back through them all. I had five Yards [an affectionate nickname for the tribal people of the highlands, shortened from the French term for these peoples, *Montagnards,* which translates as *Mountaineers*] and one other American. He was wounded pretty bad, shot in both hands. He was in pain all the time and wanted me to give him morphine, but I wouldn't do it. We couldn't carry him, and we weren't going to leave him, so he had to keep going. Everybody was wounded at least once. But there were so many grenades going off and M79 rounds exploding, it was hard to notice when you got hit unless it was pretty bad.

On the second day the interpreter came to me, and he had tears in his eyes. He said, "Are you going to make it?" So I got out my signaling mirror and took a look at myself. There was blood all over my face, little pieces of metal in one eye, and a little piece of metal sticking out of my neck. I thought, *I don't look too good!*

Our assigned AO [area of operations] was a five grid-square [five kilometers by five kilometers] area on the map. Within a day or so we were well out of it. We could hear the recon plane come over, but without the radio there was no way to talk to him. I still had a small PRC-38 [the small radio pilots carried as part of their survival equipment]. But it only had a range of about two miles, and that meant the plane just about had to be overhead.

We came to a clearing, and I decided to stay put there for a few days in the hopes that we'd get lucky and somebody might come by and we could try signaling to them. We were there for two days when I heard a couple of A1-Es [Douglas Skyraider attack planes] somewhere nearby, doing a bomb run. I waited, hoping they would come our way. Sure enough, they did. I pulled out that antenna and started transmitting. They were overhead right away, and I just stood there waving. I figured they'd strafe me, but they came by and buzzed us, over and over, then went high and orbited.

They stayed overhead for two or three hours, and then we could hear those old blades coming. The gunships came in first and orbited the clearing a couple of times, looking us over carefully. All I could do was to wave to them, but finally the "slicks" [troop-carrier helicopters] came in, and we piled on.

It was a bad operation. We must have been really close to the base camp when we were discovered. I still think about it. I still think about all the things I could have done. There was nothing gallant about the whole thing— it was just run and hide!

"You Get to Blow a Bridge!"

I came off a mission and was just getting off the helicopter when Captain Gail and Colonel Smith (I think it was) grabbed me. They said, "Dennis, have we got something for you! You will *love* this mission, but you will have to go right away!" They knew I was an engineer, and they said, "You get to blow a bridge!"

I said, "Wow, really?" That's something you train for as an engineer, but hardly anybody ever gets to do.

They took us to the briefing room, and it then turns out that they not only don't know what the bridge looks like, they don't even know where it is. "We ain't never seen it, but we know it is there!"

"How are we supposed to find it if you don't even know where it is?" I asked them.

Well, they could tell from aerial photographs that one branch of the trail crossed this river somewhere under the jungle canopy. They couldn't actually see where, but they knew that the trucks had to get across this river, and it was too deep to ford. So there had to be a bridge there somewhere. They thought it might be a pontoon bridge that they floated out there at night.

We only had two hours to plan the mission; then it was time to go. We collected all the C4 explosive we could carry, put it in the rucksacks, and off we went. The helicopters arrived, and we all piled aboard and headed for the insertion point. Since we didn't know exactly where the bridge was, we had the helos put us into the general area, and we started looking for the thing.

We spent five or six days searching for that damn bridge. We walked along the river, then moved away from it, over and over. We moved up to the water, looked up stream and down—no bridge! We could hear the trucks moving at night, but we just couldn't figure out where they were crossing.

After about six days of this, I told Sp5 John Kendenberg, "Enough is enough. We are going to get out on the Ho Chi Minh Trail, and we are going to walk down it until it crosses the river. That's where the bridge has to be."

John said, "Do you really think we ought to do that?"

Well, I was tired, and dirty, and annoyed. "*That's* what we are gonna do!"

"Well, okay," he said. So we put the point man out front, we got on the trail, and off we went. The recon plane came over, right on schedule, and we got off the road to make contact with him.

"Hey, be careful!" the recon pilot said on the radio. "I just saw a patrol walking down the trail!"

I called him back and said, "That's us." He didn't believe me that we were just walking down the Ho Chi Minh Trail, so I said, "Okay, take a look again," and we all went out in the middle of the road where he could see us.

"Holy crap!" he said. "Are you guys crazy?"

"No," I said, "but we are going to find that bridge! Come back in a couple of hours. I have a feeling that it is going to be something that we are not going to be able to blow up with what we have with us." So he left.

We kept walking, and sure enough, we finally came to the water. The point man signaled that he saw someone moving on our side of the water. Apparently the NVA bridge guards ran across the river from the side we were on. We carefully moved up to the water, on line. On the far side of the river was a bunker, and inside were four guys. They watched us and we watched them, nobody shooting.

But there was no bridge! The bunkers on our side of the river were empty, and we figured that the guards weren't sure who we were and moved across until they could figure us out. I brought the team up on line, everybody's weapons aimed at the guys in the bunker. I gave LAWs [light anti-tank weapon, a small rocket launcher designed for bunker-busting and light armor targets; a notoriously unreliable weapon] to two of the Yards and told them that if the guys in the bunker fired, to hit them with the LAWs.

John and I walked out into the water. There was a bridge, all right, but it was completely submerged. The NVA had placed four culverts in the water, then piled rocks on top of them to form a roadway. The water covered the road for a foot or so, and flowed through the culverts. No wonder the planes couldn't see anything.

Well, John and I couldn't figure out how we were going to blow this thing up. We stood there, talking, with the NVA guards watching us, and the Yards watching them. So we went back to the shore, got the rucksacks together, and put all the C4 in three of them. We decided that we could use another ruck filled with rocks as an anchor, light the fuses, and drop the charges into one of the culverts. So we set the fuses for about a two-minute delay, called the recon plane to watch for the explosion so somebody would at least know where the bridge was, and got ready to light the fuses. It was really stupid, in a way. We would hardly be able to put a dent in this thing with our charges, but we figured we had to do something as long as we had come this far. So we placed the charges, lit the fuses, collected the Yards, and started jogging back up the Ho Chi Minh Trail.

The recon plane called, "I see you," as we were running along the trail. We didn't get very far before the charges went off. It was raining rocks and mud and water. No sooner did the junk stop falling from the sky than we had the fast-movers overhead. They saw the explosion, and now they knew where the bridge was. They started bombing—I thought they were going to kill us all! "Stop! Stop! We gotta get out of here!" I was yelling on the radio. They really pasted this thing.

I always wondered what those guys in the bunker must have been thinking. They just looked out at us, like, *What the hell is this all about?* I think they must have thought we were North Vietnamese. We certainly weren't wearing American uniforms.

After we got away, I was curious about those LAWs and decided to fire them, to see how they worked. Neither one fired. I thought, "Of all the missions I have carried these things—if I knew they didn't work I wouldn't have bothered with them!" I was pissed. So that was my bridge assignment with John Kendenberg.

Eavesdropping on the Enemy

One mission they gave my team involved attaching a tape recorder to the NVA commo wire along the Ho Chi Minh Trail. They gave us a big, heavy box (it must have weighed at least seventy pounds) and explained that it would record anything the NVA were talking about. There were two wires with clips attached that I was supposed to clamp to their wire. There was about thirty pounds of explosive in the machine too; it was designed to explode if anybody tampered with it.

I was given a short class on the machine. It was supposed to be buried near the wire, armed with a key. There was a little meter on it that showed if it was recording properly. When somebody was talking on the wire and the machine was hooked up correctly, the needle moved. "Don't leave until you see the needle move!" the guy told me. The machine came with its own rucksack, and it was so heavy that I had to have other members of the team carry my gear.

Well, they gave me the coordinates where they said there were thirty or forty pairs of commo wire running along the trail; they wanted me to go tap into one. I thought, this is ridiculous. But I decided to give it a try.

The other American they assigned to go on the mission was a reservist. The guy had six kids at home, but he had volunteered to go to Vietnam, and they sent him to me. I thought, this guy does not belong here, but I spent about a week working on the team signals and SOPs [standard operating procedures] with him, checking him out. I thought I had him down pat—had him throw a few grenades in the grenade pit and test fire his rifle. He was "good to go."

We were inserted and moved up to the trail. You could see the commo wires running along it, but the North Vietnamese were walking up and down the trail, constantly. So we moved up, on line, where we could observe the trail and still be at a safe distance from it, hidden in the jungle. Finally, when there didn't seem to be anybody nearby, I moved up to the trail to attach the box.

There were wires from ground level to about ten feet up, running through the trees. I started digging a hole for the box, buried it part way, then clipped the leads to one of the pairs of commo wires. I attached the leads to the box, and right away the needle started moving! I thought, *All right!*, put some leaves over it, and left.

We waited in the brush for twenty-four hours, then moved back up to retrieve the recorder. The needle was still moving! There were so many NVA walking up and down the trail that I decided not to undo the clips, but to just disconnect the box and take it with me. I disarmed it, took it out of the hole, and moved back to the team. After I got the recorder back in its ruck-sack we started to move away from the trail—the point man first, then the interpreter, then me. The other American was toward the end. We started moving down a steep hill, and about the time I got to the bottom, I heard firing up at the top. There was a firefight going on! The rest of the team came running down the hill, and the reservist ran up to me and said, "Holy shit, they saw the wires! As soon as you left, a guy came up and tugged on the wires—so we shot him! And they started shooting back!" And then he says, "Oh, no! Did you hear a grenade go off? I think I forgot to pull the pin! I hope they don't throw it back!"

Well, we ran off and got away. When we got back I explained exactly what had happened. I waited for a couple of days, then went to the S-2 [intelligence] shop and asked them what was on the tape.

The S-2 says, "You ain't gonna believe this, but there wasn't anything on the tape—you hooked onto an electric wire! They were using that wire to run a light bulb or something; all we got was a hum."

Ghost Helicopter in the Jungle

We were on a mission to mine one of the branches of the Ho Chi Minh Trail in Laos. There was only one place in the area where we could get off the helicopter without rappelling, and that was in the middle of a stream. This was my primary insertion point. We had to jump out into the water because there was no other place to go. We got off the helicopters without any problems and were good to go. Once we got off the helicopters we waited and listened to hear if anybody was moving toward us. There was no sound, so we moved off, up to the top of a little hill nearby.

The insertion was late, and it was getting dark, so—even though we were pretty close to the landing zone—we started looking for a RON position. I chose a place and sent the team out to emplace the Claymores. The team took the mines out fifty meters and set them up. Then the interpreter came back, and he had a number written on his hand. He showed me the number and indicated that it came from a helicopter. My first thought was that we had blundered onto an NVA helicopter landing pad, and I thought, *Boy, did we goof this up!*

So the interpreter and I went back out, and sure enough, there was a helicopter in the jungle. The guns were still mounted on it, and the inside was clean as a whistle! The rotor was intact, and nothing seemed to be damaged. Just inside the door was a leather medical kit bag like a doctor would carry, but it was all decayed. Inside were medical instruments. Hanging from the machine gun was an albumen can. The rubber tube was gone, but there was a skeleton on the ground underneath, with the remains of the needle. Some of the clothing was still there, along with a wallet.

On the other side, in a little ditch, were several other skeletons, all lined up with carbines pointed down toward the river we had come from. I couldn't figure it out. There were no bullet holes in the helicopter, no signs of any kind of fighting that I could find. It was really weird!

Well, the recon plane came by not long after that. I wanted to have him relay a message about the helicopter, but I didn't want to send it in the "clear" [in uncoded, plain language]. Well, I kind of screwed up and didn't encode the whole message, but got the message off to the plane. He retransmitted it to a relay station somewhere, and I could hear the pilot telling the relay station operator the helicopter identification numbers. Then I heard the retrans operator ask the pilot, "What did they do, find a helicopter?"

Well, when I heard that I thought we were in real danger; the NVA were probably listening, and now this guy has just given away the game. I told the team, "That's it. Pick up the Claymores—we're getting out of here!"

We got down to the stream and started moving, and we kept moving downstream until midnight or one in the morning. The streams were the fastest way to move. The jungle was too thick; you made too much noise. But if you got in a stream you could move pretty quickly, without making any noise. The only problem was that the enemy was there, too, to get water. So you had to be careful. Even so it was faster than walking through the jungle. If I had to get someplace in a hurry, I used the streams, just like a highway.

We slept until daylight, then got back in the stream and took off in the direction of the Ho Chi Minh Trail to complete the mining operation. While we were en route, the recon plane came back over, and the pilot radioed, "Go back to the helicopter. The intel guys want to know more about it."

I told him, "I am *not* going back!"

I tried to ignore the order, and we kept moving toward the place where we were supposed to put out the mines. About three days after we left the helicopter, the recon plane came over with the word that if we didn't go back to the helicopter, they were not going to pick us up. We were about five hundred meters from the trail at that point, and about to set the mines, but I was mad. So I got the interpreter, and I told him that we were going to follow the stream back—and we were going to get back there in one day. So we hustled and got back there that night.

When the recon plane came by, I told him to make sure the helicopters were on the ground at the site the next morning, and we'd have the bodies for them. So we took our ponchos and collected all the bones in the ponchos. When the med-evac chopper arrived the next morning, they kicked some body bags off, and I threw them back on, along with our big bag of bones. They were furious; they wanted them all kept separate. But I did sort out the wallets, and we climbed on the helicopter and handed the wallets to the medic. He just sat there, dumbfounded, looking at that big bag of bones.

Later the S-2 told me that there had been a doctor on the helicopter and four Vietnamese, along with the crew. They had been en route to a village in

Laos to help with an epidemic, and apparently the helicopter had pooped out on them. After they sorted out the bones, they found that the doctor and the pilot were missing, and they figured that they tried to walk out.

Standing Guard for the NVA

People who didn't adapt didn't survive. You couldn't just do things the way they taught at Bragg or you would die. There were a million things you had to adapt to. For instance, when we set up a RON position, we put everybody within touching distance and not one person stayed awake. I made sure everybody was asleep. Then, if something was wrong, you'd sense it and wake up, and you could warn the people near you by touch. When that happened you could feel a kind of electric tension! When the danger passed you could just doze off again.

Our procedure for selecting and setting up at a "RON" (Remain Over Night) site was to find a place on a slope, preferably in the brush, where nobody would naturally go. We put out Claymore mines [command-detonated devices that spray steel balls across a wide sector—a bit like firing twenty 12-gauge shotguns all at once]. The guys went out about fifty meters past the end of the Claymore wires, just so they knew the terrain, then came back in.

One night (now, this was crazy) we set up late, well after dark, and the guys didn't go out as far as they should have. Sometime in the middle of the night, much later, I woke up. . . . It sounded like a herd of buffalo was moving through our RON site! You could hear them coming, crashing through the brush!

You could hear the NVA move right into our position—and then you could tell that they were sitting down! I was cussing to myself, thinking, *I know there's a trail within fifty meters, and these idiots of mine didn't see it!* We were all basically just holding our breath.

Then the brush moved a little, and the interpreter came up to me and whispered in my ear, "*Chung-si* [Vietnamese for *sergeant*], one of the North Vietnamese told me that I have guard duty next!"

I still hadn't actually seen any of them, but I thought, Boy, this is *bad*! I figured we had to do something, but I didn't know what. We couldn't set off the Claymores. I thought maybe we would just abandon the Claymores, and if they were still there when it started to get light, we would just try to move away from them. Then, just before dawn, the brush started moving again. They got up and moved out. That was close!

Boy Robin

Sgt. Mike Tremell was on ST [Spike Team, a heavy team of two or three Americans and eight or more Yards, sent out with the expectation of contact with the enemy] Colorado, and I had ST New York. Tremell was teamed with Sgt. Sherman Batman (his real last name), the highest ranking team leader we had. Naturally, since Tremell had red hair, we all called him "Boy Robin." When Batman left the team, Tremell was put in charge of the team.

Mike Tremell was also known as Magnet Ass. He never went on an operation where somebody didn't get shot—killed or wounded—so the guys didn't want to go out with him anymore. So he got put in the recon planes and would talk to the teams when the plane flew over. His first day out, the recon plane got shot down. Tremell got the pilot out, and they had to walk for a couple of days in the jungle to get out. So then the recon pilots said, "We don't want him to fly with us anymore."

After that they had him run the club. But one day while he and another guy were doing PT [physical training], they took sniper fire! Now, FOB-2 [a forward operating base set up to support the units in the field] had never taken a round of fire, ever! After that everybody said, "Keep this guy in the compound! He is bad luck!"

Well, on Tremell's first operation with the team, he got them in big trouble. Most of the team got killed off, and he had one guy with him who had never been in combat before.

My team was on ready reserve at the time, so when the call came from Tremell, they tossed us on the helicopters and shot us out there. It was getting dark, and we had to rappel in on top of his team to reinforce and maybe save them. Well, while we were riding in, I was listening on the radio, and I could hear Tremell. He said, "It's getting dark here, and it looks like we aren't going to make it. But we will fight to the last man! They will not take us alive!"

He kept this up for maybe half an hour. It was really dramatic. Then the helicopter gunships got out there and worked over the area outside the perimeter. The slicks came in and picked up what was left of the team on McGuire rigs and brought them out. Finally they showed up at the FOB, and I said to him, "Tremell, what was all that crap on the radio?"

He said, "You know what? I always wanted to do that! Wasn't that impressive? If I hadn't made it out, wouldn't you have been impressed?"

Prisoner Snatch

I was involved in three prisoner-snatch operations. My interpreter and the Yards just couldn't understand this. They thought that you ought to kill all the NVA you could find. We once caught an NVA officer. While I was interrogating him, he spit on me. The interpreter cut his throat.

I said, "Why did you do that?"

He replied, "He spit on you—disrespect!"

I told him, "I would have gotten a free trip to Taiwan and a hundred dollars if we had brought him in. He could have spit on me all day!" But by then it was too late.

The last one I caught spilled his guts—told me everything I wanted to know. When we were done with him, I told the interpreter to unlock the handcuffs, take the blindfold off, and let him go. I thought the interpreter was going to shoot him, so I said, "I am telling you, don't shoot him—let him go!"

The prisoner got up, walked off down the trail a little ways, and looked back to see if we were going to shoot him. He waddled off a little more, looked back again, and pretty soon he was gone. The other American with me said, "He's gonna come back, and he's gonna bring his buddies!" But I knew he wouldn't. We moved out of the area anyway, but I knew he was just happy to be alive.

Miller Time with the NVA

I went on another prisoner snatch mission with a captain who later earned a medal of honor. We found a trail with a lot of commo wire running along it. We could hear generators at the top of the hill and the bottom of the hill, and it seemed reasonable that there was a lot going on. We decided to cut the commo wire and wait until somebody came along to find the break. Hopefully it would be a commo guy, and then we'd have somebody really knowledgeable.

Although I thought it was a bad idea, the captain insisted that we cache our rucks at the rally point before we set up to snatch the prisoner. He and the other members of the team took the stuff while I stayed by the trail. Being lazy and hot, I lay back against a tree, put my feet out, with the commo wire right across the top, with my feet on the trail. As a matter of fact, I reached in my ruck and took out a beer. I always have some beer with me, at least a six-pack.

So I'm sitting there, enjoying my beer, and what do I see coming up the trail but two guys. I thought, *Dennis, you goofed up*! They wandered up the trail, one with a big sack, both with their weapons slung backwards where they couldn't get to them. They got to me, looked at my feet, and stopped. They looked at me, and I had my weapon pointed at them. First, they smiled. Then you could see it go across their faces: *This is an American*! I'm sure it never dawned on them that they'd ever see one. I looked down the trail, and there were more of them, and they were moving up toward me. But the rest of the team had moved up into position by now, and I felt a little better.

Another NVA came along, stopped, and saw me. He was a little braver than the others, and I thought, *Oh oh, I'm in trouble with this guy*! The rest of them were bumping into each other, and this guy started to go for his weapon. I was up on one knee, ready to go. When that third guy went for his AK, the whole team opened up on them. I used my weapon to club the first two, and they went down. I took the weapons away from them and had the cuffs on the first one. There was firing everywhere. I stuck my hand in that big sack—it was nuc mam [fermented fish sauce]! I was mad! I figured it was full of money; I thought I was a millionaire! So I punched these two guys, cut them loose, and told them to get going.

We took off down the hill, and then we called in an air strike on the positions and called for extraction. The AD-6s [another version of the Skyraider attack plane] started bombing the top of the hill and began taking lots of ground fire. One of the planes was hit several times.

The helicopters came and got us out with McGuire rigs [harnesses that allowed the team to be quickly extracted by attaching themselves to a rope hung from a helicopter]. It was a horrible ride! Every time I did it, I said, I will never, ever do that again. But then, the next time, I put it on again. You had to have a good pilot. When he plucked you out of that jungle, if he started taking hits and took off, or did anything except go straight up, you were dead.

After I got to FOB-2, I ran six or seven operations and didn't fire a shot. I saw incredible numbers of North Vietnamese, more on one operation than most guys in the 101st would see in a whole tour. If things were going smoothly I didn't have to fire my weapon.

The Prisoner

I was assigned a prisoner snatch mission along the Ho Chi Minh Trail. When we got to the trail, there were lots of NVA. But they were walking in columns, so we waited for a chance to snag an isolated straggler or somebody moving along the road alone. We put our Claymores out and just waited.

Several columns went by, and then, sure enough, along came a straggler. He had an AK, but the interpreter and I ran out in the road, grabbed the weapon out of his hands, and dragged him back into the jungle. We handcuffed him, gagged him, and picked up the Claymores. Then we all moved out.

We moved about three hundred meters into the jungle and stopped to start questioning the prisoner. Well, he was crying and was really upset. It was sad, and I started to feel sorry for the poor guy. He was kind of wimpy. We pulled out his wallet. It had a couple of minor documents in it, along with a picture of his family—his wife and kids.

I asked him about his job, and he told me that during his training the NVA instructors told them that there were Americans hiding along the Ho Chi Minh Trail, just waiting to snatch stragglers, and now that is just what happened. That's why he was so scared. The South Vietnamese had no use for prisoners at all. I had to handcuff the guy to me to keep from having his throat cut. They figured that the only good NVA was a dead NVA.

Well, the guy spilled his guts—told us everything! He was a supply sergeant, and he told me where everything was. He couldn't read a map, but he could describe locations, and we figured out where all his people and vehicles were camped. I said, "Great!" We picked up our stuff and moved out again. Then I called in air strikes on these places, and a flight of A-1Es [Douglas Skyraider attack planes] showed up and clobbered these places. Then over the radio you could hear the pilots—they were ecstatic! They were getting secondary explosions from the NVA ammunition. So I knew the prisoner had told me the truth!

We stayed in the jungle for another two or three days. Then the helicopters came to take us out. The S-2 talked to the guy. He turned out to have a *lot* of information, and it was going to take several days to interrogate him. Well, we didn't have a proper place to keep a prisoner, so we decided to keep him for three or four days. He slept in my bunker with me, in my little hooch.

I never had a problem with him. In fact, I took him to the club, and he had a few beers. He ate at the mess hall with us. He turned out to be a really nice guy. Finally, it was time for me to go on another mission, so I took the guy to the S-2 shop and told them to take care of the prisoner. They said, "Okay," and off I went.

When I got back from the operation, I had a beer; then I went over to the S-2 shop. "Where's the prisoner?" I asked them.

"You ain't gonna like this," the S-2 said, "but the Vietnamese got him, and they took him to downtown Kontum. There was a kind of riot, and the Vietnamese grabbed him, and they buried him alive."

I said, "That is *it* for prisoners! No more!" I was furious. The next one I caught after that, I let him go.

The Big Mouth

I went on one mission where the helicopter door gunners refused to go! I went on another mission where, after we were inserted, the other American started crying so bad that I had to sit on him. I tried to get him to calm down, but he just kept getting louder. I had to hold my hand over his mouth, he was crying so bad! I had the helicopters come back and get him. We weren't getting shot at or anything.

Well, I ran into that guy later on; he was still in Special Forces. We were on an AT [annual reserve component training exercise] and were on a C-130, about three years ago. He's an officer now, a captain. We were getting ready to make a parachute jump, and this guy was walking up and down, shooting off his mouth. I thought, I knew a guy like that once. Then I saw he was wearing a Special Forces combat patch. It was the same guy! I said, "Sir, were you in Vietnam?"

He said, "Yeah."

I said, "You ever been to Kontum?"

He looked at me, hard, recognized me and said "Uh . . . no, never in Kontum!"

"Well, where were you then in Special Forces?"

"Oh, I wasn't in Special Forces! I was in the 101st Airborne!"

"Then how come you're wearing that Special Forces patch? And where were you in the 101st?"

He just backed up and went and sat down and shut up.

I went back to my team and said, "That's him all right, that's the big mouth!" He never said another word on the whole flight. And I'd never have recognized him if he hadn't opened his big mouth.

Elephant Stories

We were coming into an LZ, and the grass was so high that you couldn't see the ground. The helicopter's rotor wash was pressing it down, but even so, the ground wasn't visible. I kept telling the pilot to go lower, but he was getting nervous—the blades were starting to cut the grass. Even so, I couldn't see the deck, and I was not jumping off this thing! I was thinking, *If I jump and break a leg, then I will be* really *screwed because they won't be able to get us out of here.*

The pilot and I were arguing this way, with me standing outside on the skid, when the helicopter started to move violently! I almost fell off. I grabbed something, and up we went. About twenty elephants crossed the LZ underneath us. If we had put down there, we would have been pounded into the ground!

Another time, over in Laos, we had been on the ground four or five days and hadn't seen the enemy. I was thinking, *This is an* easy *one.* We kept walking. We weren't doing anything. Finally, we stopped for a break. I was sitting there, with my back to a tree, and we heard brush crashing in the distance. I looked at the interpreter, and he looked at me, and we all got up on one knee, in firing positions behind trees, watching.

It was an elephant! It came crashing through the brush and buzzed right past us. The interpreter and I said, "Don't shoot! Don't shoot! It will give away our position!" But it came back, and came crashing through the brush again. I had laid the radio on the ground, and the elephant stepped on it, crushing it. I looked at that and thought, *This is ridiculous.*

The brush was very thick. You couldn't see more than fifty feet or so, and that made it hard to tell what was happening. The elephant repeated this performance a couple of times, screaming and yelling, crashing around, and I told the interpreter, "Enough is enough! If it does that again, we shoot!" The elephant came back again, and everybody opened up, full automatic. We shot him in the front, the side, everywhere! But he went on by and came back again. We started firing again, but this time the interpreter, who had the M79 grenade launcher, fired. He thumped the elephant with a high-explosive M79 round, and that was the end of the elephant!

In retrospect, the thing that amazed me about the incident is that we didn't manage to shoot each other. We were shooting like madmen! It wasn't a very big elephant, but it sure was a mean elephant!

Monkey Tales

I asked some of the NVA prisoners we captured why they normally operate in pairs. I assumed that it was related to some combat reason. They said, no, it was because of the monkey we call the Gibbon ape. The Gibbon ape will attack a lone man, but not a pair.

Well, we were on patrol in the jungle, out near the Ho Chi Minh Trail, and we came across what looked like a RON site. There were ten or fifteen positions where the grass had been disturbed, as if people had bedded down in a circle. We figured that an NVA patrol had slept here.

It looked like the position had been well used, and I thought, Why don't we wait here and maybe they will come back. So we set up outside the position, and we waited. We waited all day, all night, and into the next day. Around noon of the second day, we began to hear the brush move in the distance. I thought, *Good! They're coming back; I got 'em!*

As the sound got closer, I could start to see the brush moving—and out came these apes! They have white faces, and they were walking along in patrol file! They kept moving toward us, and finally they got quite close. I told the interpreter to tell the guys, don't fire. Then one of the apes saw us. It held its hand up, just like the hand-and-arm signals we use on patrol. They all stopped and looked at us.

One picked up a stick and started to act threatening with it. It moved closer, and the interpreter tried to push it away. The ape swung at the interpreter and hit him in the face with a kind of slapping punch that made his nose start bleeding. Then the rest of them started throwing things at us, so we opened up on them, and they finally took off. I was really impressed. These monkeys were using good patrolling techniques. Maybe we should have sent them to Ranger school!

Across the Northern Fence

I named my son after a friend of mine who was killed in North Vietnam, doing something around some railroad tracks. I tried to find out what happened, but I didn't come up with much.

When I look at that wall they have at Fort Bragg, and I look at those names—I know so many of those people! It means something to me, but most of the other people who walk by don't appreciate it; it's nothing to them.

John Kendenberg's Medal of Honor

John earned his Medal of Honor on a mission that I was supposed to go along on. If I had gone, he might still be alive today, and he might not have had to earn that medal.

I was just coming in off a mission. We were walking back in from the helicopters to the compound to be debriefed. John came up to me and said,

"Dennis, you've got to come with me—this is a bad one. I need to have you along."

So I said, "Okay," dumped my gear, and went to pick up some more rations.

The sergeant major and the colonel saw me and said, "Where are you going?"

"I'm going with John on this operation."

"No, you're not," one of them said. "We've got something different for you." They gave him another American, a guy on his first mission, and the helicopters picked them up and off they went.

John was killed on that mission, and I think if I had been with him he might have made it out alive. He died because of a stupid mistake.

They made contact that night, almost as soon as they got on the ground. There was a hellacious battle afterwards, and the body count was supposed to be about two thousand NVA killed, most from air strikes. We never found out what that mission was all about. John's team made contact within ten minutes of insertion and fought all night long. The NVA brought up two light-armored vehicles, both of which John's team knocked out. This was very unusual for the NVA, because the jets could make it so hot for them once their positions were exposed.

John was able to break contact and get his team out and to a bomb crater. He called for extraction, and when the helicopters came in to get the team, the NVA were waiting. The team climbed on to the helos, but then the North Vietnamese rushed out and grabbed the skids of the helicopter. It couldn't take off, there were so many hanging on to it.

John jumped off to fight them. The new American, who was carrying the radio, was supposed to never leave John's side, but he stayed in the helicopter. John shot the NVA off the skids, beating them off so the helicopter could get airborne. The NVA didn't get him in the crater; he killed them instead. But the helicopter took off, with the radio operator still aboard and John still on the ground. He moved out of the crater to hide, and an AH-1 Cobra gunship came in, firing rockets at the NVA. A rocket hit too close to John, and he died from internal injuries [on June 14, 1968].

The rule was, when the "Zero One" [the team leader] gets off the helicopter, the radio operator gets off too—no matter what. If that had happened, John would have stayed in the crater, but instead he had to hide out.

The American never came back to the compound from his first mission. They flew him off somewhere else, and we never saw him again. I never learned his name. It was a stupid mission. They should have just dropped bombs on that place.

Tools of the Trade

We made our own LBE [load-bearing equipment—also called "web gear"]. Instead of the regular magazine pouches, we used canteen covers for spare M16 magazines. We carried about nine hundred rounds of ammunition for our CAR-15s.

Some of the missions were so clandestine that I figured that the only way to survive was to carry an AK-47 rather than M16 or CAR-15. I even started wearing a load-bearing vest like the NVA wore, with pockets for the AK magazines in front and back. We tried to look as much like the enemy as possible, short of wearing their own uniforms.

That paid off for me once. We were on patrol in Laos when an NVA sentry stood up in front of us and said to the point man (in Vietnamese, of course), "If you guys are hungry, just go down this trail over here. The unit's eating dinner down there now."

The point man just said, "No, thanks, we don't need anything now," and we moseyed off.

I tried to explain to the Marines that you just can't use face paint and put sticks in your helmet without becoming conspicuous in a place like that. You have to look like the enemy, wear something like what they wear. We wore a light green uniform that was about the same color as theirs after it had gotten dirty. And we sometimes wore their hats. I always wore jungle boots, though, never those thong sandals—but some of them wore boots, too.

We tried to train some Marines to do this job once, and they started putting all that face paint on. I told them, "If you guys want to die, keep putting that stuff on. When you are moving through that jungle you have to look as much like that enemy as you can. Then, when you encounter them, they will sometimes hesitate. That's all you need!"

Half the battle was having the right gear, and the way you walked. What I taught—and still teach—is that you never, ever walk on flat ground. Never, unless you have to scurry across a valley. You always walk on ridges, and you never sleep on flat ground. The enemy is lazy. The enemy walks on flat ground. When he is looking for you, when you get in thick brush on the side of a steep hill, he will go around it. You go where he doesn't want to go. And that's how you live!

Except that there is always an exception to the rule, and one time that rule could have gotten me killed. We had mined the Ho Chi Minh Trail late one afternoon. The closest hillside was on the far side of a valley. We could have crossed it in daylight, but we would have drawn attention to ourselves in the process. I decided to stay in the valley, but instead of setting up on flat ground, I told my team, "We are going to sleep in the river."

We worked our way to the stream out in the middle of this valley and sat down in the water, using the overhang of the bank for cover and concealment. That evening the trucks started moving, and one triggered the mine. They knew what had happened, and they started looking for us. You could hear them moving around, searching for us in the night. Then their artillery started firing—at the hillside where we would have been, ordinarily.

Magnet Ass and the Radio

Mike Tremell, also known as "Magnet Ass" and "Boy Robin," was on a patrol near the Ho Chi Minh Trail. They were taking a little break during the middle of the day. Down below, in the jungle, Tremell noticed two NVA soldiers, also taking a break. They were leaning against a large, man-portable radio—an elaborate and apparently important piece of gear. Such equipment was typically worth a large reward if it could be captured and returned intact.

"Man," Tremell said, "I wonder what I'd get for that radio?" Then, after a moment, he told the other American, "You stay here with the team. There are only two NVA; I'll be right back with that radio."

Tremell snuck down the hill, to within only four or five feet of the NVA. Only then did he notice that there were not just two NVA but about two hundred or more, all strung out along the trail. He decided to let the two

NVA keep the radio. He started to sneak back up the hill as silently as possible, but one of the guards turned around and saw him. "Oh, shit," said Tremell as he opened fire. He hit both the NVA and the radio, too, and then he ran back up the hill to the rest of the team.

The entire team ran up toward the crest of the hill to escape the pursing enemy. At the top they found a large bunker complex built by the NVA, but empty. The NVA were swarming up the hill, so Tremell and the team started throwing hand grenades. Unfortunately, one of Tremell's first pitches struck a tree limb over the bunker and the grenade bounced back, right into the bunker. Despite all the NVA, both of the Americans jumped out of the bunker for a few seconds, until the grenade exploded, then rolled back in. On the way back in, Tremell's assistant, the other American, got hit in the ass.

About this time the recon plane flew over, and Tremell reported the predicament on the radio. The fast-movers were overhead shortly, bombing and strafing the NVA below. Not long after that, the helicopters arrived to extract the team with McGuire rigs.

That evening, back in the club, Tremell's radio operator and second in command was already back from the hospital, almost as good as new—but standing at the bar while giving an informal report on the operation. "I ain't going back out with that guy," he said. "First he tries to kill me with a hand grenade—then I get shot in the ass! And all from trying to steal that damn radio!"

The McGuire Rig

Sergeant First Class Charles McGuire invented this rig for extraction from places where the helicopter couldn't land. Before he came up with this thing, if you made contact you had to go someplace where the helicopter could set down—except, in a lot of areas, there weren't any.

The first McGuire rigs were just ropes that were tossed out of the helicopter doors, one end on each side. It was pretty primitive. There were all sorts of versions of the thing, but at first you had to just tie a couple of loops in the rope, stick your leg in one and an arm in the other, and hang on.

The helicopter pilot had to go straight up. If he went left or right even a little bit you would be dragged through the trees and possibly killed. Then you just had to hold on and wait until the helicopter got back to friendly territory. You flew along at about ninety knots, and you tried to put the wind on your back, otherwise the air would dry out your eyes and mouth.

It was extremely painful. You rode for very long distances, and when you landed there would be guys with stretchers waiting. When you took off that rappel seat, all the blood rushed into your legs—it hurt so bad that it was like somebody beating you with a baseball bat.

When they put me on that stretcher I always swore, in very vulgar terms, that I would never get back on that thing again. But the next time we got in trouble, I would climb right back in it again! They would call on the radio, "You can make your way to an LZ, or we will make one for you with five-hundred-pounders, or you can come out on the McGuire rigs," and I'd say, "Throw the ropes down!"

LZ Building, the Easy Way

When a mission was going well, and everything was smooth—no contact with the enemy—I sometimes would call up the recon plane and report, "I just saw two hundred North Vietnamese, a tank, and several buildings at such-and-such coordinates" and then sit back and watch. Pretty soon the B-52s would come over and wipe out a huge section of jungle. Then they'd call back and say, "Okay, now recon it."

I would tell them, "It will take a few hours." We would stay right where we were for a few hours, take it easy, and then call them up with a report. "You killed X number of NVA, destroyed X number of tanks and buildings. Great job!" If you told them they killed a hundred trees they wouldn't come back again, so I gave them this hellacious story.

We continued with our mission, mined the trail or whatever, and then moved to the area that they had just bombed. Even if there had been something there before, there wasn't anything there now, and we called for extraction. They never seemed to catch on, to put two and two together. I did that many, many times!

The AK-47 versus the M16

The AK was more dependable than the M16, but it was harder to hold on target. But I always knew it would fire. The M16 wasn't like that. As a matter of fact, on one occasion my CAR-15 wouldn't fire; we were in a fight, and it had been firing, and all of a sudden it quit. I threw it on the ground and was about to kick it when I noticed that it had a bullet hole through the magazine well that had jammed the bolt. I looked at that and thought, Holy shit!

I carried the AK for about six months, but then I quit using it. We had been using rounds we called "soap chips," part of a program we had to psychologically mess with the NVA. Part of it involved planting diaries on the bodies of enemy soldiers we killed. The other part involved planting exploding rounds in AK magazines that we left for the NVA to pick up and use.

I had a box of these rounds that had been reloaded with explosive instead of regular powder. We would put one of these in with regular magazines. Then, when we made contact with the enemy and killed some, I'd swap one of these magazines with theirs. They would pick up the mag and use it, and the weapon would blow up in their face. But then we started hearing that some Americans were picking the AKs up as souvenirs, and firing them, and some were killed by these explosive rounds, so I started to reconsider using them at all.

The diaries were a different part of the same deal. They didn't have a name in them, just a series of homesick entries. They were heartbreaking. When we killed one of the NVA, we'd plant one of these things on the body. The guy's buddies would find it and read it. We were warned not to ever get captured with this stuff on you—it would mean big trouble. So I always carried mine in a little plastic bag that I could ditch easily.

Becoming a Green Beret

It has always been extremely difficult to become a Green Beret, although that sometimes hasn't been obvious right away. It requires athletic ability plus intelligence; it demands individual initiative plus the ability to fit onto a team. Rather than the big, brutish *Rambo*-types, real Green Berets tend to be scrawny guys, built like cross-country runners rather than football linemen.

From the day in 1960 when President John F. Kennedy popularized the group, the Green Berets have had a kind of romantic aura about them that attracts many "wanna-bes." It was true during the Vietnam years and it is still true today. As a result, the standards for admission were, and are, extremely high. It is not easy to become a Green Beret.

Most people in SF are sergeants, although there is a small, hard core of officers who've made it a career. For officers it has often been just another "ticket punch" that is part of the career progression toward senior rank. But for the sergeants, Special Forces is a calling and a career that may last thirty years.

The selection and training process takes about six months today, just as it did thirty years ago. Applicants must already be in the Army, must either have been to "jump" school or ready to go, and have plenty of time left on their enlistments.

There are three phases to the training program. The first is the hardest, and isn't really training, but a selection process. Candidates are pushed physically and emotionally from the moment they step off the bus until they either break or survive the month-long initial phase. It used to be common for people to quit within a few minutes of arrival, the stress was so great.

The new SF candidates arrive at the flag pole at Camp MacCall, a remote and decayed facility on the outskirts of Fort Bragg, North Carolina. The men pile off the bus with their duffel bags. The cadre then escort the new aspirants to their new home—at a run, up a long hill, with a heavy duffel bag, in the oppressive heat and humidity. By the time the last straggler arrives in the camp, the group is already lighter by several men. They've been tested, and some have already failed.

The real purpose of the first month has always been to get rid of the people who aren't up to standard mentally or physically. There is a lot of running, but SF candidates don't just run, they wear rucksacks with a sandbag inside. And they don't just run a measured course, with a finish line, they run from point to point, not knowing how long it will be until they are allowed to stop. Seventeen miles is a common distance for one of these little waddles in the woods. This is a test of emotional and physical endurance, but mostly of resolve. It is brutal to watch. Stress fractures and injuries are common. It has always been common for men to keep running with blood squishing around in their boots. Anything less than a sucking chest wound is considered sissy stuff.

Camp MacCall is the decrepit remnant of a World War II facility. Until recently trainees lived in very old, decayed barracks or in tents. The headquarters building was a tarpaper shack. The latrine, for as long as anybody can remember, has been called the John Wayne Memorial Shitter. The old buildings have been recently replaced with somewhat more modern structures, and the old latrine was replaced by a very modern, expensive, politically correct, solar-powered building that doesn't work right but that is still called the John Wayne Memorial Shitter.

—*Hans Halberstadt*

RUSSELL MANN

Russ Mann has just retired from the Army as a master sergeant after a long career in the active duty and reserve component. He served two "official" tours in Vietnam (which means that he also went over on "unofficial" assignments that he isn't supposed to talk about). He was a medic in Special Forces and now works as an emergency room nurse, where he still gets to work on mangled bodies and gunshot wounds. These stories are from 1968–69 and the siege at the old French fortified position called Khe Sanh just below the border with North Vietnam.

Yards and Grenades

The scariest thing I did in the Vietnam war was to teach Montagnards to throw hand grenades. Montagnards were primitive tribal people who lived in the central highlands of Vietnam. "Yards," as we affectionately called them, were an ethnic minority in Vietnam. Short of stature, stocky and square-faced, they were dismissed as *moi* or *savages* by the Vietnamese, who, by contrast, were slender, lighter skinned, and lived in the lowlands and cities.

The Yards were easy to recruit. They nursed a smoldering hatred of the Vietnamese that had been nurtured by generations of prejudice, abuse, and neglect. The opportunity to kill Vietnamese appealed to them. We tried to ensure that they only killed North Vietnamese!

Hand grenades were a problem, however. Montagnards culturally do not throw. They have no games that require throwing. They don't even throw rocks at their chickens. Hand grenades are heavy; each weighs about two pounds. They aren't easy to throw, even for athletic Americans.

We had to start from scratch. We began with small stones thrown at close targets and gradually increased the weight and distance. This was all taken in good spirits by the Yards, who were more than willing to humor the crazy Americans as long as they got to kill some Vietnamese.

The final exam in hand grenade training was to throw a live grenade over a four-foot earthen berm. The student would crouch behind the berm with an American instructor, pull the pin, and lob the grenade over the berm. Not all the students passed this exam.

All too often, a poorly thrown grenade would fail to clear the top of the berm. Instead, it would come skidding and tumbling back down the slope, hissing softly and trailing a thin spiral of smoke, toward the fear-paralyzed student.

The instructor had three courses of possible action, depending on the location of the grenade and the time available—five seconds or less. He could pick up the grenade and throw it over the berm; he could kick the grenade into a nearby trench dug for the purpose; or he could grab the student and dive into the trench. The last option was the least desirable.

The bottom of the trench was knee-deep mud, a mixture of monsoon rains and loose earth homogenized by the exploding grenades. A frantic dive into the trench and the subsequent mud-soaked exit was a source of great amusement to the tribesmen. Any of the Montagnards not otherwise occupied would gather at the grenade range to socialize and to gamble on the outcome of the next student's performance.

As the lowest ranking member of the team, I usually drew the duty as hand grenade instructor. It was a pretty good trade-off: The Montagnards learned to throw hand grenades, and I learned how to stay calm in a crisis—a skill that has served me well since then. I developed a great fondness for the Yards. If it was a slow day, I would occasionally dive into the trench just to amuse them.

As a token of their appreciation for my efforts to teach and entertain them, they presented me with a necklace of rhinoceros beetle carapaces strung together. The village shaman placed it around my neck and solemnly assured me of its protective powers. "VC shoot—no die!" I guess it worked.

I am sure the conclusion of the Vietnam war did nothing to mellow the racial enmity between the Montagnards and the Vietnamese. I wonder if the Yards are still throwing hand grenades?

Khe Sanh

Khe Sanh had originally been a Special Forces camp, with an A-detachment nearby at a site called Lang Vei. The Marines got interested in it because of the airstrip that had originally been built by the SF team and the local tribesmen.

By early February 1968 there were about five thousand Marines at Khe Sanh, about four thousand inside the wire and another thousand or so stationed at outposts on hilltops and listening posts in the vicinity.

The Studies and Observation Group [SOG] maintained FOB-3 at Khe Sanh. SOG used the forward operating base to launch teams into the border area surrounding Khe Sanh, primarily to observe traffic on the Ho Chi Minh Trail across the border. These recon teams were small units, just two or three Americans and four or five Bru Montagnards.

The Bru were the local tribe, the northernmost tribe within South Vietnam. They were probably the least warlike of any of the tribes, an agricultural society less interested in hunting and less territorial than other tribes to the south, like the Rhade. They were pretty calm, not as aggressive, compared to the Rhade. But they were competent soldiers, and they worked well in large groups. They were accustomed to working together in teams in their civilian farming activities, so they worked well in platoon-sized units.Like other Montagnards, they were "salt-of-the-earth" folks, very pleasant people. They were rather like midwestern American farmers, with good work ethics, honest. They'd open their houses to you . . . and they really wanted to hear what the Americans were preaching about involvement in the government of South Vietnam where they'd been second-class citizens for many years.

The Khe Sanh Cooking School

I had a bunker on the line at Khe Sanh that I shared with two other guys; we had an old M1919A6 Browning .30-caliber machine gun in there that we crewed. Because we were under siege, a lot of rather funny "head" things happened. We couldn't do much, and some of the things that we could do assumed great ritualistic importance. We drew them out. One of these was food.

Food was the only pleasure. There was no sex, no drinking, just a little card playing, so the only really personal satisfaction available to us was food. But all we had were C-rations for about three months.

There are only twelve different kinds of C-rations, and at the rate of three a day, they get old in a hurry. So we got very inventive at taking a little from one and mixing it with some of another and coming up with something entirely different. We actually had contests to see who could come up with the most inventive thing from C-rations.

Meals became an important ritual; when it was time for lunch, we could spread it out for a whole hour of preparation. We had to scrounge all the right ingredients, collect the various cans, trade with other guys, and then open our cans and portion everything out very carefully. We'd add salt and pepper, Tabasco sauce from one of your friends, and one of the guys on the team was a Mexican, so he had some salsa; if you really begged and pleaded he would give you a little of the salsa for your meal.

When everything was all lined up, it was time to heat it up. We cooked on an empty C-ration can on top of another can, with a little pinch of C4 explosive for fuel. You'd light the C4, then put one can on top of the other, and that was the stove.

Anyway, I was in my bunker and had completed lengthy preparations for lunch. I had all the cans lined up in the order I intended to heat them, on the sill of the firing slit of the bunker. I had just finished toasting my bread and was almost ready to dive into my meal, when I heard a loud crack from the front, probably two or three hundred meters away, followed instantly by a tremendous explosion on the front of my bunker.

The bunker immediately filled with dust. When my team members ran in to get me they were yelling, "Russ! Russ! Are you okay?"

I was beside myself with anger. "Those motherfuckers! Those bastards! Did you see what they did to my lunch!" All my cans had shrapnel holes in them, and a layer of dust and dirt on top of the food. Although I had just escaped death by a small margin, that didn't seem nearly as important at the moment as what had happened to my lunch.

My Team Sergeant

I'll call him Sergeant "Smith," but (for a variety of reasons) that's not his real name. He was a fabulously interesting character, a person born to be a warrior, unable to adapt to normal peacetime society. Outside of combat he was a drunk, a womanizer—not a person you would like to be around. But in combat he was wonderful. He was a veteran of the Korean War and had gotten into Special Forces at the outset. He had been one of the early SF guys who hid out in First Group. First Group during the 1960s was loaded with characters, and he was one of them.

Sergeant "Smith" did a lot of interesting things. For example, we had been inside the wire at Khe Sanh for a long time and were getting tired of being shot at. We wanted to do something—anything! Instead of sitting there and get shot at while doing nothing we decided to go out and "do" a few of them; we'd still get shot at, but we'd at least have the satisfaction of doing something to them.

So we snuck out of our wire with a patrol early one morning, about 0300 and well before first light. We crept out the wire and managed to get out to the NVA trenches a quarter to a half mile from the wire without being observed.

We had about a hundred Montagnards and about a dozen Americans. As the dawn rose we started to fire into their trench line, and then we and the North Vietnamese traded hand grenades with each other for a while. After a while we thought it was about time to withdraw. We thought this would be a good idea to do sometime before we were flanked and then surrounded. We had gone out and made our statement, gotten their attention, and they outnumbered us by a huge proportion, so it was time to go.

We counted noses; only one man had been wounded. He had splinters from the wooden handle of a "Chicom" [Chinese communist] grenade in his face. I pulled those out, bandaged him up, and everybody was looking pretty good. So Sergeant "Smith" said, "You know what would really surprise 'em? Let's charge!"

So we lined everybody up, shoulder to shoulder, and roared back to the trenches, whooping and hollering, throwing grenades and shooting. We got to the trenches, shot them up, threw more grenades into some bunkers, and then got the hell out of there before we all got killed! We got back to Khe Sanh shortly thereafter. That was the kind of thing my team sergeant liked to do!

"Don't Bother Me, Boy, I'm Thinking"

We were on another patrol outside Khe Sanh, a small operation with about a dozen Americans and Montagnards and, well, *ambushed* isn't quite the word . . . we *blundered* into a group of NVA and began to trade fire with them. As we had been trained, we assembled in a circular defensive position. This was not, under the circumstances, a really smart thing to do.

We were enormously outnumbered. The NVA forces outside Khe Sanh have been variously estimated at between twenty thousand and forty thousand men. We were definitely playing on their turf. It didn't take long, only a minute or two, for them to flank us—and then surround us. They were pouring pretty heavy fire into us. We had a couple of folks wounded.

I looked to see where "Top" [an informal and affectionate name for senior sergeants within units] was. I turned around, and there he was, sprawled in the middle of the position, flat on his back with his arms and legs out at odd angles.

Oh, shit, I thought, *Top's been hit!* So I directed the two guys on either side of me to cover my field of fire and crawled back to him. I reached out my hand to touch his neck, checking for a pulse; as soon as I touched him, his eyes opened and he looked at me. "Don't bother me, boy," he said. "I'm thinking."

I said, "Okay, Top," and crawled back to my position.

After a little while, probably only a minute or so, he stood up—in the middle of all the NVA fire—and gave us our orders. "We're breaking out thataway," he said. We all aimed our fire in that direction, to clear a path, threw a few hand grenades, and off we went. And it worked . . . we broke contact and got back to Khe Sanh. There aren't a lot of guys who will lay down in the middle of a firefight, close their eyes to think and get their mind straight—he was an amazing guy!

Hatchet Force

In addition to the recon teams were what we called Hatchet Forces—company-sized units of Montagnards that were used to exploit information developed by the recon teams. The hatchet teams were used especially against things like NVA truck parks or other targets that weren't suitable for bombing. Hatchet teams were also used to rescue recon teams that were in trouble.

My combat experience was a little different from some guys in SF because I was assigned to a hatchet force. I have seen, shot at, and killed NVA soldiers. When a hatchet force was sent in, it went in to fight. There was a target to be destroyed or a recon team in trouble that had to be rescued. When we got the call, there was no doubt about it, there was a "hot" LZ, and we were going to fight.

We never had to go far, either. The helicopters put us very close to our objective, or, when we were rescuing a team, we were put right on top of the team and we were fighting as soon as we got off the helicopters. As a result, we went in very heavy. It was common to go in with a rucksack that weighed eighty to one hundred pounds, loaded with ammunition and hand grenades. Most of my missions were: Go in quick, fight like hell, get the hell out. Unlike some of my friends on the deep recon teams, I didn't have the luxury of watching the NVA from a distance and at leisure.

Rats

Almost anybody who went to Vietnam will have a rat story for you. I don't know what the species is, but the Vietnamese rats can be huge and aggressive. The problem we had at Khe Sanh was that the camp was being "cultivated" by enemy artillery much as if it were being plowed on a daily basis, and sanitation was pretty much nonexistent. There was no place to put the garbage—the garbage dumps were being blown up, and there was garbage everywhere. That was part of it.

The other, related part was that it was worth your life to take a shower. Anybody who was above ground drew fire. So we didn't get to do much bathing, other than what we called the "whore's bath," out of our helmets, where we wiped ourselves down with a wet cloth. We went weeks without a real shower.

Since it was hot there, we perspired a lot and the perspiration dried, leaving a salty residue that was worst in our hair. The rats, which were multiplying in typical ratty fashion, had a craving for salt. They would wait until you were asleep and then sneak up and nibble your hair to get the salt crystals. That would not have been too bad, except that they'd occasionally stand on your face in the process! It was pretty scary to wake up in the middle of the night to have this large, furry thing all over your face.

We were frustrated; the enemy was just outside the wire, shelling us, but they couldn't be seen. We had nothing to vent our fury on, nothing really personal that we could do . . . so we declared war on the rats. There was an enemy we could reach, somebody we could do something about.

We mixed poisons, and we built traps, dead falls, snares, and all sorts of other things to kill the rats. Everybody had a favorite recipe for poison. For instance, if you mixed the C-ration peanut butter with the smoked cheese, then laced it with rat poison, you were supposed to have a sure-fire combination. There were all sorts of recipes, all based on C-ration ingredients.

Some guys were really terrified of the rats. You had to watch out for those guys because if a rat started crawling around the floor of the bunker they would start blazing away at the rat. It got to the point where a lot of guys would sleep with a pistol in one hand and a flashlight in the other. If they were awakened by one of the rats, they would try to kill it with the pistol—and were quite often successful.

Some guys would go so far as to shoot a rat off one of their sleeping bud-dies rather than to risk waking him up and having the rat get scared away, spoiling an otherwise clear shot. Of course the guy would wake up, some-what startled, but it was otherwise a pretty effective technique.

All of this was based on a fear of bubonic plague. Even though most of us were inoculated against it, a lot of people were worried about the possi-bility of catching it. There were reports from guys who had investigated enemy bunkers outside the wire after the siege that there were bodies of NVA present with symptoms of the disease. It was probably a real problem for the enemy because their living conditions just on the other side of the wire were as bad as ours, if not worse.

It was an interesting time for Special Forces—it was World War I all over again. We were fighting from trenches and bunkers, living under-ground, under constant artillery bombardment, with occasional enemy ground attacks. We were living under the constant threat of being overrun. There was no question in our minds that, if they attacked with all the per-sonnel they had opposing us, that they were going to trash us, that we were all going to die. The psychological pressure was enormous.

Joining the Tribe

I got inducted into the Rhade tribe at Kontum—a monumental tale!

After the siege of Khe Sanh was over, my team was reassigned to FOB-2 at Kontum, again to a hatchet force. We had a company-sized unit of Montagnards, mostly from the Rhade tribe. They were wonderful to work with, aggressive fighters. They liked playing with guns. It was like working with a bunch of fourteen-year-old American boys—they wanted to get out there and play! And they were anxious to kill almost any Vietnamese, north or south. It was our job to keep them pointed at the *North* Vietnamese.

After a month or two, the locals decided to induct us into the tribe. It started with about twenty tribesmen playing gongs of different sizes—a bit like watching Swiss people playing bells. The tunes were completely unrec-ognizable, of course, but the music was very pleasant.

Then we consumed a barbecued water buffalo. Now, we discovered that one of the reasons we got inducted into the tribe was that the locals realized that they could get the Americans to underwrite the cost of a big water buf-falo feed, complete with all the fixings, all paid for by the Americans. It was a real win-win situation.

So the buffalo was on the barbecue, and the band was playing, and then twenty or thirty earthen jugs of their rice wine or beer they called "Ooo." It was made from a rice mash, placed in the jar with a bamboo mesh mat on top of the mash to keep it in place. Water was added and the mixture allowed to ferment. You had to drink this stuff, and it was pretty "green."

There was a little measuring device on the top, and you were required to drink your allotted portion through a long straw. Then some more water would be added and the next guy would have to drink the same amount. You had to keep up and drink your "Ooo." It was a kind of social obligation, and you couldn't lose face. You had to eat all the food, smile and laugh, and drink round after round of the brew.

Well, I was never much of a drinker! The stuff went straight to my head. I finally realized that I was going to be sick, but when the thought entered my head that I was about to be ill, it was already too late. I managed to vomit an enormous amount of barbecued buffalo and rice wine into the lap of one of the tribesmen conducting the ceremony. Needless to say, he was an unhappy camper.

I managed to find my way outside and get myself together somewhat, then went back in for the ceremony. They put the tribal bracelet on our wrists—which we also were required to supply. Ten years earlier, in the good old days, the brass bracelets that identified the various tribes were handmade with great care, decorated with markings unique to each tribe. Then they discovered that they had a kind of racket going, with this semicontinuous party as new Special Forces guys rotated into the camp, each of whom would help pay for a water buffalo. So we got brass rings made from welding rod, which we had to supply, that they bent into a circle and gave back to us.

Well, there was an interesting climax to that night. I had been celibate for the entire time I had been in Vietnam . . . up to that point. My team sergeant had always been after me to join him in a foray to the local house of ill repute, and I had declined. That particular night, however, I was exceptionally drunk, and he recognized a moment of weakness! He made the suggestion again, and this time it sounded like a capital idea to me!

Unfortunately, it was monsoon season, and it was raining so hard that everything was obscured by a curtain of falling water. In addition, there was supposed to be an imminent enemy attack of the compound, so the camp was shut down tight; nobody was allowed in or out. Well, we certainly weren't going to let little things like those stop us.

Since it was hot and raining, we were wearing just cut-off fatigues. We got our .45s and crawled out of the camp, under the wire, through the mine field (although we had no clue where the mines were) and staggered over to Flower's establishment.

Now, Flower ran a house of prostitution that was about a hundred yards from our compound. Although it was officially frowned on by the Army, we had Flower and the girls visit our dispensary once a week to be checked for VD. It was much easier to keep half a dozen girls clean than a hundred guys. So Flower already knew me because I'd been examining her and her girls. We staggered up to the door and demanded to be let in.

They realized at once that we were going to be poor customers. We were dead drunk, had almost nothing on, and we were outside a camp that was supposed to be shut down tight. "No, no—go away! Come back tomorrow!" Flower said. So we demanded our rights as American fighting men and were allowed inside, perhaps just to shut us up so we wouldn't draw any more attention.

The building was a ramshackle affair built of bits of tin, stolen US Air Force plywood and other pilfered materials. It was like a rat warren of little cubicles. I was grabbed by the hand in the semidarkness and led to the rear of the building and a small room with a bed in it.

I was still quite drunk, and not in any condition to be the aggressor in this little passion play. So I just fell backward on the bed and was the completely passive partner. The young lady pulled my pants down and had her way with me. When she was done, I detected that she expected payment. It was dark in the room, and I couldn't remember how much money I had brought with me, so I just pulled out whatever was in my pocket and gave it to her. This was probably about ten times more that the going rate. I asked her then to lead me out, and on the way, we negotiated the maze, coming at last to where my team sergeant was sexually engaged with one of the resident maidens.

"Top," I said, "I'm all done, and I'm going outside."

"Just hold on; wait a minute," he said. "I'm almost done."

He concluded this sexual congress, zipped up his pants, and we were about to leave when an MP [military police] jeep stopped outside. The MP got out, walked directly to the door, and we thought, *Oh oh, we're in trouble now!* We didn't have any identification, we were out of uniform, and we were not supposed to be out of camp.

So we asked Flower where the back door was and made a break for it while the MP was coming in the front door. Then, while he was inside, we made our way to the front of the building—and realized that he had left the jeep's engine running! We immediately thought, Isn't this interesting! Here's a piece of Uncle Sam's equipment that clearly needs protecting. So we got in the jeep and drove back to the camp.

We got to the main gate, where a Vietnamese soldier was on guard. He refused to let us in. We were disheveled, out of uniform, soaking wet, and without identification. We tried all the usual techniques: "You know us! I'm *Bac-si* [*doctor* in Vietnamese]! You gotta let me in!"

The guard said, "Nope! Orders say, not let anybody in!"

We were getting worried. We figured that it was about time for that MP to come out of the whorehouse, so we both pulled our .45s and pointed them at this guy and told him to open the gate or we were going to shoot him right then and there. He concluded that discretion was the better part of valor and opened the gate and let us in.

We drove the jeep directly to the motor pool, shut the door, and immediately painted over the identification numbers on the bumpers of the jeep with cans of spray paint. By the time we were finished, it was about three in the morning, and we both tottled off toward bed. I hit the bed, and it seemed like I had just closed my eyes when a voice said, "Sergeant Mann, wake up. It's time for guard duty!" I had forgotten that I had guard duty that night. I was supposed to have the shift from 4:00 AM to 6:00 AM.

"God! Can't somebody else take it for me?" I begged.

"No. It's your turn; get up!"

So I got up and pulled my shift on guard duty, but when the sun came up I was one sorry young soldier! And that's how I was initiated into the Rhade tribe.

The Scrounger

Scrounging in the military is a fine old tradition. In Special Forces it's an art form. The scrounger at Khe Sanh was a guy named Craig Rowe. Craig was a good-looking guy in the Hollywood version of a Green Beret: about six-foot-four, one hundred and ninety pounds, well-proportioned, with a strong jaw and clear, glinting eyes. He was a persuasive speaker, and he could sell anything to anyone.

As a result, Craig was detailed by the sergeant major at Khe Sanh to go get stuff at depot installations like Da Nang. The sergeant major would say, "Craig, we really need another 'duce-and-a-half' [the Army two-and-a-half ton heavy truck]. See what you can do."

So Craig would fly down to Da Nang, where he would trade a few Viet

Cong flags and a few AK-47s for, say, a jeep. Then he'd take the jeep to, maybe, the 4th Infantry Division who didn't have any jeeps—because we'd already stolen them all. Craig traded the jeep for an ambulance, which he then drove to one of the medical companies where he would say something like, "I know you guys are short of ambulances. You probably don't need that duce-and-a-half over there; why don't you trade it to me?" And then he'd have the duce-and-a-half. Then he'd do some more trading, and come up with a supply of booze, sexual favors, or something of similar intrinsic value that was then used to get the crew of a C-130 to transport the truck to Khe Sanh. This was Craig's job, and he was superb at it.

Hangover Repair

Sergeant "Smith" and I shared a fighting position. He liked to have his medic nearby in case he got hit, but more importantly, he wanted me around for hangover repair. Although not so much at Khe Sanh, where booze was mostly unavailable, but elsewhere, I could expect to be awakened by my team sergeant telling me that I was going to cure his hangover or he was going to kick my ass!

Our fighting position was just big enough for two men, just forward of the trench, with a step and cutouts for storing grenades. Well, at the sergeant's direction, we had stored about two hundred hand grenades in this position, all removed from their little containers and sleeves, ready to throw.

For the floor of the position we had several twenty-pound satchel charges that we made from C4 blocks, with ten-second fuses and fuse lighters attached. We probably had about one hundred sixty pounds of C4 under our feet in this fighting position. The satchel charges were assembled on the expectation that we would, sooner or later, be overrun, probably by tanks. The camp at Lang Vei nearby had recently been overrun by NVA tanks, and we expected that when the North Vietnamese came—as we were sure they would—we were all going to die.

I was unsure just how we were supposed to die, and asked Top for a little clarification of exactly what his plan for us was supposed to be. He said, "The satchel charges are for the tanks. When they come, we'll just duck down and light the fuses on these things, then stick them up on the tank treads. They'll roll past us and the charges will go off. If they're real close, we can just throw the charges on top of the tank."

"Well," I said, "what about all the hand grenades?"

"When we get overrun, you and I will just hunker down and we are going to take turns throwing hand grenades in all directions. I figure we can hold out for two or three hours this way!" It was not a bad plan. But he was very matter of fact about the way we were going to die.

Coping with Combat

There was a enormous difference at Khe Sanh between the Special Forces personnel present and the Marines. Now, I don't mean to say anything bad about the Marines, because they were good soldiers—but they were kids! They were seventeen to twenty years old, most of them, and had maybe four months of training before they were shipped off to fight the good fight in Vietnam. They were really mentally unprepared.

Special Forces, on the other hand, were not kids. The average age was probably about thirty! We had three Korean War vets on my team, and so we had that maturity. Also, there was a much higher level of professionalism. We weren't there for a short haul, anxious to go home; this was our profession, this was what we did for a living. We expected to keep coming back to Vietnam until the war was over, because we were professional soldiers. And when that war was over, we'd be sent off to another one someplace else. It was a different head space. While this wasn't true for every guy in Special Forces, it was certainly the pervasive feeling.

Even the youngest guy on the team (as I was) had a lot of experience. I'd been in the Army two years before I went to Vietnam, a year and a half of which had been training, rather than sixteen weeks. And it was high-intensity training! Even before we deployed to Vietnam, we got a full month of training as a team, to get our teamwork together—much like a football team has its pre-season practice. We had a chance to identify the strengths and weaknesses of each guy on the team.

For example, I was a young "buck" sergeant [three stripes, lowest ranking real sergeant rank] and assigned to lead a night patrol out of the wire to set up a listening post. Well, a listening post at Khe Sanh was an enormously scary operation; you were supposed to sit out there and wait for the enemy to overrun you. When they did, you were supposed to make a lot of noise to let the guys in the camp know that you were being killed (delaying them not at all), and the camp could then get ready to be attacked. It was a kind of "throwaway" position.

I had not been in combat before; I had only been in the country for a month or so. I was adrift from all my friends, utterly alone except for two or three other Americans and five or six Montagnard tribesmen—surrounded by maybe forty thousand enemy. It was a very scary feeling.

The other two Americans were both SF engineers. We all crept out of the wire under cover of darkness, not too far . . . maybe a half a mile or so. We snuggled into the jungle for the night in the only good defensive position around, an old graveyard, a small position about twenty yards across and containing about a dozen headstones. The headstones were the only cover around, and we snuggled in behind them and lay there quietly. One of the other Americans was next to me, our boots touching so that we could warn each other without speaking in the event of danger.

In grand Special Forces tradition, we had taken Dexedrine (a.k.a. "Green Beret candy") so we could stay wide awake all night. We were wired! We were watching intently for any enemy movement, hoping that we would have enough warning to call the camp on the radio, report "Yep—they're coming!" and run like hell.

While we were lying there quietly, we heard a tremendous explosion! The explosion jarred me for a moment, and then I thought, "Aw, shit, now they've found us! They're dropping mortars in on us!" I looked around for the guy on my right, and he was gone! I thought, "Oh, no, I'm in the middle of forty thousand NVA, and my sidekick runs off the first time we take fire!"

Then I heard a kind of low moaning sound, which turned out to be coming from one of the Bru tribesmen. I started examining him by touch since this was not a place where I wanted to use a flashlight. During this examination, I discovered that one of his arms was no longer attached to the rest of his body.

I called to the team, all of whom were within a ten-yard perimeter. "We gotta get out of here! We've been spotted. They're mortaring us. We've got to run for it."

I directed the other American to take the Montagnards to another position and set up a base of fire, while I used them as a screen to evacuate the Bru casualty. So I patched this guy up as well as I could, attended briefly to another Bru who had been less seriously wounded, and got ready to go. The rest of the team crawled off as I had ordered them to do and prepared to set up to screen me as I hauled this guy back to base. Well, I knew there was no way I could drag him all the way back to the wire. It was too far to crawl while dragging him—I would have to stand up.

Unfortunately, the noise we created attracted the attention of the guys back inside the wire at Khe Sanh, and they started sending up flares, thinking that they were under attack. That was the last thing that I wanted! There I was, out in a clear field of fire, in a virtual spotlight from the flares. I picked up the Montagnard and threw him over my back and stood up. This was probably the only consciously brave thing I have ever done because I knew that when I stood up I would be "skylighted" and an obvious target. But I couldn't think of any alternative; if I didn't get him back to base he was going to die. So I just gritted my teeth, thought, Fuck it! and stood up with this guy and ran back toward the base.

We all made it, except for the guy who had been next to me and had disappeared. I assumed that he had just cut and run—I couldn't think of any other reason for him to be gone.

During our debriefing, the guy questioning me said, "What the fuck happened to you?"

I said, "Nothing, I'm fine."

"Look at yourself," he said. Only then did I notice that my right side was coated, about a quarter of an inch thick, with hamburger—which was all that was left of most of the guy who had been next to me. I knew it was him, because he was a black guy, and there were little pieces of black skin. I realized that something truly awful had happened.

We went back the next morning, in force, to see if we could find any more of his remains. We recovered his head and one of his legs. It appeared that he had either had taken a direct hit from a mortar that had set off the Claymore mine he was carrying under his shirt, or that something else had set it off accidentally.

A lot of the guys theorized that this latter possibility was what had happened. I couldn't believe it myself. He was an engineer, and the use of explosives was his specialty. He wouldn't have been so stupid as to carry the Claymore "primed" [with a blasting cap installed in the device]. I have always liked to think that he took a direct hit from something that set off the Claymore.

Water Truck Follies at Khe Sanh

We tended to see humor in things that other people might find horrifying. One of the funniest things at Khe Sanh was the water truck. FOB-3, our camp at Khe Sanh, was perched just outside the Marine wire and didn't have a direct source of water. We were dependent on the Marines for water, and we had a water truck to go get it. It was a five-ton truck we'd scrounged from God-knows-where, and it had a great big water tank on it, and that's what we used.

This truck was one of the few things that rolled in our camp, and anything that rolled at Khe Sanh was a target. While that included helicopters, C-130s, and people, it especially included our water truck. Whenever any of these things moved, it attracted the attention of the NVA artillery spotters who then called down fire upon it. As a consequence, our water truck was a much-wounded veteran. A great many artillery shells had gone off in its vicinity, and it had been patched many times.

We had a guy in the unit whose name I never discovered, but who was universally called Gomer. He had a mechanical bent, and so his only jobs were to keep the generator running to power the lights in the bunkers, and to keep the water truck running. He did most of his work at night.

The water truck was covered with patches he had welded on, all over this truck. The job of actually driving the water truck was highly dangerous and was rotated among the junior sergeants in the unit. I drove it twice.

There were two problems to driving this truck. The first, of course, was that you were a target. But the second was that, unlike anywhere else, you couldn't hear the incoming round that the enemy had fired at you and consequently could not take evasive action. Normally, when their artillery fired, you had three to five seconds to find a hole. But while driving the water truck you couldn't hear the round, so you had to watch the other soldiers and Marines along this dusty road. If they suddenly broke into a run, then you had to throw the transmission into neutral, jam on the brakes, and dive out the door (if you thought there was time), or lie down on the seat if you thought impact was imminent. Then, as soon as the round exploded, you jumped back into the seat, slammed it in gear, and roared off until it happened again.

Several guys were wounded while driving the water truck. It was always a little scary to climb in and discover that the dark brown stain on the seat was the blood of the previous driver.

The Marine water point was just under the airfield control tower. Both of these things were like aiming stakes for the NVA gunners. The heaviest concentration of artillery rounds impacted in and around the control tower. The Marines had huge rubber bladders to hold the thousands of gallons of water, a pump and filter set up, plus a Marine water purification specialist to run the whole thing. People came to him all day to draw their water.

For some reason there was only one guy to run this water point at any one time. And he got killed on a regular basis because of the high density of artillery fire on this location. As soon as one of these specialists got killed, the Marines radioed back to Da Nang for another one. So the new guy would show up, be shown the pumps and tanks and other equipment, and then he'd invariably ask, "So, what happened to the last water point guy?"

"*Which* other water point guy?" the reply tended to be.

"The water point guy before me?"

"Oh, *him*. He got killed."

"Well, what about the guy before him?"

"He got killed too."

"And what happened to the guy before him?"

"He's dead too."

"Uh . . . how long did they last?"

"A couple of days, sometimes a week or two."

I can't understand why the Marines did that, why they didn't rotate these guys and let them try to survive a week or so, then let them go back to Da Nang and bring in somebody else—but they didn't. Apparently the TO&E [Table of Organization and Equipment] said that there was supposed to be one water point specialist, and one it was, until he got killed.

I will never forget the look on the faces of these water point guys. They were the walking dead; they knew their life span was limited. They could go in the next minute, or they might last a week or two, but they knew they were dead men. There was no doubt about it. But somehow they bore up. They would do their job and dispatch the water. But they were pale, with sunken eyes and a kind of hunted expression.

Well, we'd get our water and drive back to our part of the camp, then drive around the line and distribute the water. Every fifty yards or so there was a drum to put the water in, and the troops filled their canteens from these drums.

So driving the water truck was pretty funny. And it got to the point where the Marines knew that if our water truck was moving, it was going to get shot at. Well, when they saw the water truck coming they didn't bother to wait for the NVA to shoot, they just jumped into their holes. But the driver saw all these guys jumping in holes and assumed that artillery was on the way in. He'd bail out, find cover and—when nothing happened right away—conclude that it was a false alarm and hop back in and drive off a ways further. But he would only get about fifty meters up the road before a fresh batch of Marines would again jump in their holes and the process would be repeated. It could take all day sometimes to drive the mile to the water point and back.

Ambush

I don't know how much patrolling the Marines did around Khe Sanh, but we were pretty active outside the base. And we kept getting asked to do these goofy things. Somebody had decided that Special Forces would be the ideal place to test new gadgets.

On one occasion we were supposed to go out and plant some vibration sensors; they were shaped like small trees and resembled foliage. As we were preparing for this mission, somebody came to us with a request. He said, "Since you guys are going out on patrol, why don't you take along these nifty new squad radios? Try 'em out and let us know how they work."

They were really slick little radios and came in two parts. Each was about the size of a pack of cigarettes, with a loop of wire between them. They attached to the shoulder portion of your combat harness, with the transmitter on one side, the receiver on the other, and the wire across the back. We said, "Okay, we'll give them a shot."

"These things are still in the developmental stage," the guy said, "and they are super secret! Nobody knows about these things. This is their first field test. Be careful and don't lose them!"

Well, this was my very first combat patrol. I'd probably been in the camp only a couple of weeks. So we got together, planned the mission, and hooked up the radios. They seemed really neat! And then off we went to put in these sensors.

When we'd gotten the sensors installed in the designated spot, we began to work our way back to the camp. We had been taking a little break by the side of the trail and were just getting ready to start back when this little attack began. We were only about a mile out when we started to come under sporadic small arms fire, and then mortar fire, from an enemy force that clearly had a good look at us. It wasn't much of an ambush, and wasn't well organized—just a hasty ambush—but they were clearly shooting at us and rounds were coming really close to us.

Well, we all got up and took off at a dead run toward the base. We had gone about a hundred yards when the assistant team leader, a lieutenant, suddenly realized that he had left his radio back where we had been resting. "Shit!" he said, "My radio's gone!"

I was the last guy in line, "tail-end Charley." I said, "Okay, cover me. I'll go back and get it." So I ran back the hundred yards to where we had been. In the meantime, the NVA had moved up on both sides of the trail after us. As I ran back, it was like running a gauntlet. They fired at me from both sides of the trail, all the way back. I found the radio, picked it up, and ran back to the rest of the team, all of whom were standing there with their mouths open with an amazed expression on their faces.

I'm sure the NVA were shooting each other while I was running up the trail, but they all missed me, out of sheer luck. When I got back to the group my team sergeant said, "Boy, what the fuck do you think you're doing?"

We got back to base without any casualties and with all the radios. When the enormity and stupidity of what I had done finally struck me, I resolved to never do anything so foolish again. And I didn't.

But when you are in combat for the first time, there is a kind of John Wayne syndrome. We've all seen combat movies, and the good guys never get killed. There is shot and shell everywhere, and yet they manage to get through unscathed. So the first time I was under artillery fire, I was astounded. I just stood there, looking around, saying, "Wow! Look at all this. They're shooting at us!"

Meantime, the rest of my team was all underground, in our bunker. Finally, the senior medic yelled, "Get out of there, you! You dumb son of a bitch! Get in a trench!"

Going Wild

I won't tell you this guy's name, but this is a true story.

A close friend of mine was an SF medic assigned to a team in the highlands, a regular A camp out in the bushes. He was working with the Montagnards, one of whom had become a good friend and whom my friend was training to be a medic. My friend was invited to this guy's house, was made a member of the tribe, and they had a close relationship.

The relationship between the Americans and the Yards was good, but relations with the Vietnamese LLDB [Vietnamese special forces] was uncomfortable. For some reason the LLDB had this Montagnard killed.

My friend became totally unbalanced. He adopted the Montagnard attitude: The only good Vietnamese was a dead Vietnamese. He packed his rucksack, collected his weapon, left the A camp, and disappeared into the jungle. He went wild for several months. He killed every Vietnamese he saw, regardless of what side they were on. If they were Vietnamese, they were dead.

Eventually he was "convinced to return" to American military control. My friend was smuggled out of South Vietnam, was sent back to the United States, and was then promptly discharged from the Army. Special Forces took care of its own. Only an SF soldier could do something like that—disappear into the jungle for months, alone.

Medical Chase

This is something I try to use today when I train paramedics who sometimes whine about the stress of their work, dealing with life and death on the streets. While that stress exists, I like to tell them a little story to show that their stress isn't at the level that they think it is.

While I was assigned to FOB-2 at Kontum, I (along with the other medics in the camp) had the job of medical chase. This was a dangerous job. When a team was being inserted, across the border or wherever, the last helicopter in the flight was the medical chase ship. If the LZ turned out to be hot, if the team got hit when they landed, then the medical chase ship had to go in to pull the wounded guys out.

This was not like a conventional med-evac anywhere else, where the LZ would be secured before the helicopter could be called in. Anywhere else you'd have one or two companies of infantry fighting off the NVA while the helicopters came in for the wounded. But when our medical ship went in, the LZ was always hot.

On one of these missions, the team was inserted and then was hit pretty bad. The LZ was pretty hot, with fire coming from both sides of the LZ. As we approached the ground I could see the Americans converge where the helicopter was going to land. Well, before the skids hit the ground, while we were still a foot or so in the air, these guys rose out of the grass like apparitions, and they threw their dead and wounded into the helicopter. We were on the ground no more than about five seconds before we were off again, airborne.

I had a half-dozen dead and wounded people on the deck of the helicopter, and that is not a very large space. Even though the seats had been removed from the helicopter to provide more room, I had what amounted to a pile of people to deal with.

I had to decide what to do first. They were bleeding; some were crying out. It seemed like an eternity, but it was probably just a few seconds before I concluded that I must figure out who was dead. I did quick, cursory examinations and identified the dead ones. I put them on the bottom, so I could stand on them while I was working on the living.

You can do all the basic stuff in a helicopter: ensure an adequate airway, stop the bleeding, plug up any chest wounds, and start IVs to replenish fluid volume. About fifty percent of combat medicine involves plugging up holes—holes that are leaking blood, or brains, or lungs. That's about half of it. Then if you can get in an IV, that's a bonus.

But these are young, healthy guys you're dealing with. You don't have to worry about cardiac problems or long-standing cardiopulmonary disease conditions. It's just pure trauma to young, healthy guys. Plug the holes, set up an IV, administer morphine if the guy is in a lot of pain—pretty easy stuff. But you have to get your head in the right place and approach it as if you were a mechanic working on a car. You can't afford to get emotionally involved. You find the problem, fix it, and move on to the next one. You can get emotional later.

And it worked out okay; at least the wounded guys didn't die on the helicopter on the way back. Modern paramedics aren't used to the idea that there are times when you might have to stand on dead people to help living ones.

Montagnards and the LLDB

The South Vietnamese had some good units: the ARVN (Army of the Republic of Vietnam) Rangers, ARVN Airborne were pretty good—but the LLDB was two-faced.

First, they got the money that was supplied by the US that was supposed to be used to develop the camps where the Montagnards lived and the money that was supposed to pay the Montagnard soldiers. Well, wrong answer! The Vietnamese kept the money.

Vietnamese society ran like that. And I don't think that we can just apply American standards to Vietnamese society, that we can say that since they aren't like us that they are all screwed up. Their society runs differently than ours; anything you need to get done requires a bribe. That's just the way it is. The higher you are in the Vietnamese government or military, the more money you make from bribes. That's the prime benefit of promotion.

As a result, the LLDB played all sorts of games with the payrolls for the Montagnards. The program had been set up by the US with the LLDB paying the tribesmen in an effort to make the Republic of Vietnam government look good in the eyes of the Montagnards. But the effect was the opposite. The LLDB's handling of these programs made the Vietnamese government look like dog shit in the eyes of the Montagnards.

On Being a Vietnam Veteran

I'm always suspicious when I meet someone and the first words out of his mouth are, "I'm a Vietnam veteran." These are people who've never left the 1960s, whose whole lives are wrapped up in that experience. That's all they are ever going to be, and they believe that they deserve something because of that.

Well, the statistics say that the ratio of front-line combat troops to support personnel was about one to ten. And yet, in all my experience, I've only met one or two guys who claimed to be Vietnam vets and would admit to being a cook or a truck driver! They all were combat soldiers! It is bullshit!

I think a lot of the so-called delayed stress syndrome has to do with the extreme youth and immaturity of many of the people who served in Vietnam, along with a lack of training. I can't think of any people within my circle of friends from Vietnam who has anything like delayed stress syndrome. Now, this makes no sense to me because we in SF had some of the hairiest missions over there.

The experience for me, and the guys I was with, went in stages. First, there was disbelief that any of this could harm you; it was like watching a movie where you have an emotional separation from the event. It was not particularly frightening. Then the reality gradually strikes home as you become more exposed. It is now scary, but there is still that detachment that tells you that you are not going to be one of the people who gets hurt. You think, *It's scary, but I'm not one of the guys who is going to get hit.*

Then some of your own friends get killed, and you start to think that perhaps your own death is not as far off as you previously thought. Then you become scared, have nightmares, and begin to worry about what will happen on the next patrol.

If you can get past that, you occasionally get to a point where you start to need a "fix," even though after every patrol you think, *I am going to do everything in my power to avoid ever having to do that again.* But a week or two will go by, and life begins to get a little flat, somehow. There is something missing. The other guys come back from patrol and tell their stories—with embellishments, of course—and you start to think, *Yeah, I could do that again.* And before you know it, you're over at the sergeant major's office saying, "I'm ready! Send me out again!"

My team sergeant did that to us once. We had just gotten to Kontum after the siege at Khe Sanh, and we were really enjoying the place. We were digging trenches, building bunkers (we were the camp experts on bunkers), and having a great time. We were going to the club at night, getting drunk, and watching movies; and nobody was shooting at us. It was wonderful.

Well, the team sergeant came into the hooch one night and announced that he had volunteered us for what we all considered a *very* dangerous mission. We were aghast! Somebody said, "Top, why did you do that? We have just survived a terrible siege; we're getting a little rest now!"

He replied, "I'm bored. We haven't been shot at in two weeks! Let's go do something!"

Special Forces Medics

If you ever get run over by a truck, pray that the paramedic who reaches you first or the technician in the hospital emergency room is a former Green Beret medic and not a garden-variety doctor. Most SF medics, particularly the ones with any combat experience, are superbly skilled trauma physicians. Many Green Berets would rather have their team medic treat their wounds than risk the uncertain abilities of a "real" physician. That's a bit surprising when you consider that doctors spend years learning their craft while a Special Forces medic is trained in only six months.

The difference, of course, is that the SF medic's training is somewhat limited. Even so, he can perform surgery, administer anesthesia, and dispense powerful drugs. Green Beret medics aren't supposed to open the chest cavity, although they are well qualified to stuff the contents back in if necessary. They can set bones, remove shrapnel, control bleeding and treat infection. And they are, without exception, the premier trauma specialists; gunshot wounds are their stock in trade.

But how do you take a bright young man and in six short months turn him into somebody who can save your life when your essential juices are draining away? It has always been done through a challenging, extremely intense program that combines academic training plus a lot of hands-on training.

Rather than have neophyte surgeons practice on human beings, the medic program originally relied on the use of animals. These were once (but are no longer) dogs from the pound that were going to be put down. Because of the emotional attachment many people have for dogs, this part of the program produced a lot of negative publicity, particularly during the time when the antiwar protests were at their most strident. The program was radically revised and dogs haven't been used in the program for many years; the pound now just puts them to death.

"Dog Lab existed," said one graduate. "It was hidden back in a cluster of old abandoned barracks. The first thing they told you was that you never talked about dog lab! That was the Number One rule.

"Number Two was, you never give your dog antibiotics. They were really serious about that; you couldn't work on your dog without having somebody there to keep an eye on what you were doing.

"We first anesthetized our dog, then inflicted a gunshot wound right behind the femur. Then we took the dog into the operating room and cleaned up the wound, flushed it, and then took care of the dog while it was healing. The instructors inspected the wound every day and critiqued you on the progress of the injury. If it got infected you were in deep shit!

"After the dog recovered, we put it to sleep, but only after we were able to learn several important procedures on the animal. It was taken to the operating room, anesthetized, and then we did amputations, some people learned to put in chest tubes, and I got to do my first 'cut down' [cutting through the skin to find a large vein in order to insert a large catheter] on my dog. One guy in my class did an appendectomy.

"One of us functioned as the surgeon, another as the assistant, somebody else would monitor the anesthesia.

"I got a pretty good dog, fairly healthy. I fed him well, brought him extra food to get him strong—and he rewarded me by never getting infected or dying.

"It was a learning experience. I didn't enjoy the idea that the dog was going to die, but we all rationalized it because the dog was going to be put to sleep otherwise, and everybody took really good care of the dogs, fed them well, and gave them a lot of attention."

—*Hans Halberstadt*

JOHN PADGETT

John Padgett, like many Special Forces medics, uses his military skills in a civilian medical profession. John is a physician's assistant in a group medical practice. He is still in Special Forces, serving as a captain in 3d Battalion, 12th Special Forces Group. His friends in Special Forces still call him by his old title, the one all Vietnam-era medics seem to own, Bac-si, *meaning* doctor *in Vietnamese.*

My Wife, the Assistant Machine Gunner

I was with a Mike Force [a quick-reaction combat team of Montagnards led by SF troopers]—4th Battalion in II Corps—and we were moved from Qui Nhon on the coast up to Kontum, up in the highlands. We took over a compound next to the B detachment up there, B-24.

The road from Qui Nhon had long been a treacherous one, up through the Mang Yang Pass, past the graveyard where hundreds of French soldiers were buried standing up, facing France. We drove that road many times and often would see the remains of recently ambushed vehicles alongside the road. I remember coming down out of that pass once, passing a burning gun truck.

At that time I was going with a Vietnamese lady who would later become my wife. She worked in a pharmacy in Qui Nhon, and when we were still based in that town it was easy for me to see her when I was in from the field. But when we were moved up to Kontum it was more difficult, because she still lived and worked in Qui Nhon. But she made every effort to see me.

That created problems for both of us. She normally had to take public transportation to get from Qui Nhon to Kontum, up that dangerous road. On this occasion the section of the road between Pleiku to Kontum was closed because of enemy activity, which did not deter her. She rented a motorcycle and drove up this closed road to Kontum.

But she arrived safely, and I was very glad to see her. We proceeded to spend some private time together. Later, a couple of hours after full dark, an enemy mortar team infiltrated the area and set up between our compound and the ARVN compound about 500 meters to the northwest. This team started lobbing mortar rounds into both camps, some at us and some at the ARVN. Their tactical plan seemed to be not only to harass and damage us, but to get us shooting at each other.

Now, there wasn't a lot of love lost between my Montagnard Mike Force troopers and the ARVNs. They tended to get in fights downtown, to take pot-shots at each other, and worse. Once, our guys came running back to the compound; they grabbed LAWs, machine guns, grenade launchers. I thought, What the hell is going on? I didn't hear any firing, and it didn't look like we were under attack, so I asked what was up. It turned out that they had gotten in a fight with the ARVN, and the ARVN told them they were going to go get their tanks, and they were going to assault our compound. And apparently they meant it! But we got on the radio to the ARVN advisors, and they shut that down. But tensions were high. So when the enemy mortar team started lobbing rounds in both directions, they apparently were trying to use the bad feelings in both camps to their own devices.

As soon as the first rounds went off our alert warning sounded, and we all went to our fighting positions. I told my girlfriend to get down and to stay put. My fighting position was a machine gun in a bunker on top of a wall, and it faced the area where the enemy mortar was firing from. Of course it was our policy to not fire automatic weapons after dark at an assumed target, but in this case I could see the mortar's muzzle flashes, and I knew where he was.

I started "firing him up," using short bursts to try to silence the mortar. An M60 machine gun is a crew-served weapon, normally operated by a gunner and an assistant. I was dimly aware while I was firing that my assistant was keeping me supplied with ammo, and doing a good job. Finally, the mortar stopped firing, and I looked over at the assistant gunner. It was my girlfriend. We were not yet married, but I thought, this has got to be the woman for me! And so, after another difficult year of courtship, I married her.

Bong Son was my first camp, and it was a neat place. It was in the middle of an area that was allegedly pacified, and it was decided that it was time for us to pack up and move, and to let the 1st Cav take it over. So we were closing it down and getting ready to move to Ha Tay. But for the few months I was there, some very entertaining things happened.

We had a quite good internal security net in the camp. At one point we learned that an assassination plot was in the works, that some of the Vietnamese in the camp were going to try to kill the Americans. The security guys "tumbled" a CIDG [Civilian Irregular Defense Group] member who was in on the plot, and he was interrogated. He gave up the others, including the leader—one of our hooch maids, a sixteen-year-old girl.

This girl was delivered to the Vietnamese interrogation specialists, who started to question her. Suddenly, from out of nowhere, she produced a bottle of poison and consumed the contents before anybody could stop her. Guess who was then brought to the dispensary for the medic to work on? I didn't have any Ipecac syrup to induce vomiting, but I put together something from scratch. It did the trick.

But I can remember thinking a couple of things while I worked on her. In America, sixteen-year-old girls are thinking about prom dates and dresses, and this one was planning an assassination. What kind of society is it that selects and trains its children to do this kind of thing? Secondly, this girl looked at me—while I was trying to save her life—with such intense hatred that I will never forget it. This young girl, an otherwise probably sweet, somewhat attractive young woman, hated me. If she had had access to a weapon then, she would have killed me first, then herself.

But I brought her back around, and they took her back to interrogation. I don't know what happened to her after that; I think she was turned over to the national police. I prefer to think that she was. But this is what we learned from her.

This girl had been trained in North Vietnam for about a year. The plan was simple. They were going to wait until the wee hours of the appointed night—which happened to be the very next night. Then they intended to shoot the guards on our team house and bunker, then roll grenades inside. If anybody got out, they would be hosed down with machine guns. They would stand their ground as long as possible, then split. Fortunately for us, they never got the chance.

Super Snake

We closed down the camp at Bong Son and moved to a new place called Ha Tay, at the junction of the road coming out of the 506 Valley and a small spine of mountains coming off the larger coastal range. It was a site that controlled a lot of the territory outside of Bong Son. There was an American fire base there, in the process of closing down, and we were taking over part of it for our Camp Strike Force (CIDG) camp. Special Forces was, of course, an American unit, but our troops were indigenous people and the unit an irregular paramilitary group. We tended to think of conventional US military formations as "the Americans," as if they were a different army.

Naturally, the first thing we built for the new camp was our club; once we put in our bar and got comfortable, we could proceed with the rest of the camp. My dispensary site was one of the old American artillery ammunition bunkers. We planned to build a proper facility, with concrete floors and fully timbered; but in the meantime I was to function out of the old ammo bunker, which provided both some protection and a central location.

I went down to the bunker to conduct a preliminary inspection. It was dark and dirty inside, so I got out my flashlight and peered inside. There was a large cobra toward the back, and it saw me and reared up with its hood out, ready to strike. I thought about that for a moment, and concluded that, No I don't really want to go in there just now.

This presented a tactical problem; there was still some ammunition in there, and I couldn't adjust my line of fire to shoot the snake and miss the ammunition. I couldn't roll a grenade in there because it would detonate everything else. I thought, Well, what do I do now? And I concluded that the best option was to roll a tear-gas grenade in there to possibly subdue the snake. Maybe it would force him out where I could shoot him, or maybe it would just knock him out in the bunker. I wasn't sure if either would work, but I got a CS grenade and rolled it in there.

The bunker filled with fumes, and I waited outside for about twenty or thirty minutes while the gas slowly dissipated. Finally it cleared. I put a "drive-on rag" over my face, pulled my pistol, shone my flashlight down in the bunker, and saw one really pissed off snake! The gas hadn't seemed to knock him out or phase him in the least, and it was obvious this snake was now really mad.

Well, I couldn't go back and tell my team sergeant that I was afraid to go in my bunker because of a snake; it wouldn't look good. Finally, one of the Montagnard soldiers who had been watching this whole performance came over and asked what I was doing. I took him over, shone the flashlight on the snake, and showed it to the guy. He said to me, "Wait a minute; I'll be right back," and disappeared.

Ten minutes later the guy reappeared with a box. He opened it, shook it, and out popped a mongoose. He herded the animal over to the door of the bunker. The mongoose got one whiff of that tear gas and went in the other direction. The Montagnard brought the mongoose back two or three times until the animal finally got a whiff of cobra. His tail shot up, and he dove into the bunker, out of sight. Finally, we just had to see what was going on. So we aimed the flashlight into the bunker, and there was the mongoose with the cobra in its mouth. So I guess modern science and technology have their limits; the old ways are usually the best.

Building a Mike Force

The city of Qui Nhon was taken by the Viet Cong during the Tet Offensive in February of 1968. When the place was retaken by a force of Montagnards (after an attack by the ARVN and the Koreans failed), it was decided that the place needed its own Mike Force. For political reasons, this Mike Force was going to be a two-company battalion, including a recon platoon and a headquarters element. One of the companies was to be made up of lowland ethnic Vietnamese and one of tribesmen from the highlands. I was one of four Americans assigned to go up to the highlands to recruit this company from among the Jarai tribe.

We traveled to the camp at Phu Tuc, an old fortification built by the French and slightly improved by the Americans later. This camp was in the heart of Montagnard territory. The territory around the SF camp at Phu Tuc was extremely secure; the relationship between the Yards and the SF soldiers in the camp was excellent—a "love-love" relationship. Nothing moved in that area of operations without Special Forces knowing about it. If a lizard shit ten miles from camp, there would be a report about it delivered ten minutes later.

We arrived in mid-week, a Wednesday or Thursday, and met with some of the tribal elders and chiefs in the village outside the Special Forces camp. We told them what we were doing, and they asked, "How many men do you need?" At that time a Mike Force company was about one hundred and twenty men, according to the TO&E. So we asked if they could come up with, say, one hundred and fifty candidates, since some would probably be unfit for duty, and we'd have to weed out a few.

"We will have two hundred men for you in five days," they told us.

Five days later at eight o'clock in the morning, after our coffee in the SF camp, we hopped in a jeep and drove down to the runway. Two hundred men were standing in formation, at parade-rest, waiting to be inspected. Some were in loin cloths, some in old fatigues. Some had weapons, some didn't. The ones with weapons had machetes, spears, crossbows, and old French rifles. It appeared that our recruiting mission was not going to be as difficult as we had originally feared!

We interviewed the men, paying particular attention to the leadership, and together with the tribal elders we determined who would be in positions of responsibility in the unit. They voted on their officers, and we were allowed to approve or disapprove of their choices. There were few disagreements, and those were minor, and we essentially accepted their command structure. We selected the best one hundred and twenty of the group, and thanked the rest, who then faded away.

We trained them for about a month in weapons and small-unit tactics. But most were already experienced in paramilitary operations and were already natural soldiers. We had to teach them about "fire and maneuver" and introduce them to some crew-served weapons like the mortar and machine gun, but they were already familiar with the carbine. They learned to use the M79 grenade launcher, and other, more effective weapons. Then we took them out on training combat patrols, in the vicinity of the camp, and they did very well.

Honorary Jarai

We were very happy with them. Well, they were sufficiently impressed with us that they wanted to induct us into their tribe, to make us honorary Jarai.

On the appointed day, we put on our best and cleanest uniforms, put on our berets (which we normally never wore in the field), polished our boots to a high luster, and marched down to the village. The ceremony involved a visit to each of the tribal elder's homes for a drink of rice wine—a *large* drink. The proper and traditional presentation is in very large ceramic urns. Rice is placed in the urns, some water is added, a layer of banana leaves is placed on top, and the top is then sealed. The urn is buried for a while, and the stuff ferments. When the time arrives, it is dug up, water is added, and it is ready to drink. It is a very potent brew!

The wine or beer is drunk through a long straw, and each man's portion was measured by a carved ceremonial stick placed across the top of the jug. Your mission, as a new member of the Jarai tribe, is to drink until the surface of the wine in the jug clears the bottom of the stick. That is about a quart or more of this exotic potion—at each house.

After the fourth or fifth visit, getting up the little ladder to the long house became a challenge. The floors of Montagnard houses are about six feet off the ground, a lattice of bamboo that allows a kind of natural ventilation and that keeps everything up out of the mud and dust. These ladders, though, are just logs, notched for steps, propped up against the end of the house.

After all that alcohol, climbing the logs became very difficult! But we made our round of social calls, talked and visited. At one point, I remember vividly, one of our group said "Excuse me for a moment," went to the side of the house, and barfed his guts out. Then he came back in and took up where he had left off.

Finally, it was time for us to be initiated into the tribe. We were asked by the shaman to remove our boots and socks. Then he placed an old bronze ax head on the ground. We gathered around the ax head, and he put the bracelets on the ax, then our bare feet on the bracelets. He took some of the rice wine, and, with some raw local cotton, he began painting our feet, the bracelets, and the ax head, all in one continuous motion.

During all this he was chanting incantations, and the painting process was repeated several times for each of us. When he was done, he placed the bracelets on each of our wrists, telling us that they would protect us from bullets. And—interestingly enough—none of us was ever struck by a rifle bullet, although we were all peppered with shrapnel, and one guy lost his leg to an artillery round. But, as he promised, none of us was hit by a bullet!

After the ceremony, we all proceeded to get even more drunk. When we finally headed back to our camp later that evening, our fatigues had somehow been replaced by Jarai loincloths and ceremonial hand-woven shirts. That's how I became a member of the Jarai tribe, and I still wear my bracelet today.

"Sorry, Nothing There!"

The Montagnards considered their experience with us to be training, not just for the missions they knew they would be conducting with us, but for the ones to come in the distant future, the operations against the

Vietnamese communists or the lowlanders in general. They knew we would eventually leave, and they would be on their own. There were occasions when we sent patrols out to known cache sites where we pretty well knew the VC had stashed weapons, and they came back to report, "Sorry, nothing there!" I figured that they were simply marked for future use by the Montagnards against the Vietnamese, after we were gone.

Chase Medic

Before I moved across the river to take over the C&C Central remote dispensary in the old Mike Force compound, I was a "chase" medic for C&C Central, working out of the main compound at Kontum. My job was to get on the first helicopter going in to extract a team that had been in contact with the enemy, to start treating casualties on the ground or in the air. The wounded were picked up first, everybody else after they were out.

During Operation Tailwind, I was sent out to pick up a team that had been in heavy contact with the enemy and had a number of wounded. The helicopters and crews were supplied by the Marines, two big Sea Stallions out of Da Nang. They staged out of Dak To, picked us up, and we headed into Indian country to collect our guys. These particular Marines, though, had never heard a shot fired in anger. They had simply been ferrying cargo from ship to shore and back out again, low-stress logistics supply "milk runs." They had never done such a mission, but they had been tasked with this mission, and—like good Marines—that's what they were going to do.

On the way in we started to see something I'd only encountered before in the movies: flak. There were little puffs of flak going off, just like in *Twelve O'clock High*.

The other SF medic and I told these guys, "Look, when you go into that landing zone, go in hot; fire up the tree line. You don't have to have a target. Just don't hit any of our people, who will all be in the immediate vicinity of the LZ. Anything beyond that is fair game. Fire it up!"

Well, when we got to the LZ, the pilots started a slow, deliberate approach, just like they were used to doing on to the landing platforms of ships. While we SF medics laid down fire with our CAR-15s, the gunners didn't fire a shot. Then, many bullet holes began to appear in the fuselage, in rapid succession.

While we were still in the air, a few feet above the LZ, I was trying to reach a patient who was being handed up to me, a wounded guy wrapped in a poncho. The ground fire must have become too intense just as we were about to land, because the pilot pulled pitch and rotated a little to his right. As we started gaining altitude, a B-40 [NVA rocket-propelled grenade] came through the bottom of the helicopter and up through the fuel tank. It didn't explode, but it punched a big hole in the tank, and now fuel was gushing out, all over the inside of the helicopter.

The crew chief was looking out the window and didn't notice. I banged on him to get his attention, then pointed to the fuel. His eyes got very wide. He reported all this to the pilots who were trying to get us out of there. We only lasted for two or three kilometers, then crash-landed. The other SF medic and I grabbed our weapons, and as soon as we were on the ground, we dashed out and tried to set up some security. This was a good thing since, as we soon discovered, we had landed directly on top of some

NVA bunkers (which were, thankfully, unoccupied at the time).

I looked back at the helicopters, and the Marines were all huddled around the tail of the aircraft, looking rather bereft and forlorn. So the other medic and I had to go back, tell them to get their machine guns, and we set them up in defensive positions in some sort of perimeter around the aircraft.

It seemed like an hour (but was probably more like twenty minutes) later, another helicopter finally arrived to get us out of there. They dropped a rope ladder from a hover. We hadn't received any unwanted guests during the interim, but when the second helicopter dropped that ladder they also started receiving fire. The Marines didn't want to climb the ladder, but I thought, the hell with this, I'm getting out of here, and I started up the rope ladder. I held on with one hand and tried to return fire with my rifle with the other. Even over the noise of the helicopter, I could hear the .51-caliber rounds from the NVA hitting it, but finally everybody was hanging from the rope ladder, and off we went.

But the helicopter was damaged enough that we only got twenty or thirty kilometers with this one before it, too, had to land. Finally, a third helicopter arrived and picked us up and carried us back to Dak To.

I was really upset. We'd been through all that and still had to leave the wounded guys out there. We rescued them later, but at that moment I didn't know what would happen to them. I dumped my flak jacket, CAR-15, web gear, and aide bag on the floor. When I took off the flak jacket I noticed a shrapnel hole, right over the heart.

Party Time

The medics liked to party as well as anybody else. When bad weather closed in, or when we had no teams out in the field, we knew that there wouldn't be any incoming casualties—and that was our signal to start partying! We took the precaution of having a "designated medic," like the designated driver of today, who stayed sober just in case, but the rest of us kicked back and had a drink. A favorite cocktail was canned orange juice from the mess hall combined with medicinal alcohol to make a screwdriver. But, one thing about military men when they start drinking—they start thinking about women!

We tended to combine our cocktail parties with visits to the local "ladies" who were loaded up in the back of our ambulance and transported back to the camp for "dermatological studies." The next morning we loaded them back in the ambulance and made another medical run back downtown to take them home.

Phase II training for medics, when I went through the OJT [on-the-job training] part of the program, was assigned for the first time to Fort Gordon, Georgia. But the people at Fort Gordon didn't really know what to do with us young Special Forces medical trainees. They didn't know who we were, what we were doing, or what to do with us.

The hospital at Fort Gordon at that time was a complex of long, wooden barracks buildings connected by what seemed to be miles of covered walkways. We were provided with one of these barracks for our living quarters. It was great; we had comfortable hospital beds, we had our own kitchen, and it was all our own. And it was particularly interesting when we first opened it up because it hadn't been used since the Korean War, and in the bedside tables we found a lot of magazines from the early 1950s that made amusing reading.

When we graduated from the medic OJT program at Fort Gordon, my class had a real knock-down, drag-out party. We had a good time! We had water fights and everything! But the next day we were all supposed to leave, to go back to Fort Bragg for Phase III [a team exercise in the woods, the last phase of SF training after which we would finally become real Green Berets. A couple of us looked around at the mess and said, "We gotta clean this place up! This place is a disaster!"

Of course, as might be predicted, we were met with a chorus of "Fuck you!" The consensus seemed to be that there were plenty of "legs" [non-jump-qualified people] around. After all, we were almost Special Forces. We could walk on water, and we didn't have to clean up after ourselves!

Well, I wasn't about to do it all by myself. Since we had already signed out, they couldn't do much to us unless they actually caught us—so we left! Some of the guys got on busses, some of us climbed in our cars, and we "exfiltrated." But I will never forget that, just as the last two of us cleared that messy building, the hospital's first sergeant was walking across the facility toward our barracks with fire in his eyes! As he was headed up the stairs, we made our getaway—and we didn't look back.

"I Love You, Bac-Si!"

Here's a story about one of my favorite patients. When we moved to the new camp at Ha Tay the first thing we needed to do was to secure the area, and that means that the security patrols go out immediately. While I was putting my dispensary together, one of these patrols came back in one day with an eight-year-old patient. He looked five. He was malnourished, with protruding abdomen and very thin arms and legs. The patrol had found this child hiding in what was left of a village.

The Viet Cong had gone in four or five days previously and, as an object lesson, wiped out the entire village. They apparently decided that the people were a little too cozy with the government, or they weren't sufficiently supportive of the VC, or whatever reason, so they killed everybody they could find. Then they killed all the livestock, and they left the place. This one child managed to find a place to hide, and he escaped death. He had survived for those four or five days on what little grain and foodstuffs were around the bodies of his parents and neighbors.

When he arrived at the dispensary he had pneumonia, parasites, and malaria. But slowly I was able to bring him back to health. The child quickly became a regular fixture of our camp. The ladies who we hired to do our cooking took him under their wing; they made sure he was fed, and they began to teach him reading and writing. Gradually, he came around.

He was fascinated with the running water in the showers we had installed. He would stand in there and turn the water on and off endlessly. He loved taking baths and did so at any time of the day, so he acquired the name "Tam," which means bath in Vietnamese. The team sergeant more or less adopted him at that point, and it was time for me to move on to another camp.

A year later, my assignment was with the Mike Force. As it happened, our new unit's first really big toe-to-toe fight with the North Vietnamese Army was in the 506 valley, right at the edge of the area of operations for the force in the SF camp at Ha Tay. We were called in because the NVA were building up for a hit on this camp. We went out there and found them, and they found us! It was a real epic battle, with one company of camp Strike Force and one company of Mike Force against two battalions of North Vietnamese.

I was actually on another operation with the other Mike Force company across the river, but we were ordered to stop our mission (a raid against the NVA secure areas) and come back to camp to get on helicopters to go out to take part in the battle. We were lifted onto a ridge overlooking this battle and had to wait all night before we could come down from the mountain to try to relieve our people.

It was interesting. You could see our guys' positions below, surrounded by the muzzle flashes and tracers of their weapons firing outwards and the positions of the NVA firing in. With all the artillery and airstrikes, it was quite a light show. But at first light we moved out and were able to break through to them. The enemy had pretty well dissipated with the light. They knew the gunships would be able to see them, and they left. When we broke through, that was the final straw for them, and they broke contact.

We resupplied, got the wounded out, and rested for a while before moving out. The plan was to move up, out of the valley, to a plateau where the helicopters could come in and extract us. So now the remnants of the camp Strike Force, Mike Force, and the group that I had brought in were all together. As we moved out of the valley, the NVA let the first group through, then opened up on us from their bunkers.

I had joined one of the groups of Montagnards that had been hit pretty hard, and now they were getting hit again. My recon platoon leader was right beside me. He got up on one knee to give the hand and arm signal to order his unit forward—and was immediately hit by one bullet in the arm and two in the chest. I dragged him to cover and started treating him (he survived, by the way), but we all reached the same conclusion at the same time. We were not going to be able to hold the position. So we started retreating back down the mountain. I put the platoon leader on my back and moved out.

When we got to the valley floor it was obvious that we were surrounded; it was kind of like Custer's Last Stand. Luckily, we got some close air support on scene, and they dropped their ordnance between where we were and where our other company was, on the hill above. The FAC [forward air controller, a coordinator for artillery and air fire support] called me up and said, "You've got a lot of movement around you. There are a lot of people moving toward your position from the west. There are some to the south, too!"

I thought, shit! I started looking around, and I was looking for a place to die—a place to make a stand, and to make it count. We headed for a little rise, a little high ground. We wanted to get there before the other side. That was going to be the place I would be killed.

Then I heard a call on the radio: "This is so-and-so . . . I've got eight slicks and two gunships. Can you use us?" One of the gunships was brought down by enemy fire, but they managed to get all of us out of there, and they dropped us all at Camp Ha Tay—the camp that I had helped to build. We got off the helicopters, and after the debrief, I headed for the club.

I walked into the club with my CAR-15 in one hand, the aid bag in the other. My fatigues smelled like smoke and sweat, and they had blood all over them. I sat at the bar and ordered a beer. There was a little commotion from the back of the room, out of my line of sight, and I heard, *"Bac-si! Bac-si!"* It was little Tam, who remembered me from a year or so before, when I was treating him. He crawled up on the stool, planted himself on my lap, threw his arms around my neck, and said, "I love you, *Bac-si!*"

When people ask me why I spent four tours in Vietnam, that's the story I use to explain my attachment to the place and the people.

Later, I learned from intel sources that we had killed over two hundred and fifty of the NVA and wounded many more, so we pretty well decimated the two enemy battalions—but at a price for us, too.

Martha Raye Kicks Butt

The first time I encountered "Maggie" was by radio, right around Christmas or New Years of 1968. Maggie was traveling around Special Forces camps with a few girls, putting on shows for the guys, and I had the radio watch when she called me up from the helicopter.

"Hi, Doc," she said, "I'm gonna come up to your camp and bring my show." I told her that sounded great, and she was welcome anytime.

"I have some problems with transportation," she said. "You'll have to be satisfied with the old broad!"

I radioed back. "Maggie," I said, "an old broad is better than no broad!"

"You sorry son of a bitch," she said. "I'm gonna come up there and kick your butt!"

I said, "You know we love you, Maggie!"

"I love you too, but I'm still gonna kick your butt!"

And that was my introduction to Martha Raye.

A couple of years later I was down at C&C Central and ended up being one of Maggie's unofficial escorts. She had a lot more freedom of movement than other visitors and could go just about anywhere she wanted. We ended up over in the recon team's billets about midnight, drinking and telling war stories and drinking some more. The last thing I remember was that Maggie was still going strong . . . and I was *down for the count!*

The IV Class

One of my very strongest early memories as a Special Forces medic is the IV class.

I wanted to go into Special Forces when I joined the Army in 1965, but I was told there was no guarantee for SF, just for jump school. I could volunteer out of the Airborne school and take my chances—which I did. I was lucky enough to be selected for SF training, which I attended right out of jump school. Then they sent me to Fort Sam to get my basic medical training—as a basic medic first, then advanced medical training, then OJT, then Dog Lab [the phase of SF medic training where the students practiced medical techniques on dogs from the local pound], and finally the last phase of SF training.

Part of the basic medic program was a class on IVs, setting up drips and transfusions. The Army, then, was enthusiastic about "training models"—if you wanted to learn how to give an IV, you practiced on your buddy. We had some hard partners in my unit. Some of the guys would go downtown at night, get really intoxicated, then come back in at seven or eight in the morning and still be drunk. So there I was with my fellow soldier, who was still drunk and shaking, trying to stick a fourteen-gauge needle in my vein! For a long time after that class, whenever we appeared in our "Class B" short-sleeved khaki uniforms, we looked like a bunch of heroin addicts, with all those bruises on our arms.

Then there was the famous and ever popular nasal gastric tube class! You know, the one that is inserted into the nose, down into the throat, into the stomach. Of course, this was also normally done after an evening of partying, so the stomach contents—beer, and breakfast, combined and fermented—took some of the fun out of learning to be a medic.

Capt. Arnie Estrada and the Full Body Cast

Arnie Estrada joined the reserves after he left active service, and the training jump that crippled him occurred after the war. His response to this injury, though, is rather typical of how Green Berets cope with what other people might consider debilitating injuries. Arnie is currently a competitor in the Wheelchair Olympics and took home a silver medal and two bronzes for the shot put and the javelin at the 1993 meet in Madrid, Spain.

Arnie Estrada's reserve parachute deployed prematurely during a training jump, and he was sucked out of the C-130 and struck the tail. His back was broken, and he was crippled for life. He was scraped up and carted off to Letterman Army Hospital. The staff put Arnie's major subgroups back in their approximate correct positions, then wrapped young Arnie in a full body cast. The plaster was not quite dry when Estrada decided what he really felt like doing was to go fishing. In the ocean. Now.

Two of the things those of us in Special Forces do particularly well are *infiltrate* and *exfiltrate*—at will. Consequently, Arnie concocted a scheme that would allow him to go fishing. He had his wife park their camper outside in the parking lot. Then, he enlisted the help of some of the hospital orderlies who moved recently deceased patients down to the morgue. They put Arnie on a gurney and covered him with a sheet, just like a corpse. Then they rolled him down the hall, into the elevator, and out to the parking lot. They helped his wife load him into the back of the camper, and off the happy couple went for an afternoon of surf fishing at the beach.

Mrs. Estrada propped her husband up near the water's edge, stuck a surf rod in his hand, and went back to the truck to read for a while. Arnie fished for an hour or so before he noticed that the surf line was getting closer; the tide was coming in. Then the surf was actually splashing on him. He called to his wife, but she couldn't hear him. He called again, louder, and still no response. Then he was fully engulfed by one of the waves. About this time, Mrs. Estrada noticed his predicament and retrieved her soggy husband. According to Arnie, she is supposed to have said, "Why didn't you move?"

By now the cast was soggy and starting to deteriorate, so it was time to get back to the hospital. His wife took him back to the hospital emergency room entrance, maneuvered him onto a handy gurney, and left him lying in the afternoon sunshine. A couple of orderlies noticed him out there, unattended, and investigated.

"What are you doing out here?" one asked.

"Just getting a little sunshine," Arnie replied, smiling.

They collected him and rolled him back up to his room. Later that night the nurse noticed a funny odor in Arnie's room.

"Is something wrong?" she wanted to know.

"No, nothing! I'm fine, just fine, thanks!" Arnie replied.

By the next day the sea water and seaweed had fermented sufficiently to make a tremendous stench. When Arnie's doctor dropped by on his rounds, he opened the door, noticed the strong fishy smell, and yelled, "What the hell is going on here!" He assumed Arnie had a badly infected wound.

It took six hours to put the original cast on, and it took longer than that to take it off and apply a fresh one, but it was done. And the hospital staff was mad. So, when Arnie was taken back to his room this time, a guard was assigned to keep an eye on him. Who else but a Green Beret would need a guard to keep him from escaping—even while in a full body cast?

Happy Hour at the Hospital

Arnie maintained an illegal stash of liquid refreshment under his hospital bed, and every afternoon at the usual hour he would have a cocktail. Arnie and one of the nurses became friendly, in a kidding, teasing sort of way. For Arnie at the moment, this was about as friendly as he could get.

The nurse had a supply of popcorn, and Arnie wanted some. The nurse knew about his bar and told him, "If you can come up with the drink I want, I'll let you have some popcorn."

"Okay," Arnie said. "What will you have?"

"I'll have a beer," replied the nurse. "And not just a beer, but a cold beer!"

"No problem!" Arnie said, and he handed her a cold one.

Well, Arnie did a little "intel" work on this nurse, and he found out what her favorite drinks were. So the next day the nurse came in with the popcorn and the same demand. Only this time she said, "Today I want some wine, and the wine I would really like to have is Mateus."

"No problem!" said Arnie, and out came a bottle of Mateus. Arnie got his popcorn. The nurse was impressed.

On the third day the same nurse came in at happy hour again and said, "Okay, if you can repeat your performance again, I will keep you in popcorn for as long as you're here. You will never want for any popcorn!"

"Okay," said Arnie. "What'll you have?"

"Today, I want a margarita."

"No problem," said Arnie. He produced a glass from the bed stand, some ice from his ice chest, a little lemonade and orange juice, then pulled a flask of tequila from somewhere, and assembled the margarita. After that Arnie had all the popcorn he could handle.

Sergeant Psycho and the Alien Life Form

Several of us from 3d Battalion, 12th Special Forces Group, were tasked with training some ROTC [Reserve Officer Training Corps] cadets from the University of New Mexico in small-unit tactics—raids, ambushes, and patrols. Several of the senior NCOs, myself included, were assigned teams of these trainees. After several days of joint training, we each took our teams on training missions out in the desert.

Those of us in 3d Battalion knew Staff Sergeant "Rod" had a short fuse. So, naturally, we did all we could to provoke him. We enjoyed ambushing him on occasion, and harassed him just to get him started.

One night we were operating in teams of ten or twelve out in the desert, three or four teams, far from civilization. My team encountered something extremely strange. The point element reported back to the main body that they had something odd in sight, so I did a little "leader's recon" and went forward to investigate. The point team was on a slight rise of ground. Ahead of them, in a slight depression, was a very strange green metallic glow. Behind the glow we thought we might be able to see another shape, but couldn't tell for sure.

I came off the berm and consulted the other NCOs. It didn't seem to be part of the training program; it was too strange for that. Staff Sergeant "Rod" was called on the radio, and he and his troops moved to our position. I led him to the top of the berm and showed him this phenomenon. He couldn't figure it out, either. We studied this thing for a while, and none of us could make any sense of it.

Finally, in his typical, well-reasoned, diplomatic way, Staff Sergeant "Rod" declared, "Fuck it! Let's assault it!" He put all the troops on line, and down the hill they all went, blazing away at whatever this thing was!

I was thinking, this looks like a UFO to me. If this is our first contact with an alien life form, we are *not* going to make a good first impression.

Well, the assault was unopposed. When we got down to the glow, it turned out to be a reflection from some streetlights of the camp, miles away, from the polished blade of a bulldozer parked in this little depression, miles from nowhere. But that was his style. He didn't have the slightest idea what it was, but he was going to kill it anyway.

We camped that night nearby, in the open desert. The next morning, as we prepared to move back to camp, the cadets started calling him "Sergeant Psycho." So I asked them, "Would you guys like to know what would really piss Sergeant Psycho off?"

"Yeah!" they all said with eager anticipation.

"Let's ambush him!"

So we planned our route back to camp to intersect his. Just as he and his team departed the bulldozer site, we hit them. He was really angry. "Dammit, you aren't supposed to do that!" he screamed.

We said we were sorry and we wouldn't do it again.

Then we hit them again, about two kilometers back toward camp. He got so mad that, if he had had any real ammunition, he would have shot me.

Why I Served

I was in my third year in college and doing well, but Vietnam was heating up and I heard my country's call. My family has a tradition of military service that goes back to the Revolution; every generation has had at least one member under arms since that time. The battle in the Ia Drang got everybody's attention, and it was obvious that a buildup was under way. Even though I was in college, I felt I had a duty and a family tradition, and it was now my turn to go. I felt a responsibility to serve.

One of the things I tell my colleagues today in the Veterans Caucus of the American Academy of Physician Assistants (of which I am the current president) is that they ought to be proud of what they did, however and wherever they served. Those of us who went chose to fulfill a difficult obligation of citizenship when others chose not to do so. It didn't matter if you fixed airplanes, took out the garbage, or stood toe-to-toe with the enemy and slugged it out. You served.

John Wayne and *Rambo*

A lot of Americans have learned everything they know about the Special Forces community through films like *The Green Berets* (starring John Wayne) and *Rambo* (starring Sylvester Stallone). The consensus in the community is that the first portrayal is okay and the second sucks.

The Green Berets is actually a pretty accurate description of SF work in the highlands. Unfortunately, John Wayne's character is a colonel, but they have him doing sergeant's or captain's work. Although there were certainly a lot of bad actors in Vietnam, *The Green Berets* makes things look even worse than they were; this movie has some of the worst acting in the history of motion pictures—except for Wayne, who was a pro. The rest of the cast appears to have been selected by somebody standing on a street corner, asking, "Hey, buddy, wanna be in a movie?" Even so, the SF community liked Wayne (who actually visited Vietnam and the highlands) and the movie for its attempt to accurately describe the missions and situations of people in the camps—for part of the movie, anyway. Wayne became extremely popular with Green Berets in Vietnam, though, because he wore the tribal bracelet ever after, even in his cowboy movies! The Montagnards loved his heroic roles, and with that bracelet . . . well, they were fired up, big time!

Rambo, on the other hand, has the same type of bad actors plus a story line that is just plain silly. That would be okay, except that the story is alleged to be about the SF community, and a lot of people think it's a documentary. Green Berets mostly hate *Rambo* and are quite fed up with being associated with this story and its bone-headed, renegade central character. Oddly, though, the *Rambo* movie and the commie-killing Rambo character are extremely popular in (I'm not kidding) Russia!

—*Hans Halberstadt*

KENN KUBASIK

Kenn Kubasik left active duty after a long and varied career but still serves in the Texas National Guard as a lieutenant colonel. He operates a private investigation business with his wife and is active in Special Forces Association and Special Operations Association.

How I Became an Officer

I was commissioned in April of 1964, but before I went to OCS [Officer Candidate School], I had the distinction of having been busted back to private six times and court-martialed twice. I received my first court-martial when the regimental commander (I was his driver) published the policy that nobody under the rank of E-7 could be out on the streets after eleven at night—and I missed bed check the very first night.

I got hauled up in front of the colonel the next morning. "You know," he said, "if I had to bet on the one man in this entire regiment that would screw this thing up for me, it would have been *you*! I have no recourse but to give you a summary court-martial."

I was busted to private, fined, and confined to quarters for thirty days. Finally, when the thirty days wereover, I was released and was on my way to an important softball game (I was a hell of a softball player) when my section sergeant, Sergeant Jennings, intercepted me.

"Where are you going?" he wanted to know.

"I'm playing softball."

"Oh no you aren't," Sergeant Jennings said. "We've got a detail for the mess hall and you are now on it."

I tried to tell him that I had just come off thirty days of details, but he just told me, "You're not off confinement yet as far as I am concerned!"

The witnesses at my court-martial shortly thereafter all testified that I did not, as Sergeant Jennings claimed, actually say those nasty things about him then and there, and consequently I was acquitted.

So I had this long list of Article 15s and the two court-martials, and I was not exactly prime OCS material. But a few of us were in a bar, and while I was in the rest room, the other guys got to talking about OCS somehow. When I came back there was three hundred dollars on the table. Two of the guys bet I couldn't make it, and the other two bet that I could.

So I went to OCS on a bet.

The Sergeant Major's Moment of Glory

At one time we were sent over to Vietnam and Laos on six-month TDY [temporary duty orders]. A few months after we had rotated back to Fort Bragg, the Army got around to giving us our TDY per diem pay—fifteen to twenty-five dollars a day—an important event.

I was in Delta Company, and we had a sergeant major whose real name I have forgotten, but for this story I'll called him Sergeant "Smith." How this guy got in Special Forces was a mystery to all of us. He was a sergeant major, but they only used him for "site beautification" [mowing the lawn] because he was so incompetent, otherwise. But one day the command sergeant major was a little short of help and assigned him a real military mission: He was to form up the troops and give them their TDY pay. After doing nothing but landscaping for months, this was his moment of glory. The company was assembled and formed up in ranks.

"Okay, men, when I call your name, sound off smartly. I'll tell you how much money you are due. Then fall out of the formation and into the group to march down to finance to collect your money." We didn't need much encouragement.

He studied his list of names, then called the first one. "Brown!"

"Here, Sergeant Major!" was the reply as Sergeant Brown fell out of the ranks and started the formation that was to receive TDY pay.

"Three hundred dollars. Fall out. Smith!"

"Here, Sergeant Major!"

"Two hundred and eighty-five dollars. Fall out. Green!"

"Here, Sergeant Major!"

"Four hundred and twenty-eight dollars. Fall out. Kubasik!"

And so it went, down the list. Finally, he got to the bottom of the list. "Totals!"

Nobody said anything. "*Totals!*" the sergeant major roared again.

Still no response. Then, "GODDAMMIT, TOTALS, WHEN I CALL YOUR NAME YOU BETTER SOUND OFF!"

By now we all realized what he had done, and the whole formation started breaking up, laughing. "At ease, dammit!" Sergeant "Smith" yelled. "Totals has more money coming than all of you!"

An Officer and Gentleman

I got my commission through Officer Candidate School, and after six months I got shipped back to my old unit—something normally not done. I was a young kid, with my "butter bars," and there were still a lot of World War II veterans in the NCO ranks. I was waiting for a salute from somebody, when Sergeant Faffik turns around and says to me, "Goddammit, I oughta whup your ass. If you ever think I'm gonna give ya a goddamm salute, you're crazy!"

An Officer and Gentleman, Part II

Colonel Kelty liked to keep dogs, and he took them to the office with him. He liked them, but he called them names. "Hey, son of a bitch, get over here," was typical of his style of communication with his pets.

Walker Davis is retired from the Army now, but on this particular day he was a brand-new second lieutenant, and he was reporting to the same unit he had left when he went to OCS six months before. Sergeant Major Benzoni looked at him and said, "You were a goddammed Spec 4 when you left here, and as far as I'm concerned, you're *still* a goddammed Spec 4!"

Walker, a little flustered, saluted the sergeant major, even though the sergeant major hadn't saluted him, and said, "Sergeant Major Benzoni, I'm here to see the colonel. I've been assigned to A Company."

"Take a seat," Benzoni said. "He'll be with you in a minute." Then he announced Walker's arrival to the colonel.

Colonel Kelty's Dalmatian was sprawled across the doorway opposite the chair where Second Lieutenant Davis was seated. Kelty noticed the dog blocking the entrance and bellowed, "Get in here, shit head!"

Walker Davis (who, after all, had just spent six months at OCS) popped to attention, stepped in the office just as he had been taught at OCS, and smartly announced in a military manner, "Sir, Lieutenant Davis reporting for duty!"

"We Are All Dead. Out."

It happened on my birthday, December 29, 1964. I had been in the country for about a month. I was a somewhat green second lieutenant, the XO at Camp Ben Cat.

There were three of us in the camp who took the patrols out: Capt. Andrew "Buzz" Erickson, the commander; myself, the executive officer; and the team sergeant, Sgt. William Segrist. We took turns in rotation, so every patrol had one of the three senior leaders. A patrol was scheduled to go out on my birthday, on the twenty-ninth of December, and it was my turn to lead it.

We had a Strike Force made up of Nungs, Cambodians, and Montagnards, and these troops hadn't been paid for a long time. They refused to go on any more patrols until they were paid, so this issue became an important one. It was my job to be paymaster. Since I couldn't pay the troops and get ready for this patrol at the same time, Sergeant Segrist and I traded turns.

Segrist, Sgt. Reino Peanula, and Sgt. Roy Jacobson took the Strike Force out, about three hundred men total. They got to the little town of Ap Ban Dong So. Sgt. Elliot Wilson took another element around to the north, toward a town called Bau Bang. Some Vietnamese Special Forces—the LLDB—went too.

Sergeant Segrist's Strike Force got to Ap Ban Dong So about twilight, and they decided to spend the night in the town. We were all pretty new to this stuff, and didn't know or use the tricks we did later on that might have saved them. They decided to camp right in the middle of town, and when they did the Viet Cong came up out of their holes, formed skirmish lines, and attacked.

Sergeant Segrist called me on the radio. "Sir," he said, "put three hundred rounds on top of our position!"

"I can't do that," I told him. He was asking me to kill him and all the strikers, too.

"Sir, please, you have got to put three hundred rounds of artillery on our position, NOW!"

"I cannot do that!" It was hard to communicate with him, for several reasons. One was the VC started mortaring our camp just as they hit the Strike Force. Their shells used VT [variable time] fuses, set for air bursts. These things were going off outside, right at rooftop level.

While all this was going on, I was on another radio, talking to a major in Saigon, trying to get some air support and some supporting artillery. I had Segrist yelling at me on one radio, and this major down in Saigon telling me, "Calm down, now, lieutenant, get control of yourself. You're getting overexcited; the VC don't even have VT fuses."

About that moment one of the rounds detonated right over the ARVN regimental commander's house, and it took out the whole roof. The local Vietnamese artillery unit was doing their best, but the air bursts from the incoming mortar rounds produced a kind of metal rain that was falling all around us. That made it virtually impossible for the ARVN gunners in our compound to fire their guns, although they tried hard and managed to get some rounds downrange. Whenever there was a little break in the attack, those gunners got off a few rounds. We didn't get any support from anybody until the next morning, and by then it was all over.

I gave up on the major in Saigon and hung up on him. Then, Sergeant Segrist called the last time. "Sir, they are coming through the gates now! Put three hundred rounds on top of our position. We are all dead. Out." That was the last I heard from him. The radio went dead, and so did he.

Buzz Erikson, the commander, was in Saigon drinking and whoring around when this happened, so I was in charge. I flew in to Ap Ban Dong So the next day. I had a gunship overhead to provide cover, and I didn't let anybody else go in with me at first.

There were bodies everywhere (our bodies only; the VC had removed all of theirs). The VC took the boots from all our guys. I had tried to get Peanula to leave his pistol and save the weight, but he had taken it anyway. They had emptied it into his face. He and Sergeant Segrist were lying together, inside the town. Jake [Sgt. Roy Jacobson] had wandered out of the jungle, alive but without his boots or weapon. The Vietnamese LLDB commander, Lieutenant Toi, had survived without a scratch—which made us all wonder about him.

With the gunship overhead covering us, I got the surviving Nungs and Cambodians to start loading bodies on the other helicopter. We sent out about fifteen helicopter loads of bodies. The strikers had to load the bodies of their friends on the helicopters—the wounded first, the dead second. There were thirty dead, thirty wounded, and thirty captured by the VC.

I was very upset about the whole thing. It was a patrol that I was supposed to lead, and I didn't lead it. I had liked Sergeant Segrist. He had been a good man and a good soldier, and now he was dead instead of me. He had told my wife, when we left, "Don't worry, Mrs. Kubasik, I'll bring your husband home, safe and sound." We had been over there for a total of three weeks, and I had let him down. He had a wife and two daughters. It was as if I were responsible for his death, in a way. I had big problems with this thing, for a long time. And they focused on Sergeant Jacobson.

When he showed up, it was without boots or weapon. He had been hiding in the jungle. It looked to me like Jake was a coward, had run and hid in the jungle instead of standing with the other guys and fighting. When Jake got the Bronze Star, I refused to attend the ceremony. It really bothered me. It ate at me all these years, until this year, at our convention in Nashville.

I hadn't seen Jake since I left Ben Cat. He had looked me up and called me a couple of years ago, but I didn't say anything to him about the way I felt. All I said was, "Jake, someday we'll have to talk." But I made up my mind that, if we ever met at one of these conventions, I was going to ask him about it, face to face.

Thank goodness Joe Stringham (Brigadier General Stringham now) was there. I asked the two of them to take a walk with me. I wanted Joe to hear this, too, because I hadn't talked to him about this before. I don't mind telling you, I cried my eyes out. I faced the man and told him that I had carried with me all these years the idea that he had been a coward. Now I wanted to hear from him directly what had happened that night.

It turned out that they were all heroes, including Jake. What he told me was that they were all running together, trying to get to cover, when Sergeant Peanula and Sergeant Segrist ran back for something. Jake didn't know what or why. And then I started putting the pieces together, and a picture of what might have happened appeared. [Sgt. Roy Jacobson's account of this battle and his escape are presented in the story "Bad Day at Ap Ban Dong So."]

The Littlest Guy in SF

Tully Strong was quite a character. He was supposed to have been the shortest man in the Airborne, and somehow he managed to end up in Special Forces. I was working for The Agency in early 1968 as a USAID employee, a captain in civilian clothes, when the NVA offensive struck during the Tet holidays. I was the CORDS [Civil Operations and Revolutionary Development Support] advisor to the PRU [Provincial Reconnaissance Unit], the Revolutionary Cadre, and the Census-Grievance Committees [three of the programs from which the Phoenix program was developed]. During the mop-up after Tet, my sergeant, who was the PRU advisor, was killed, so I was sent a new replacement NCO—who turned out to be Tully Strong.

A CV-2 Caribou landed at the strip at Song Be. I was standing there, looking for something that looked like a PRU advisor, and this little thing gets off the plane and comes up to me. He says, "My name is Sgt. Tully Strong, and I am here to kill Viet Cong!" He had a Cambodian woman with him, and I don't want to say anything bad about her, but she looked like five miles of bad tank trail. But he loved her, and that was his business. Nobody had told me that Tully had a little trouble with his drinking.

There were two military compounds—the SF facility at one end of town and another camp, the old SF camp that had been overrun years before—and a USAID compound in Song Be. We lived in the USAID compound, but often ate and drank and watched movies at the old camp, now used by MACV [Military Assistance Command Vietnam]. The MACV compound was in the south, the USAID compound in the center, and the new SF compound in the north.

Until Tully arrived, I had a jeep, a Bronco, and a moped to get around my province. One night, not long after Sergeant Strong had arrived, I was down at the MACV camp for dinner and a movie when I got a phone call. It was Major Nelms, the commander of the B-team [the company-level command and control]. He said, "Come down here and get your PRU sergeant. He is trying to tear up the camp."

I arrived to find Major Thompson, a *very* big, good man, with his one hand on Tully's head, holding him off. Little Tully was trying to fight him, but his arms were too short. It looked like something out of an old comedy film, with Tully yelling that he was going to whip Major Thompson's ass. I collected Tully and took him outside, told him that he was a bad boy, and that he couldn't do that sort of thing.

Less than a week later, I got another phone call. "You better come and get Tully," they said. "He just put your Bronco into the wire." Sure enough, Tully had gotten drunk and had driven my Bronco off the road and into the wire. It was destroyed.

"Okay, Tully, we can't have this sort of thing anymore. This has to stop," I told him.

But not long after that I sent him off somewhere on my little moped, and then the phone rang again. "The medic is down here working on Tully," they said. "You better come down and get him." Drunk, he'd run the moped off the road and into the concertina wire, and he'd gotten both stuck and cut quite badly. He had now ruined my little moped.

"Okay, Tully, that's it. No more driving for you." From then on Tully was restricted to walking or using a bicycle.

Not long after that a new sergeant arrived. He had just arrived in country. On the evening of his very first day, he was walking down to the MACV camp for the movie when he noticed a moaning sound coming from the moat around the camp. He stopped to investigate. Down at the bottom was this tiny little figure in an American uniform, moaning, "Help meee . . . help meee . . ." It was Tully, drunk again. He had run his bicycle off the road, into the moat.

The new guy went to the mess hall where the movie was going to be shown, and he said to me, "I want to go home. I've seen enough of Vietnam! I've had it! I just saw a midget trying to get out of the moat!"

Everybody looked at me. "Kubasik," one of them said, "you better go get Tully." So a bunch of us went out there and looked in the moat. It was about ten feet deep. There Tully was, trying to climb up out of it, calling in a pathetic, drunken voice, "Help me . . ." We pulled him out and sent him to bed. That was the end of the bicycle.

Shortly after that the town was under threat of attack by the NVA, and we started making preparations. I was looking for Tully, to get him out in the field to see what was going on, but I couldn't find him. We were out by the airstrip, talking about it, when the interpreter started laughing.

"What the hell is so funny?" I asked him. The rest of the Yards were laughing, too, but they didn't want to tell me why.

"Andy," I said to the interpreter, "give me the straight scoop. Where's Tully?"

He said, "Sir, first God-dammed plane in, Tully take his wife, he get on plane, and he *di-di-mau!*"

Only then did I discover that Tully, who was beloved by the PRU, never went on the three-day operations that I had sent him on. Instead, he sent the PRU off while he went behind a building somewhere and crashed. When the PRU got back, they gave him some information and he gave it to me, completely fabricated. We never saw him again, but his memory lingers on. Even today, when those of us who were there get together, the guys kid me about Tully. I swore I would kill him if I ever got the chance. We put out a chair for him, just in case Tully shows up.

The Boy Captain

Joe Stringham would later become a brigadier general, but when he was my boss at Ben Cat, thirty miles north of Saigon, I called him the "Boy Captain." Joe didn't really know how to play cards very well, so we used to lure him into card games and take all his money.

We were playing poker one night in the team room. A young sergeant from the MACV compound across the road was visiting and playing poker with us. He was also a Stringham (no relation to Joe), so we called him "Joe, Jr." We played several hands when, in the distance, we heard the unmistakable sound of an enemy mortar firing: *Whump! Whump! Whump!*

Now, under normal circumstances, we would all immediately start running because we all knew that, in about fifteen seconds or so, those mortar rounds were going to come back to earth, probably in our compound. But the Boy Captain kept studying his cards. Since he was the senior man, nobody moved. Joe Jr. started to look a little apprehensive.

"Uh, don't you think we ought to go to the bunkers, sir?" Joe Jr. asked.

"We'll, get there . . ." the Boy Captain said, still contemplating his poker hand.

We were all getting a little shaky at this point. I'm not that brave to begin with, but I was not going to leave until somebody else did. The Boy Captain continued to ignore the prospect of imminent death.

After another eternity, Joe Jr. meekly asked again, "Sir, are we going to go to the bunkers now?"

"NOBODY MOVES UNTIL THIS GODDAMN HAND IS OVER! Do you hear me?" the Boy Captain roared.

Joe Jr. was really getting worried, now, because the impact was due any second. He pleaded with the Boy Captain again.

But this time Elliot Wilson, our weapons sergeant, said in his slow, southern drawl, "I'll tell ya how it is, Stringham: we'll probably go to the bunkers when we see the Nung guards doing hand-to-hand combat with the VC at the doorway."

Captain Stringham said again, "Nobody moves till this hand is over!"

And then the first three mortar rounds hit, not too far away: *Blam! Blam! Blam!* Now the Boy Captain was a little shook up. "Everybody lay your hands down on the table! Nobody touch them till we get back!" And we all took off for our bunkers.

We were back in forty-five minutes. Nobody got killed in the attack, not a lot of damage got done, and we picked up the game where we left off. We'd been playing Deuces Wild. Joe turned over his cards; he had a straight flush, normally a winning hand. But one of the other guys laid out five aces and beat him. He had figured that he'd finally get back all the money we'd taken from him, but he lost again!

And Joe Jr. never ever came over to play poker again.

Flower Power, SF Style

Now this is a true story. I was a second lieutenant at the time this happened, and momentarily the commander of the camp at Ben Cat. Our defenses were virtually nonexistent. If the VC wanted the place, we probably would have had to give it to them because we had no sand bags or barbed wire to fortify the compound. We had been making requests for wire and bags for a long time, but nothing materialized. Finally, Col. John Spears, the 5th Group commander, authorized the request for the wire and bags, and the materials were prepared for delivery by air.

Without telling us, somebody decided to put this stuff on C-123s, in bundles, and drop it on our camp. About the time the aircraft appeared overhead, an ARVN convoy came motoring up the road through the camp. Without warning, the Air Force started kicking the bundles of sand bags and wire out the back, without parachutes, and these things were falling everywhere.

I sent my radio operator, Sergeant Reeves, out to the road. He cut the convoy, trying to hold it from the drop zone. He managed to stop one of the trucks, and that cut the convoy in half—something convoys are *never* supposed to do! Sergeant Reeves almost got run over by one of the ARVN trucks, and he stepped out of the way. The rest of the ARVN trucks zoomed past, trying to catch up with the front of the procession. They were scared!

The last plane came over, and I don't think they were actually aiming for it, but the pallet they dropped landed right on the back of the very last truck in the convoy. It flattened the truck like a pancake and killed all the ARVN soldiers riding in the back. Blood was running everywhere.

Then, out of nowhere, came the villagers screaming and yelling. The bundles had landed on houses, gardens, pigs, crops, and buildings. The next day, Joe Stringham, the camp commander, arrived with a large pile of piaster notes. He gave them to me, and it was my job to pay off the villagers for the damage done by the air drop. One guy lost two pigs. Okay, three thousand piasters. Another guy lost his garden: five thousand piasters. Another man was preparing pineapples for market; he got out of the way just before they turned to pineapple juice. He got two thousand piasters. I distributed about three hundred thousand piasters at a time when they were still worth quite a bit.

Finally, I got them all paid off. They didn't love us, but they had their money. And we had our sand bags, a hundred thousand of them, and concertina wire.

About this time a Col. Jeff Wilson became III Corps commander. He was not jump qualified, and proud of it. Wilson was notorious for his dislike of the Airborne community, and he hated Special Forces especially. He and Colonel Spears, our 5th Group commander, didn't get along.

We were busy using the sand bags and wire to fortify our camp when Colonel Wilson arrived for an inspection one day. "What are you doing with all these sand bags? What is this wire supposed to be for?" he wanted to know.

"Sir," I said, "we have to fix our defensive positions."

"Lieutenant," he said, "do you want these Vietnamese to think we are cowards? This gives the American Army a bad image! It makes us look like we are afraid of the VC!"

He went on like that for a while, then said, "I am leaving here today. I want *every* foxhole filled up! I want every sandbag emptied! And I want all of this concertina wire removed!" Then he looked around and continued, "This place looks shitty! It is an eyesore. I will be back in two weeks, and I want to see *flowers* growing in this whole area!"

His MAAG [Military Assistance Advisory Group] advisor was devastated. Nobody knew what to say. But Colonel Wilson wasn't through. He concluded, "You *will* have flowers here in two weeks, or I will relieve you. And don't think that I am not your commander, either! You are in III Corps, and you belong to me! Fill these foxholes up, get rid of that wire, and get this place landscaped. I want to see flowers!"

So we filled the holes and took up the wire. We made a deal with the Vietnamese and gave them all the bags and wire. There was nothing he could do about that. Two weeks later, Colonel Wilson came back, and he was amazed. I had the nicest flowers in III Corps—all plastic. I sent some of my people into Saigon, and they bought up every plastic flower they could find. We stuck them in the ground, all over the camp. The very next night after Colonel Wilson's visit, we received a mortar attack, and we didn't have a damn thing to hide behind.

"I Think He Wanted to Kill Me!"

A guy came wandering down the highway and into our camp one day, asking to speak to the American commander. He had a note and handed it to our interpreter. They talked for a minute, then Joe Stringham [the camp commander, known as the "Boy Captain"] asked the interpreter, "Well, what does the note say?"

We all knew that interpreters didn't like to tell us bad news. They didn't lie, but they would avoid answering if they could. The guy said, "Oh, no problem. Nothing to worry about."

Joe said, "What is in the letter?"

"Nothing important," the interpreter said. "No big deal."

This just made Joe highly suspicious. "I want to know what is in the goddammed letter!" he said.

Finally, the interpreter opened the note and read: "To the American commander of forces in this area. If you take any more troops and attempt to move north of Lai Kai plantation, we will cut you off and annihilate you." It was from the VC commander in the region.

Joe turned to me and said, "*Te-uy* [Vietnamese for *lieutenant*], that son of a bitch can't threaten me like that!"

"Joe," I told him, "don't do it!"

"Goddammit, they can't tell me to stay home! I'll show them!"

The interpreter and the guy who brought in the message were shaking in their boots. They thought we were going to kill them. The interpreter said, too, "*Dai-uy* [Vietnamese for *captain*], this VC commander, he means business!"

Joe said to me, "I am going to go up that road, kick some butt, and take some names. They are not going to do this to *me!*"

But of course Joe had to go. And he wasn't stupid about it. We had a good ARVN artillery unit in the town, and Joe developed a very detailed fire plan for his mission. He took it down to the artillery unit and went over it with their advisor, in detail. This fire plan covered the entire route from our camp north for about five miles. Anyway, Joe took a large force (about half the camp) out on the road and up to the north.

They had been gone only about three hours when, off in the distance, you could hear the *Whump! Whump! Whump!* of artillery and the sounds of machine guns and rifles firing. Then Joe called me on the radio. "Send in the pre-planned fires!" he said, giving me the coordinates. His fire plan gave him covering fire all the way back. Joe and his force were coming back to camp, on the run.

While I was working the radios, coordinating the artillery support, a helicopter carrying Lieutenant Colonel De La Pena, the detachment commander, arrived. He had a new major with him, his XO [executive officer]. This major, new to the combat zone, was trying to make sure that military courtesies were observed. "Where's the camp commander?" he demanded of my sergeant.

"Well, sir, the commander is in contact right now, but Lieutenant Kubasik is in charge of the camp."

The major came over to me while I was still on the radio. "Lieutenant . . ." he said, but I cut him off. "I'll be with you in a minute, major," I told him.

"I want to talk to you *now!*" the major said.

"I'll be with you in a minute," I told him again. "My commander is in trouble!"

"Do you realize that the colonel is here?"

"That's great. I'll talk to him later!" He was telling me that I was supposed to be standing at attention, and I was telling him to get out of my face. He was saying that he was going to have me court-martialed when Lieutenant Colonel De La Pena grabbed him and pulled him out of the way.

Well, it took Joe and that force of his three hours to move up the road, but it only took them forty-five minutes to get back! They must have run all the way. Joe was sweating heavily when he finally arrived. When he caught his breath, he said, "You know what, *Te-uy,* that goddamm guy out there was serious! I think he wanted to *kill* me!

Ambush at the Rubber Plantation

We sent out a patrol into the French-owned-and-operated Michelin rubber plantation at Lai Kai. Of seventy-two guys on the operation, sixty-nine were killed, including one American. We were mad. We figured the French knew about the ambush and could have warned our guys, but they wanted to avoid trouble with the VC and didn't.

We could hear the firing. It was only a couple of miles from the camp. Joe Stringham wanted to take a relief force out, but I wouldn't let him. The VC routinely prepared ambushes for relief forces in situations like this, and it got lots of guys killed unnecessarily. If we could have gotten air support, it would have made sense, but not otherwise.

"If you try to take a force out of camp, I will take command and have you detained," I told him.

He didn't go, thank goodness. Then, afterwards, we had to go out and collect the bodies.

There were two towers at the plantation. One was a radio facility, and the other was a lab. Joe and I both figured that they used the radio to signal the VC. We all felt the French were in collusion with the VC.

I don't remember just whose hair-brained idea it was, Joe's or mine, but we decided to blow up the radio tower as a warning to the French plantation owners not to let this happen again. But of course we couldn't actually do it ourselves; that would not have been nice. So we paid our Cambodian soldiers a hellacious amount of money to do it for us. They collected their gear and off they went.

It was about midafternoon when the explosion went off. A huge cloud of smoke and debris filled the sky above the plantation in the distance. Even at that range, we noticed a large quantity of what looked like paper floating in the air. I don't know how much C4 they placed in the tower, but they certainly blew the hell out of it.

Within minutes the Frenchman who ran the plantation arrived in his ancient Citroen, waving American fuse-lighters and blasting materials in our faces, insisting we were responsible.

"Don't be silly," we told him. "We've been right here all afternoon, and besides, the VC have more of those things than we do!"

He departed, and then we finally figured out that the operation wasn't quite the success we had thought it had been. The Cambodians became confused and set the explosives in the lab, not the radio station.

CORDS

We were just putting the CORDS program together in 1967 when I was working for The Agency, and it really wasn't that effective in my area around Song Ba at the time. The PRU cadre were better, and so were the Census-Grievance Committees.

There were four programs under USAID at the time: Phoenix, PRU, Census-Grievance, and Revolutionary Development cadres. The PRU were the Provincial Reconnaissance Unit, and they went out and gathered information; they were both Vietnamese and Montagnard. The Revolutionary Development cadres went around building pigsties, schools, and things like that. The Census-Grievance program used the village elders, who were supposed to ask for building materials for civic improvements. But they also kept a big book in the back room with a map of the town showing each house and family, indicating who was pro- and anti-VC.

I had a problem with this. I thought, If I lived in this town and somebody in authority didn't like me, I could be history. But one time the Census-Grievance Committee in the town indicated to us that one of the men in the community was a VC tax collector. So we started doing some more investigation about the guy, and we got concrete proof that the man was in fact a VC agent. Well, I was instructed to "neutralize" the man—to make him disappear. That was kind of harsh, but I had to do something. I wanted to get him out of the tax collection business, one way or another, and I didn't really care who did it or how.

We filled up a can with piasters in small denominations, the kind of money the guy would have been collecting for the VC. The can was "discovered" by some children who were playing under the man's house, digging in the dirt. The news of the discovery quickly spread, and we didn't have to do a thing to the guy. The VC figured (just as we expected) that the guy was holding out on them, and he disappeared.

The Census-Grievance program as we operated it was essentially an intelligence gathering operation, and it was just getting off the ground. I didn't have to take care of any of these people myself, thank goodness, and most of the cases were pretty clear cut. And it seemed to be working, too.

The Boy Captain, Part II

Our camp at Ben Cat got hit pretty hard one night, and Joe and I and the radio operator, were all in our hole. Well, actually Joe was standing up beside the hole. He would never get down, no matter what was happening. Stringham wanted air support, even if it was the middle of the night, and he wanted it *now*. He was yelling into the radio, "I want to talk to Ben Hoa . . . I want to talk to Ben Hoa!"

He wasn't getting any response at all. "Goddammit," he roared, "I can't hear anybody!"

The RTO, Staff Sergeant Pressler, was normally a rather excitable young man, but he looked up from the pit at Joe standing above. "Well, Sir," he drawled, "if you'd get your goddammed foot off the antenna we might be able to communicate with somebody."

BDA Mission

We got a mission to go in after a B-52 strike to do BDA [bomb damage assessment]. It was just like in the movies: sealed orders to be opened only at midnight. Well, our maps were old, our smoke couldn't get through the triple-layer canopy jungle, and we were lost the whole time we were out on this operation. The VC seemed to know just where we were, and where we were going; they were coming up out of their holes to snipe at us all during the mission.

There were three groups of us led by Spargo, Stringham, and me. And we were separated by a few hundred meters. Spargo called on the radio, "I'm making contact now. I'm pushing them to the east."

Well, that was toward Joe Stringham, and then Joe calls, "Yeah, I see 'em. Maybe I can push them over that way, too."

That's when I chimed in, "Dammit, why don't you push them straight ahead. You're pushing them all toward me!"

Finally, we made it to the pickup zone, and we could hear the choppers inbound to get us. I could hear firing from the other two sectors, but mine was quiet. I figured that I had a clean pickup zone. I had the helos in sight in the distance and "popped smoke." Then I heard the voice of Colonel De La Pena on the radio: "I see your smoke. We'll be there in zero five."

Well, the VC actually had us surrounded and were just waiting for their opportunity. As soon as the helicopters came in over the tree line, all hell broke loose. I waved them off with the only smoke grenade I had left—WP, white phosphorus. The helos pulled up and out of there, and I called, "We are in contact. We need help!" I started yelling for gunship fire support. "If you see my smoke, I need fire put fifty meters to the north!"

"I can't do that, sir," one chopper pilot called. "We have to maintain a one-hundred-meter buffer!"

"I want it fifty meters to the north of that smoke!" I told him. "I don't want you to put it behind them and chase them toward me. I want you to chase them away!" But he wasn't going to do it.

Then the voice of Dick Jarret came on the radio: "I'll take this mission. That's a friend of mine down there. If anybody's gonna kill that son of a bitch, it ought to be me!"

Sherman's Second March

I took the strikers out on a patrol, and, to stay off the road, I put everybody out in the rice paddies in a big skirmish line. As we moved along, we noticed several figures about 300 meters away, dressed in black, and possibly carrying something that might be a rifle, but we couldn't tell for sure.

Then the Nungs started yelling at my sergeant, Willy [Sgt. Elliot Wilson] "*Chung-si, Chung-si*! Get away, get away!"

Willy looked down and noticed a 155-millimeter artillery round, rigged as a command-detonated mine. Then he looked up at me, and in his slow, southern drawl remarked carefully, "Goddamm, *Te-uy,* ah think they're trying to kill me!" All three hundred of my guys opened up on the figures in the distance—and nobody hit them!

To make certain there would be no more surprise, I had the troops spread out in a line, and we set fire to everything in front of us. When we arrived in Ben Cat, I was met by Capt. Joe Stringham, who inquired about all the smoke trailing us. When I explained about the booby-trap bomb, all he said was, "I thought it was Sherman's second march to the sea."

The White Star Program

I started out in the White Star program in Laos as a radio operator and as an advisor with the 14th Mobile Combatant of the Royal Lao Army. We were trying to develop one hundred guerrilla companies to operate across the southern portion of Laos. We were trying to build up the forces and take back the villages that had been captured by the Pathet Lao.

I also worked for Capt. Elliot Sydnor as his radio operator in the jungles of the Plateau du Beaulevens. We trained and equipped guerrilla companies—tribesmen in loin cloths, with crossbows. We trained them to use World War II weapons. They were primitive, but they weren't stupid! I remember giving one of these men a BAR [Browning Automatic Rifle—a very heavy weapon], and he just couldn't manage to hit a thing with it. Then we gave him a carbine, and he hit every target. We figured he just didn't want to lug the BAR, but we made him carry the BAR anyway.

Rest & Relaxation

Ben Cat was a real hole of a camp, and we tried to get out whenever we could. Normally, that meant a trip to Saigon about once a month. Since we always had to have at least one officer in the camp at all times, that also meant that Joe Stringham and I alternated. And when I went, it was usually with Elliot Wilson. We tried to go on a Friday afternoon, and planned on catching a flight back on Sunday or Monday.

We didn't drink in camp—or at least, I didn't—so that was an important activity for our first night in town. Willy and I got down there, and we had a ball! On Monday we went out to the chopper pad at Tan Son Nhut, and there were no helicopters to take us back to Ben Cat. So we went back to town, had a drink, and stayed another night. Our interest in returning to camp began to diminish.

Messages started arriving at all our local Saigon haunts (the SF camps and offices where we might possibly drop in, as well as at our regular "safe bars") from Joe Stringham, instructing me to call the camp to report on our status. We didn't think this was tactically sound, so I didn't do it. We spent the week partying.

Lo and behold, we came staggering out of a bar, and down Tu Do Street marched Joe, with fire in his eye. It was one of the few times I have ever seen him really mad at me. "Goddammit, *Te-uy,* we have been trying to get you everywhere. I had to come to town for a meeting, and there isn't an officer in the camp!" We were standing on the corner of Tu Do and Louis Pasteur streets, in the shade of the many tall trees that lined the avenues of that part of town.

"Gosh, sir, I'm really sorry," I said, "but we tried and we tried but we just couldn't get a helicopter! We tried, every day." Joe started to calm down, and he even looked like he might be beginning to believe me.

But Willy ruined that. "Goddammit, *Dai-uy,*" Willy slurred drunkenly. "Do you have any idea how difficult it is to get a goddamm helicopter at this intersection?"

Joe suddenly began to lose confidence in our sincerity. Willy continued, "We come out here ever' mornin', look up at those trees, figure ain't no helicopter gonna land, an' we go back in the bar to wait till tomorrow . . ."

"You son of a bitch!" Joe roared. "You get your ass back to Ben Cat—if you have to walk!"

I was really scared; Joe was sincerely angry. But it was late in the day, and there really wasn't any practical way to get back to Ben Cat until the next day.

Willy looked at him. "We can stay the night?"

"Well, you can't get out tonight, so of course you can stay the night. But I want you out at the helicopter pad first thing tomorrow morning!"

Willy looked at me. "Sir," he said, "the old man says we can stay in town tonight. Do you think he'll loan us twenty bucks?" We were both broke by now.

"Uh, sir," I said to Joe, " . . . uh, do you think you could loan us fifty bucks?"

Joe blew up again, but he pulled out his wallet and loaned us the money.

Trade Bait

I flew into Tan Son Nhut airport one time in 1965. While I was waiting for a vehicle to pick me up, I noticed a large number of air conditioners stacked up on the ramp, down the flight line. Now, we didn't really need any air conditioners—our hooches were just screened-in enclosures—but they would make excellent "trade bait." So I was standing there when an Air Force chief master sergeant came out and said to me, "Can I help you, lieutenant?"

"Yes," I said, as casually as possible, "I was supposed to pick up some air conditioners. But I don't see them."

"We've got them for you, sir. They're right down there, at the next loading dock. Did you want to pick them up?"

"Well, I can't right now, but we'll be back for them."

So I sent a sergeant downtown to Camp Goodman to pick up a two-and-a-half-ton truck—and a clip board. He came back with the truck and the clip board, and we went back to the Air Force logistics office. The chief master sergeant wasn't around this time, and I had to start over. Another airman came over and said, "What do you need, lieutenant?"

"I was supposed to pick up twenty air conditioners, but I don't see them. They told me they'd be at Dock 65." We were at Dock 20.

"Well, sir," he said, "they must have given you the wrong dock. We've got air conditioners here. How many do you need?"

"Twenty," I said.

"We've got two hundred; they must have made a mistake on the paperwork. These have to be yours!"

"Okay," I said. "But it will take us a while to load these things."

"Don't worry about it, sir," he said. "We'll get you a forklift." Within a few minutes, the guy had loaded twenty of someone else's air conditioners on the back of my duce-and-a-half, and we were out of there.

We took those things and traded them for steaks and beer and stuff for the camp. It started out as a joke, but when everybody fell into place, I figured that twenty air conditioners were good trade bait.

The Mutiny

Do you want the *true* story, or the *funny* story about this that I tell? Okay, this is my version of events. In Morley Safer's book, *Flashbacks*, he said that Joe Stringham was the bravest man he'd ever met, and I'd agree with him. But the incident he described didn't quite happen the way he remembered. Here's the way it really happened:

Ben Cat, remember, was so poorly protected that we would have given it to the NVA if they had just asked for it politely. It was theirs for the taking. Our normal routine was to batten down when the lights went out, and we prayed for daylight.

Morley Safer and his cameraman, Alex Briar, were visiting, and this happened just before it was time for them to leave. The local Vietnamese special forces, the LLDB, got a brand-new second lieutenant as a commander. This guy was a jerk; that just goes to prove that second lieutenants are the same in every army.

Our camp population included two major groups, one of ethnic Chinese Nungs and Cambodians, the other of Vietnamese. There were two companies of each. These two groups were billeted in buildings facing each other across a square. The two groups didn't get along at all.

The Nungs were mercenaries, and they got paid better than the Vietnamese. That made the Vietnamese angry. The Chinese Nungs didn't care who they killed. They had no love for the Vietnamese at all, even before the new lieutenant arrived.

The new lieutenant (in the tradition of his breed) went downtown and encountered some of the Nungs. He decided that they were out of uniform and started chewing them out because they didn't salute him. The Vietnamese officer was offended and angry, and he returned to our camp. He had all the Chinese fall out into the square, on the north side of the plaza, into formation, and started raising hell and chewing them out. The Nungs responded by laughing at him.

About this time Morley and the cameraman started filming. They knew there was going to be trouble.

This dumb-ass lieutenant drew his .45 (I didn't see this part) and was about to fire into the formation. His first round went over their heads, which was all the excuse the Chinese needed. They came up shooting! They nailed him, right next to the building. He went down, but he was still alive.

I was coming in the gate when all this started. I was wearing my tiger-stripes and carrying my M16 and walking toward the group when the shooting started. Joe screamed at me, "Throw that weapon away!" With the weapon, I would look like a natural target to either side, and anybody could shoot me. Suddenly, it felt like a red-hot poker, and I threw it in the air. It landed in the back of a truck.

I dove into our storehouse building for cover. Two of the other guys, Jake [Sgt. Roy Jacobson] and *Bac-si* [Sgt. John Burns], went out to the lieutenant. The Nungs were screaming at them. They didn't want to kill him, they wanted him to die slowly, and they didn't want anybody interfering. Finally, our two guys got back inside, and then the shooting picked up again. This time it was the Vietnamese troops from the other side of the compound who started firing up the Nungs.

We really didn't want to be involved. I went into the supply room for cover. I used some of the piles of empty sand bags (the ones that Col. Jeff Wilson wouldn't let us fill) for cover. Somebody's machine-gun bullets came through the window. I didn't know this at the time, but they hit a bunch of big number ten cans of ham and lima bean rations that were stored in there. The big cans were falling on me, and the thick juice was running out, all over me. My eyes were closed, so all I really knew was that I was getting hit with these solid impacts, and I could feel something wet. I really thought that I was being killed! I thought I was being shot and I was bleeding, when actually it was just the cans falling on me, leaking their juice!

Well, I decided it was time to make a break for it, and I dashed out of there, headed for the MAAG compound. When I got outside, I ran right into one of the Vietnamese officers giving orders. I ran over, screaming, and crashed into him. The collision shook him up, and it shook me up, too. That collision stopped the fight. The Nungs stopped firing because they didn't want to hit me, and the Vietnamese stopped because they didn't want to hit their commander. I was yelling at him, and he finally ordered his men to cease fire. Joe Stringham went over to the Nung commander, so Joe and I were now between the two forces, and that calmed the situation down.

A couple of days later my father-in-law was sitting in a bar in Philadelphia, and was watching the news on the TV over the bar. He was watching the report from Morley Safer. "That guy looks familiar," he said. Then, they tell me, he fell off his bar stool when he recognized me.

Later, back at Fort Bragg, I was called in to see the commanding general, and I was presented with the Soldier's Medal, the highest decoration you can get for an action that does not involve the enemy. The citation makes me sound like a real hero, but I was actually one mighty scared SOB!

Montagnards

I've never met anybody who knew the Yards who didn't love them. They were tiny, tough, cheerful, smart, honest, and faithful—and in sharp contrast (sad to report) to the dominant culture in South Vietnam. They were, besides all this, the victims of many centuries of oppression from the lowland Vietnamese who call them *moi,* meaning *savage.* The motto of Special Forces is *De Opresso Liber,* or *Free the Oppressed,* and it was pretty much love at first sight between these two communities. When one of the big Green Berets led a gaggle of them off on patrol, it looked like the Boy Scout troop from hell, what with all those guns and grenades, and they looked like the were going to have some fun!

There are (or at least were in 1973) eleven major tribes in the highlands, including the Hmong, Jerai, and Rhade. The Montagnards are ethnically different from the Vietnamese. The Montagnards' origins are Malayo-Polynesian. They are different, too, in language, culture, architecture, and religion, and the Vietnamese remind them of this constantly. The dominant Vietnamese loathe them, and since the victory of the NVA over the ARVN and the Republic of South Vietnam, the Yards have been slaughtered by the tens of thousands, their language and tribal culture suppressed, their lands taken away by the lowlanders. Most SF people I know didn't especially care about the fall of South Vietnam—the lowland Vietnamese people of the south just weren't willing to fight for their cause. But the Yards were a different story.

—Hans Halberstadt

ROY JACOBSON

Roy Jacobson, Joe Stringham, and Kenn Kubasik all served together at Detachment A-301 at Ben Cat, north of Saigon along Highway 13. Roy, a sergeant, was the only American survivor of the company-size patrol that was ambushed on December 29, 1964 by what was probably a brigade-size force of hard-core VC. He spent most of the period from 1964 to 1972 in Southeast Asia, including several years in the employment of the CIA's Air America in Laos and Thailand.

The first story is a good illustration of the problems ARVN units had, and why SF teams generally disliked working with the lowland Vietnamese. (In the story "We Are All Dead. Out," Kenn Kubasik tells about this same disastrous mission from his perspective, back at Ben Cat listening to the calls for support from the team sergeant on the radio.)

Bad Day at Ap Ban Dong So

We had only been in country a couple of weeks. We had very little experience in combat or in Vietnam. Although the team senior radio operator had been in Korea, and Kenn [Kubasik] had been with White Star in Laos, neither had been in really heavy combat.

Our team leader at the time, who shall remain nameless, was a real son of a bitch and was shipped back to the states early. He didn't provide team leadership—Kenn had to do that as a new second lieutenant. Kenn had ten years as an enlisted soldier, but there is a real difference between being a staff sergeant and being the officer in charge of a team in a combat zone.

Things were so bad at Ben Cat that we weren't even patrolling when we first got there. The team we were relieving had only been at Ben Cat for a couple of months. Instead of the deliberate transition period that became SOP later, the other team just pulled out when we arrived. Bang, there we were, new as a team, new to the country, all by ourselves with an incompetent commander.

Our first patrol was a short, unambiguous excursion that didn't accomplish much, but the second one was done with the Vietnamese LLDB. The whole operation and the Vietnamese company was led by an LLDB lieutenant named Toi.

Our team sergeant had been around for quite a while. He was a senior master sergeant and a decent enough guy, with a lot of time in 10th Group in Europe. "Top" (as we called him) was in the nominal position of command, by advising the LLDB captain.

Sgt. Reino Peanula was the other guy; he and I had gone through demolitions training together.

I was an E-4, and I had command of 346 Company. Despite my low rank, our team leader gave me command of this company of ARVN infantry. Their lieutenant was a guy named Nguyen-something, but I called him "Cowboy." He spoke decent English—a nice guy, and the lover of the Vietnamese nurse in the camp. He was kind of a wise guy, and maybe I was assigned to him because I was young and a wise guy, too. We got along fine, although it was a very short-lived relationship, because the company got wiped out.

I have strong memories of that patrol. We moved out of camp at night and marched to the east of Highway 13, through the jungle toward Ap Ban Dong So. It was not a silent move. We had a headquarters element with Lieutenant Toi, Top, and Reino, then a heavy weapons platoon with mortars and machine guns, and the two companies of ARVN infantry. We left Ben Cat and marched north.

But the march was typical of the ARVN—transistor radios playing, pots and pans banging, laughing and smoking. An occasional sniper shot would stop us for a few minutes, then we would move north again.

During a smoke break, about halfway to Ap Ban Dong So, Reino was fooling around with his AR-15 and lost a part of the bolt. He wasn't really concerned about it; he still had his Browning Hi-Power pistol. Although Reino wasn't worried about his rifle, I was, for a different reason. Mine kept jamming, and after this operation I turned it in for an old M2 .30-caliber carbine.

Another thing I remember was our march rations. The troops used to get a piece of very fatty pork rolled in sticky rice, all wrapped in a banana leaf. I changed that for my ration—I had them give me a piece of well-cooked chicken instead of the pork fat.

Sgt. Elliot Wilson had a company of ethnic Chinese Nungs, 349 Company, and with him was one of our medics, John Burns. They moved independently of us, around to the north to a town called Bau Bang.

We arrived at Ap Ban Dong So in late morning, posted guards, and went to a little restaurant. Dong So was a nice town, clean and pretty, and people were friendly enough. It was on the northern edge of the huge Lai Kai Michelin rubber plantation. We drank beer and had some noodle soup. It's funny what comes back after thirty years. I remember thinking how beautiful it was—nice smells, a clear, crisp day.

I remember the spicy cooking smells, the interpreter kidding me as I brushed my teeth. I was with Peanula and Top and Lieutenant Toi in a small house in the town. After we ate dinner, posted guards, and scheduled guard duty among the Americans, we turned in.

About midnight the interpreter woke me up to tell me that there were many VC around the town. He had some weird, concocted story: the VC had Thompson submachine guns with red-painted stocks! They were led by a white man on a white horse! Then runners came in from around the town with reports for us.

There were only about one hundred and twenty of us in this company, not very well trained, not very heavily equipped or organized around quite a large perimeter.

We were aware that there were VC on at least three sides of us at that point. We got reports from the north and east and the south of sightings and contact with the VC. There was a hell of a flurry of activity then. Within minutes we were being shelled by mortars and rifle grenades, right there in the center of Dong So.

We were out of range of our own mortars back at Ben Cat, and we heard artillery firing somewhere to the south. We figured that the camp was getting hit at the same time we were in contact. Top contacted Denzel on the radio. I was in the same room with him and the radio, and my company and I were all part of this big, loose perimeter. I didn't know where Cowboy was. In minutes, we were under extremely heavy fire. All of a sudden we had a *lot* of casualties. I hauled a couple of wounded guys into the building where we were, which turned out to be no good, because we had to leave them, anyway, when we took off.

The troops were firing into hundreds of VC running right down the middle of Highway 13 and the middle of the streets. I later heard a Vietnamese report that there were four thousand enemy soldiers attacking us, and I don't doubt it. They were pouring though the town gate, roaring into the place. They were moving into the place in a kind of continuous stream.

I don't think they really knew where we were because many ran right past us. Initially there was a lot of firing and confusion. I didn't know where Peanula was, but I did know Top was in the building behind me. We threw hand grenades. Then I went back and told Top, "The VC are among us in town!"

He and I talked, and he called in artillery as I was standing there. Then he told me, "Throw a grenade under the radio," and we both rolled grenades in there. At that point he and I both took off from the house. The fighting from then on was very fragmented and leaderless—just individuals or groups of two or three. And it was over very quickly.

About that time some heavier artillery came in, and there was a tremendous series of explosions right in front of us. I don't think I was knocked out, but the artillery disoriented me. When I regained my senses, I noticed a large group of VC running north, right up the highway. I don't know why they did that, if they were reacting to Willy [Sgt. Elliot Wilson] who might have been moving to react to the attack with his Nungs. But one large group was obviously moving under the control of somebody, and they moved right past us, without searching the houses for us. They headed for the north side of town.

Then Top and Reino and Lieutenant Toi came running past, and the LLDB were with them. Top hollered that we were going to move toward the west. Lieutenant Toi reported at the same time that there were no VC to the west. At that point, as far as I could tell, there were VC everywhere. Reino gave me all the magazines he had for his useless AR-15; I put about six in a sack and another two in the cargo pocket of my pants. There were bullets cracking around us, but we'd lost our night vision and couldn't seen anything.

We were walking away from town, to the west. I remember that we were moving through a pig pen when an automatic weapon opened up on us from about fifty feet away. There were about twelve of us, marching single file in a column. The sudden fire split the group into two sections. That was the last time I saw the other two Americans alive.

Now there were five of us, still marching to the west, with shooting all around. The sound of firing was very loud, with loud cracks from the bullets going by. The cracks meant that the bullets were really close!

Then Andy, the interpreter, fell headfirst into a well. He screamed, "Help me, Jake!" I had two of the other guys hold my ankles, and I reached in and hauled him out. At that point we realized that we'd been separated from the rest of the group, and we agreed between us that we would continue to move toward the west. By this time, we were in "escape and evasion" mode, and we decided to move into the jungle and wait for daylight.

There were groups of VC moving around us, in both directions. While we moved to the west, Vietnamese air force fighter-bomber planes arrived on the scene and started dropping bombs around Dong So. Well, at that point the VC were in the town. The strikers who were still alive were in the jungle, so our guys were getting bombed.

We made it to the edge of the jungle about three kilometers from Dong

So. There were VC everywhere, moving in groups of two or three, moving along. We crawled into the jungle, and I took an assessment of the group. Nobody was unscathed. We had cuts, bruises, bleeding, concussions. Andy was bruised and cut all to hell from his fall into the well; he thought both his arms were broken.

I had an AR-15 with about a half-dozen magazines, including the ones Reino had given me. Andy had an M1 carbine with one magazine. There was one tall striker from the 346 Company, and he had an M1 rifle with a half-dozen eight-round clips. The other striker had no weapon or ammo. We had one hand grenade.

We all lay in the jungle in a star formation. The unarmed striker started to cry. Andy, the interpreter, was lying next to him. He took his bayonet and put it to the guy's throat and told him to stop making noise, or we would all die. He stopped crying.

Then we heard engines coming. We were only a few feet from the edge of the jungle, and we happened to be near a place where a VC unit was exfiltrating from the battle. The noise was coming from many little Vespa-type scooters. Some of them were halted just beyond where we were.

One of the VC gave a series of orders to the others, then stepped over to the edge of the jungle to take a piss. He hit both Andy's and my boots! Then he and the little scooters left, back in the direction of Dong So; they were clearly hauling something out of there, to the edge of the rubber plantation.

We just laid there until first light. Then we moved back to the east, toward Dong So. We saw workers leaving Dong So, heading to the rubber plantation—the start of another normal day, I guess! And as we walked toward the town, I had one of the Vietnamese (a civilian who'd been along to crank the ANGR-9 radio generator) flag down a bus. This guy was in civilian clothes. I pulled the pin on that last grenade and gave it to him, with instructions to hold the spoon firmly down unless he had to throw it in the bus.

He got the bus to stop. The driver said that everyone was dead in Dong So, including two Americans. There were no VC, he said, but there were some "imperialist" soldiers still in the town.

We saw Lieutenant Toi and a few of the strikers, and we moved into the town. Lieutenant Toi took me behind the house where we had been the night before. Top and Reino were both there. It was obvious they were both dead; they were gray and stiff. Both had bullet holes in the head.

The little restaurant was still there—and it was open! We went in, and I ordered beers for the guys. We had Beer Larue, not Ba Muy Ba ["33" brand, the Budweiser of Vietnam]. About that time, Kenn came over in a helicopter and landed. He told me that he'd been in the town earlier that morning and that nobody was alive.

I remember the battle vividly, but after that things go blank in places. I remember riding back on the helicopter with the remains of Top and Reino. Kenn and I had words, because I thought the wounded guys ought to go out first, before the dead Americans. But, in hindsight, that didn't matter. Nobody was going to die by then who hadn't died already.

I was taken by helicopter to a Vietnamese LLDB compound called Thu Dau Mot. There were no Americans there, but a Vietnamese brigade headquarters. I recounted my story—essentially what I have just told you. I was there for a few hours, and I was interviewed by a Special Forces major. I was sent to Ben Hoa, where our C-team [battalion-level command and control] was, and then to a TOC [Tactical Operations Center] in Saigon, where I repeated it again. By this time I was getting sick of it.

Finally, after they were done with me, a master sergeant from the intel section took me out drinking and left me with a pretty girl for the night. It was a good way to heal. She was a nice young person, and we were married for the night. It was just what I needed at the time—a good load of beer and a girl. When I got up in the morning, I went back to Ben Cat.

I had some questions about the whole thing when I went back. Lieutenant Toi said that Top and Reino went back to try to find me, apparently after we got separated. I have a hunch, not based on any real proof, that Lieutenant Toi was VC. Of the two times in my life where I have come very close to being killed, and where a little bad luck would have made the difference, both involved Lieutenant Toi. Both times he looked very surprised when I showed back up again. Besides, I thought it was bad form on his part to be reporting me captured when I hadn't been.

I have no survivor's guilt about that operation. The battle probably lasted about four minutes. Actually, there was no battle—it was an immediate, overwhelming annihilation. I was very young and inexperienced. Knowing what I knew then, and now, there wasn't anything different I could have done.

Bad Day at Ap Dong Xoai

Capt. Joe Stringham and I were the only two survivors of six on this patrol. We were the Mike Force. We were so new to the program that we didn't yet have the recon team, but were simply sent in to augment camp security at the camp at Dong Xoai (pronounced "Dong Sway") after an entire Vietnamese airborne ranger unit was decimated in June of 1965. It was quite a battle, and one of the Americans at the camp earned a Medal of Honor.

After the battle, we went in with two companies of Mike Forces, with no recon team element, as was normal later. Joe took Willy [Sgt. Elliot Wilson] and me with him. We were the only Americans. We arrived late in the evening, and we awoke the next morning to discover that directly beneath the thin floor of our hooch the ground was covered with scorpions.

The camp was still being built, but we were putting out patrols. We made one patrol to the north—the memorable part of that one was wading neck-deep up a creek. We found large quantities of weapons from the battle that had annihilated the ARVN airborne unit. The more influential of my Nungs came away from these patrols with AR-15s, helmets, and other equipment left on the battlefield; it was quite a cache.

We went on a patrol to the west of Dong Xoai: Joe and I, two Cambodians, and two Vietnamese. We'd received information that elements of the VC 325C Regiment were present about eight or nine klicks [kilometers] from our camp.

We'd become accustomed to hearing warning shots during these patrols; they came from VC who observed us and marked our progress and location by firing their rifles. That was disconcerting, but we got used to it.

When we reached the assigned area, we approached a house in an open field. The two Cambodians went forward toward the house. The two Vietnamese were about fifty meters to the south of the house, and Joe and

I were to the north at the edge of the clearing. As the two Cambodians approached the house, we all came under sudden and intense automatic weapons fire. The Cambodians were killed immediately, shot down right in front of the place. The other pair took off to the southwest, and Joe and I took off almost directly into the attack, where they'd least expect us to go. That was actually the only thing we could do.

We ran hard for the first few hundred meters. We could hear the NVA yelling to each other; we understood enough of the language to tell they knew we were Americans. I remember tripping and getting my feet tangled in a vine. Joe asked, in an almost conversational voice, "Could you please hurry up?" I chuckled at that, even then.

We made our way back with minor contact with the enemy. The other two guys, the Vietnamese, were killed by a patrol of strikers from our own camp—they were in black pajamas and didn't identify themselves properly and weren't recognized. Joe and I also had trouble entering the camp, but ultimately we identified ourselves and made it back inside.

The same Lieutenant Toi appeared at Dong Xoai, and this was beginning to be too much of a coincidence. Once again he looked surprised to see me. It was one of the closest times I have ever been to death, even more than at Dong So, which was much more intense. At Dong So the confusion and darkness provided a kind of cover; at Dong Xoai there wasn't any protection at all. Joe and I ran the whole way back, about eight or nine kilometers!

Dong Xoai Cooking School

The camp wasn't yet set up to support the multipurpose reaction force. At the beginning we didn't get a proper resupply of food. We did manage to get one planeload of ammunition, but after a few days we were out of rice, and everybody was hungry.

One day a vendor appeared with a supply of sugarcane on the back of a little horse, and I bought the whole load for the strikers. Every single person in the force was soon chewing on chunks of that sugar cane. The vendor started to complain about the price; he had decided that he ought to have bargained for more money. But he stopped when I started looking at his little horse in a way that we might want it, too, for dinner. The troops were very annoyed that the horse walked out of town!

We got on the "horn" [radio] and finally got through to the B team and convinced them to get Capt. Bob Saltzman [the S-4 logistics officer] to send us some supplies. The troops would rebel if they weren't paid or if they didn't have food. So, finally the Caribou flew over and dumped several pallet loads on the camp. We got enough C-rations for one meal for everybody, about one day's food for each man. The strikers weren't familiar with the little P-38 can opener, and for the next few days we had a lot of guys with knife wounds to the hand, received when they tried to open the cans with bayonets. The Nungs didn't like the ham and lima beans, or the cold scrambled eggs and ham, any better than the Americans did. We radioed back to headquarters and said, "We've got to get better food!"

The next day another Caribou flew over and dropped us some chow. We got a pallet of Aunt Jemima pancake mix, a pallet of canned salmon, a pallet of asparagus tips, and a pallet of Tabasco sauce! The Mike Force strikers were very disgruntled as we gave them their pancake (cooked on a section of tin roofing material), a can of salmon, a can of asparagus, and a bottle of

Tabasco sauce. Off they went to stab at the damn cans again, mixed with Chinese cursing as the guys flung the cans as far as they could throw them. It became so serious that we finally called for an evacuation; we'd been there long enough that the guys were really pissed!

Ambush at Tieu Ea Da

Our Mike Force got called to the airstrip at Tieu Ea Da one day, and you could tell that something was up—there was an urgency in the air. A Vietnamese artillery lieutenant with three "tubes" had been assigned to set up his battery to provide supporting fire for a Delta unit operating near the border. He took a wrong turn and ended up at a wrong set of map coordinates. It was at the same time that a Vietnamese airborne ranger battalion was being committed and later annihilated.

One of our FAC spotter planes noticed the VC converging on these tubes, and we got the call to urgently get out to this little unit to get them some support. We took off and moved to the west of the camp, six or seven kilometers. I took my recon platoon, and we ran down the highway. On the way we investigated some potential ambush positions along the highway. I wanted to put a reinforced platoon in one of the most likely places, a banana plantation, but got overruled. We pressed on to find the artillery.

When we arrived a big argument developed. The lieutenant didn't think he ought to be taking orders from an American NCO. It took all afternoon to convince him that he ought to leave this position. Both conditions—the lost little lieutenant and the attitude—were typical problems we had to deal with.

I sent my platoon on a patrol. At that moment we were light on manpower, and both my team sergeant and interpreter were unavailable to me. My platoon at that point was only eighteen other guys, all Nungs. We had a few compasses and no good radios.

The biggest hazard to the teams was getting shot by our own guys as we reentered the perimeter, so we had ways to minimize the hazard. One was that we would come back in at a certain point at a predetermined time. I elected to stay at the rally point, alone.

While I waited, I thought about how beautiful this particular area was, how much it reminded me of the part of Wisconsin where I had grown up. I resisted the desire to take a nap in this beautiful, peaceful place. Even the roads reminded me of the logging roads back home. I was lying behind an earthen berm, motionless and virtually invisible.

The first team was due back in and was supposed to enter from due south of my position. I saw a guy walking toward me on the right azimuth at the right time, and carrying the right weapon (a US-issue M1 carbine). What I didn't notice at the time was that he wasn't carrying a rucksack or other gear. He kept walking until he was quite close to me before I moved slightly, and then he noticed me. At the same moment, I realized I was looking at a VC, and he realized he was looking at an American. We looked at each other. We both tried to bring our weapons to bear, but he disappeared before I could get a shot off at him. I don't know if he was lost and looking for his unit, or had come up out of a hole, or what, but he was alone and that was the last I saw of him. I fired one shot in the air to alert the boys—we used the same technique as the VC.

The patrol came in shortly thereafter, crawling because of the warning shot. They hadn't seen the lone soldier, but they had seen large numbers of VC massing in the area. The VC knew where the artillery tubes were, and they seemed to be getting ready to take them.

We headed back to camp, slogging through rice paddies and then through the banana plantation. There were fresh foxholes everywhere. We reported the holes over the radio, and we were told to press on. We proceeded, but off the road, in the cover of the plantation.

The artillery finally started to move—right down the road, without any flankers out for support. As they were driving down the road, a VC recoilless rifle opened up on them and shot up the Vietnamese unit very badly.

We got pinned down by a fairly small force and took cover in a rice paddy. I thought we'd have to wait till dark, but some gunships and fast-movers arrived, and at least one of the gun tubes was fired into the ambush by an American sergeant.

Green Beret Weapons

The basic weapon issued to Green Berets was the CAR-15, a compact version of the M16 with a shorter barrel and a collapsible stock. It fires a high-velocity bullet about a quarter inch in diameter, singly or in bursts. It, like the M16, is fussy about ammunition and about cleaning; problems with either result in stoppages. Stoppages in combat, I can tell you, are not a lot of fun.

One quite popular weapon with SF is the AK-47, and it didn't come through the normal supply channels; if you wanted one you normally had to kill the guy who had it first. It is a very different weapon from the M16, and much admired by Green Berets for its reliability. This seemed a little odd at the time, since everything the Russians made was supposed to be crude, coarse, and unreliable copies of US technology. Its major flaw may have been a noisy safety; whenever SF teams heard the distinctive metallic *klatch* coming from the underbrush they knew the next few minutes were likely to be filled with action-packed adventure.

Another favorite tool was the M79 grenade launcher, a little shoulder-fired 40-millimeter artillery piece. It looks like a rifle that has been in a bad accident; it's short, with a big barrel and a funny stock. It throws a kind of grenade up to about three hundred meters in an arc, and with it you can beat up on the opposing team way over there, behind the dike. Besides the high-explosive warhead, the M79 fires smoke, illumination, tear gas, and the "bean-bag" projectile. This latter device was no more than a bag with sand inside, but if you needed a prisoner and wanted a live one, the bean-bag round delivered a solid punch that would knock a guy down for the count without having him leak all his essential juices. Then you could invite him back to meet the folks at home and to have a little chat with the intel weenies.

—Hans Halberstadt

CHARLES BERG

Charles Berg served two and a half tours with Special Forces in Vietnam before losing a leg in combat. He left the Army as a captain, and he now works for the Veterans Administration.

Mike Force

My first tour was with the Mike Force, working with the Nung tribesmen, mostly out of Nha Trang, before they became the Mobile Strike Forces assigned to each of the four corps areas. These were the soldiers that later went on to the projects—Omega, Sigma, and the rest.

The Mike Force was a kind of "in-house" program developed by SF. Normally the indigenous soldiers in Vietnam varied from okay to very bad— some were almost Viet Cong units. Well, SF had no real way, before the Mike Force, to provide reinforcements if a camp got hit, or to react to any opportunities that might develop. So SF recruited a force from the Nung tribes—a group traditionally hostile to the Vietnamese—who were of ethnic Chinese ancestry and who were essentially mercenaries in the hire of SF.

We trained the Nungs to function very much like an American Army rifle platoon. We gave them a solid basic training program, trained them in reconnaissance, and sent them to SF camps all over the country. We used them very much like a Hatchet Force, thirty-two to about seventy men, loaded with all the food and ammunition they could carry. We used them to relieve places that were under attack or being overrun. They would carry twice the ammo an American would, and went out loaded for bear. And we weren't planning on bringing any of it back with us, either! When it came to carrying bullets or food, bullets were better.

The regular Vietnamese army units were so often infiltrated by Viet Cong that they were quite unreliable in combat, but the Nungs were extremely loyal to SF. When we used them, we sent them in fast; they did what they were supposed to do, and then we pulled them back out again quickly.

The Mike Force program proved to be so successful that it was expanded from the single original unit that operated out of Nha Trang into Mike Force units for each of the four corps areas. Man for man, pound for pound, those units were probably as good as US Army infantry. They were strong, they weren't afraid of the jungle, and they had a personal commitment to the unit and to SF. They were good at reading sign in the jungle and good at following the trail of the enemy—in that they were better than the US soldier.

Although they were successful, there was a lot of animosity and resentment among the regular ARVN soldiers about the Nungs. There was resentment, too, among American military personnel, because the Nungs only followed orders from SF, nobody else. They were usually commanded by Green Beret sergeants rather than officers—who were few and far between in SF.

Studies and Observation Group

When SOG got started, it was with the idea of using the same system, but with the Yards as well as the Nungs. In fact, by the time Studies and Observation Group got started, the Nungs had been pretty well used up. A lot of them were starting to think that the war might not be such a good deal. I can't blame them.

Studies and Observation Group missions were usually five days long. A soldier can't carry enough food for longer than that, and that's about the limit of endurance for a man in that kind of situation. After five days of humping through the brush, off the trails, you could get pretty well worn out. And once you got compromised, you just ran, even with that rucksack on, to get away.

Water Buffalo Don't Die Easily

My first mission with the Mike Force was just outside of Nha Trang on what was supposed to be a relatively safe operation. During the night, while we were in our positions, we started hearing a lot of noise moving toward us. The Nungs had good fire discipline, though, and held their fire. It sounded like a whole company of NVA moving through the jungle toward us. The Nungs finally opened up, and somebody sent up a flare. Then we could see the "enemy"—a herd of about twenty water buffalo. Well, let me tell you, water buffalo are big, and they don't die very easily.

When the sun came up the next morning, there were all these water buffalo in various stages of demise. I thought it was awful, but the Nungs were delighted! They were trying to finish the animals off with the little M1 carbines they were issued at the time, but the bullets were bouncing off the buffaloes' skulls.

They butchered the animals, and we called for the helicopters to come in and get us. The Marines showed up with CH-46s, dropped the ramps, came down, and then all the Nungs started coming aboard with what looked like bloody, mangled bodies. The crew chiefs were looking at all this blood and raw meat—and happy, smiling Nung faces—and just didn't know what to make of it.

The aircraft commander knew that we'd called for extraction and figured things had gone sour in a big way. Then we all came aboard with what looked like a lot of mangled bodies. When he found out what had really happened, he was pissed. He hauled us back to the FOB and landed right in the middle of the compound, creating a huge dust storm that engulfed the whole camp.

Unfortunately for the aircraft commander, though, a delegation of senior MACV officers was inspecting the place at the time, and the dust storm was not appreciated. As a very junior NCO, I took this opportunity to exit stage left and tried to become invisible. We took a lot of kidding about that operation for a long time.

OP 34 & 35

I had been back in the States for about five months when I realized it was about time to go back to Vietnam. I volunteered and went to work with Studies and Observation Group. I was assigned to OP 35A, 35B, and 34 [these were experimental, super-secret programs in covert operations].

One of these involved our training Vietnamese hoodlums and gangsters, straight out of prison. We taught them basic military skills, and how to function as small, three- or four-man teams. Then we took them up to North Vietnam, where they were parachuted into enemy territory. While our success rate with these guys wasn't very high, it was pretty good under the circumstances. Some of them lasted quite a long time and did some good work. But others were "rolled up" right away—they were either captured or they immediately surrendered to the NVA.

The actual operations involved these hoodlums teamed with Vietnamese airborne or rangers. The gangsters were well paid, and there wasn't a whole lot of choice for them; they had to go into the Vietnamese army one way or another, or stay in prison. Most of them became pretty well motivated, although one-third of them were VC infiltrators. They were weeded out, one way or another (Detachment B-56 or -57 court-martialed a couple of guys for their "weeding" techniques). You dealt with them the best way you could—including telling the Vietnamese to take care of them, which they did, by killing them. I don't know if many Americans did that.

In theory and in fact we really were advisors in this program because we didn't jump in with the teams, we just took them up there and dropped them off. There was a Vietnamese team leader for each operation, and the only control we had was the radio. Once they were inserted, though, I didn't have any more contact with them. Any communications with them were in code. I never saw any of the guys I trained come back out.

Most of them were compromised, often by a lack of logistic support. And, it really wasn't too tough for the NVA to figure out what was going on when the bombs started dropping on their convoys and troops in the jungle. The teams were operating in the NVA's backyard, and it didn't usually take the NVA too long to beat the bushes and find the teams. These guys were dropped with the old, hand-cranked radios, and the only way they could get out of North Vietnam was to walk out.

One of the ARVN sergeants I worked with in the program had walked out of North Vietnam three times! He told me, "You fight and then go home. I have been here all my life. I have to fight, and then fight again."

It was a different perspective than we had, and I can't blame some of them for being reluctant to keep at it. They were in a meat grinder, and they knew it.

I worked with these guys for four or five months before being assigned to a recon team up at FOB-1. I did that for a few months, and then I got assigned to Special Projects at Khe Sanh, just before the Marines took over. While on a recon over in Laos in February of 1967, I got wounded in the legs and got med-evaced back to the States for an obligatory two-and-a-half month hospital stay.

Khe Sanh

When I was ready to get out of the hospital, I started making phone calls to go back to Studies and Observation Group. I figured that I could get a good assignment, to NKP, over in Thailand, where we had a launch control unit. I was trying to get assigned to work with the FAC, to go along on the helicopters, putting teams in and taking them out. It was supposed to be a good deal—you got to sleep in a real bed every night. Well, I was in-processing in Da Nang and discovered that SOG had grown up while I was gone; they now had launch sites all over the place.

Even so, I had just about convinced the guy behind the desk that I ought to be assigned to NKP when I heard a voice behind me say, "Welcome to hard times!" It was Sgt. Maj. Dick Piegram—a man who had about six years in the country by that time and was already a living legend. He said, "I got a job for you up at Khe Sanh." I whined and sniveled, but he said "Let's go," and off I went.

It rained and rained at Khe Sanh. It was muddy, and it got muddier. It was miserable. The siege began. That was in January of 1968, and it was incredible. There we were, in the trenches. I was thinking that it was just like World War II—this was *not* what I went into Special Forces to do. It was awful.

The TDY teams from Okinawa started coming in to support and reinforce us. Russ Mann [his stories are elsewhere] was one of these, and so was Sgt. Bob Scully. We watched the town of Khe Sanh get hammered, day after day, and then finally overrun. We were living in the trenches and bunkers, getting hammered by the NVA artillery night and day. We could listen in on the NVA artillery spotter's radio traffic, and it was clear that they not only had us surrounded, but they could also see everything that was going on inside the camp.

There were a lot of wounded, and artillery coming in, and we got a report of an American getting hit and needing to be collected and brought back to the casualty evacuation station. Bob Scully and I grabbed a stretcher and headed out of our bunker. These bunkers were well constructed— designed to take a B-52 strike, since we intended to call them in on the camp when and if it got overrun.

We got about twelve steps out of the bunker when I heard the artillery coming in on us. When the rounds are close but not right on you, they have a kind of distinctive warbling, whistling sound; but the one I heard didn't. I knocked Bob down with the stretcher and then the round went off right in front of me. I was knocked flat on my back.

When this happens to you, you go through a little checklist, working through your systems one at a time. I opened my eyes, and I could see. I checked my ears, and I could hear. My nose was okay, my arms were okay, my right foot was okay . . . but my left foot didn't move too well. I knew I had a problem. Then I looked down and could see that I was badly hit.

I crawled back to the bunker and just fell down the steps. I went down head over heels, and when my leg came around and hit me on the back of the head, I knew I had a serious problem. The leg was just attached by a little skin at the front of the thigh, the bone shattered at the hip. I looked up at young Sgt Mann, who had just arrived at the camp, and heard him say, "You're going to be okay!"

And I remember telling him, "No, I'm not!" Bob Scully and Russ Mann did the amputation, and they did a super job, right at the hip. When I got back to the States, the doctors were amazed that I had even survived. After a year and a half in the hospital, I got out of the Army, went back to school, and got on with my life.

Special Forces: A Short History

There are two major parts to the history of US Army Special Forces: before John F. Kennedy and after John F. Kennedy. The parentage of the modern organization is officially traced to World War II and two rather different units, the Office of Strategic Services (OSS) and the US Army Rangers. The OSS mission was highly clandestine; tiny groups of men and women were parachuted into enemy held territory where they help organize, coordinate, and direct the efforts of resistance groups, mostly in France and Burma. There was nothing very covert about the Rangers, a small infantry combat organization selected and trained for the most challenging missions; entire Ranger companies were consumed by the German defenses on D-Day. The OSS and Rangers were never popular with the Army's senior staff, and were disbanded after the war.

The real birth of Special Forces happened at Fort Bragg's Smoke Bomb Hill in 1952, and Col. Aaron Bank was the proud father. Colonel Bank didn't buy the notion that future wars were going to be just like World War II, but with even more tanks, airplanes, and nuclear weapons. Col. Bank had been an "operator" behind the lines in France during the big war, and was sure that there were some lessons to be learned from the experience, applicable to whatever war the United States might fight in the future.

Well, the Army didn't think much of these odd, unmilitary people when they were called the OSS, and they hadn't changed their minds. The new unit, christened the 10th Special Forces Group (Airborne), was a bastard child, unloved by anyone except the lunatic fringe. Naturally, the unit attracted every hard-core oddball in the Army—and there were plenty to choose from. Bank insisted on the unit being all-volunteer (no draftees, thank you) and all Airborne (that means "paratrooper" to all you "legs" in the audience). Volunteers needed to have several years in the Army, and be on at least their second enlistment. This was quite different from the massive formations of two-year draftees in their starch and polish, counting the minutes until they were discharged.

Just as the conventional force generals feared, 10th Special Forces Group instantly became home to every weirdo in the ranks, people who just refused to play by the program designed by and for very conventional strategies and tactics. Colonel Banks' little rat pack was often used to play the role of adversaries in war games, and in highly insubordinate fashion, refused to fight fair or by the script. The "guerrillas" used all sorts of ruses and disguises to sneak up on the commanders of the conventional units, then "killed" or "captured" the generals and destroyed the battle plans. It drove some officers, particularly in the 82d Airborne Division, nuts. God, it was fun!

When John F. Kennedy became president in January 1961 he learned of this organization from an aide. He was intrigued and fascinated; it was just the sort of novel thinking that matched his own. He visited Fort Bragg to inspect both the 82d Airborne and Special Forces. He knew about the prohibition of the green beret at Bragg (it was worth a court-martial), but as commander in chief, he had the power to change that, and he did.

Kennedy sent SF to Vietnam as a kind of experiment, to see if the basic theories that the OSS used in France and Burma would work against a communist enemy in an unconventional war. It quickly appeared that it did, especially with the tiny mountain tribes who lived on the key terrain to the conflict. Kennedy championed and protected SF from the rest of the Army, then he was assassinated. He is still revered and mourned within the community, particularly among the old soldiers, and that visit to Bragg over thirty years ago remains a benchmark moment in SF history.

Since the end of the war in Southeast Asia, the Army's interest in special operations has waxed and waned, and the emphasis on the unconventional warfare mission has ebbed away to near invisibility. Since then Special Forces have largely retreated from the limelight, into the shadows of covert operations. But small SF training teams still assist the armies of many nations around the world with professional development—the same kind of instruction offered by those OSS operators in Europe and Burma half a century ago.

The ranks of today's active duty SF companies and teams include few veterans of Vietnam, but many of the attitudes and traditions of the organization remain. It still cherishes its characters and it is still a place where individual integrity is the prime qualification for admission.

—*Hans Halberstadt*

The Legend of the Green Beret

The green beret has always been a symbol of a guy who was a bit different from the people in other Army units. Over the years it was a symbol that had to be earned the hard way, by each individual. Then, in the new kinder, gentler Army of the 1980s, somebody decreed that everyone assigned to a Special Forces unit, qualified or not, wore the same headgear. That policy has recently been revised back to the traditional Q-course graduate limitation.

The first berets came from a ladies' apparel shop in Fayetteville, North Carolina, in 1952 and looked just darling. A trio of young sergeants bought them to wear out on maneuvers against the 82d Airborne; they were playing the role of partisans, and wanted to dress the part, and berets were definitely partisan uniform issue during World War II. A guy named Don Gabe got the green one. Green is the traditional infantry color and green berets were items of uniform issue in the Canadian, British, French, and other armies of the time, and somehow the idea caught on as a kind of private little tradition for field operations. Then guys started wearing them in garrison, and the poop hit the propeller.

Wearing a green beret at Fort Bragg was worth a court-martial right up until about ten minutes before President John F. Kennedy arrived in 1961. He'd heard about the prohibition, and (earning the undying gratitude of the community) ordered the SF soldiers he was to inspect wear the beret. Somebody made a mad dash to Canada, and the Canadian Army supplied the eight hundred berets.

It is a rather useless piece of headgear, except for impressing women or getting into fights. It doesn't keep the sun out of your eyes, it doesn't keep your head warm, and it makes "liberals" wonder how many babies you've killed this morning. It is never worn in a tactical environment, and when you see photos of people sneaking through the brush wearing berets, you can bet it is only because the visiting idiot civilian journalist has sniveled and whined, "But nobody will know you're Green Berets if you don't have them on!"

The beret does have one useful function: when you are bouncing around in the back of a C-130 on a low-level insertion mission and you start to get airsick—it makes an excellent barf bag.

—*Hans Halberstadt*

GERRY SCHUMACHER

Gerry Schumacher is a colonel in the reserves now and still spends a lot of time on Army business. Like many career SF officers, he started out with a tour as an enlisted soldier, went to OCS, and built a career in Special Forces.

Full Circle

I came into Vietnam as a twenty-one-year-old captain and was assigned to a MAT [military advisory team] team. I'd previously served a tour in Korea as an enlisted man, then following OCS, spent several years in Germany as a platoon leader and company commander. In spite of my young age, this background gave me a fair amount of experience—more than most young officers coming out of OCS going straight to Vietnam. Well, they assigned me to a MAT team, but I wasn't really sure what a MAT team really was.

While I was in-processing in Saigon, I got on a bus with all the other MACV people, and we were all taken off to the supply room where the supply people would issue us our gear. Everybody else was getting clipboards and a handful of innocuous stuff. But the supply clerks were loading me down with tons of survival gear: knives, nets, all kinds of stuff. It took three people to help me carry all this stuff back to the bus, and all the other people were looking at me like I was some sort of freak. Nobody else had anything like the collection of gear that I had been issued, so I knew something funny was going on.

Then we all went off to Finance. A finance clerk got up in front of us, delivered the standard spiel, and then asked, "And by the way, is anybody here assigned to a MAT team?" I looked around the room; my little hand was the only one that was up.

The clerk looked at me with a little smirk and said, "Well, I'm glad to see that at least one of you will be earning his combat pay!" This was the second signal that something was wrong with this assignment, but I still didn't know exactly what MAT was.

Now it was supper time, and we went to the mess hall. I sat at a table, and across from me was a first lieutenant. His hair was singed, he had blood all over him, and his face was filthy. There were burn marks on his fatigues. He looked like somebody who had just walked through an incinerator. He sat there, eating his meal with that classic 10,000-yard stare, while the rest of us (all in our clean, neat, fresh fatigues) were sitting there looking at this guy like he was an alien from another planet. We had been in country for about a day, and we were all intimidated by this guy.

I decided to break the ice. I asked him, "Where are you coming from, lieutenant?"

He looked at me for what seemed like an eternity, and finally replied, "The delta region, sir."

Well, since I was going to a MAT team in the delta, I asked "So, what were you doing?"

"I was on a MAT team—until last night," he said.

"You *were* on a MAT team?"

"They're all dead now," he said. "I'm getting my fucking ass out of here. I'm leaving. My tour is over."

"I'm going to a MAT team in the delta; what is it like?" I asked him.

"I wouldn't know where to start," he said. "There isn't anything any-body can tell you. Just watch your ass." I didn't have the balls to ask him any more, and that was the end of the conversation.

Well, my orders got changed. Instead of going to the delta, I was assigned to take over a team in II Corps. Actually, the whole team was wiped out, so it was being reconstituted, with me as the team leader.

After catching rides on a succession of airplanes, I was finally deliv-ered to a very remote little RF [Regional Forces] compound way out in the jungle. As the helicopter came in, there was no smoke, no greeting com-mittee, nobody there! I expected five men, standing there at attention, say-ing the usual, "Welcome aboard sir, glad to have you." But there was nobody there at all!

I walked through the main gate unchallenged; there was no guard to be seen. I looked at the chain-link fence surrounding the strong points; the tail-spinners from the B-40s were still stuck in the fence. There were some dud rounds stuck in there, too. Nobody had even policed-up the compound since it had been hit.

I felt a bit like I had just landed on Mars, very uneasy. But I could hear some Vietnamese voices, then some American voices. I looked around and finally discovered a long, lanky first lieutenant. He had his feet up on a table, and there were two NCOs pushing each other around—all drunk as a skunk.

"Well, God damn, *Dai-uy*. I sure am glad to see that you're here, 'cause I sure can't handle these two guys!"

Another guy walked up. This one was wearing black pajamas and car-rying an AK-47, and he had camouflage makeup on—the third member of my MAT team. He'd been in Vietnam for seven years! This guy loved Vietnam; the other two enlisted guys had just been assigned, one from the Americal Division, the other from the 173d Brigade (which was the largest airborne formation in country). Then in came my medic, Sgt Sattamore—a classic SF type, a guy who could patch up people blindfolded and who would carry needles in his earlobes. These guys had all just been pulled into the camp from other parts of the country. So this was the group I was going to go to war with! I was thinking, *I'm in* big *trouble now*!

A year later it was time to go. I'd survived, somehow. The last night before I was to leave, my compound got hit hard and we fought all night. I headed down to Saigon, filthy dirty, with nothing to wear except the cam-mies I had fought in. I looked like hell. I got to Saigon and I was starving. I had fought all night. I walked into the mess hall—the same mess hall—sat down at a table, and started to eat. Several very clean, very fresh-faced young officers sat down at the table across from me. They were studying me. Finally, one young captain said, "Gee, captain, where are you assigned? What is it really like out there?"

I couldn't think of anything to tell them.

Shortly thereafter, I was on my airplane, heading back home. I slept pretty much all the way across the Pacific. When I finally started to wake up on the plane from San Francisco to San Diego, a large argument had developed over me between some anti-war kids (who wanted to know how many babies I had killed) and a group of older World War II veterans (who took offense to their line of questioning). The whole thing was extremely

continued on page 129

A typical recon team in the central highlands: three Special Forces troopers (one who wears his beret for the occasion) and eight Montagnard tribesmen. The rifles are CAR-15s; the man standing holds an M79 grenade launcher. *Don Green*

Capt. Larry Trapp (left) with the late, great Sgt. Walt Shumate. Shumate is shown after shaving off his famous handlebar mustache. (See Larry Trapp's story "Walt Shumate Shaves His Mustache.)

That's Viet Cong (VC) territory on the other side of the wire in January of 1963 when this photo was made, but the little Montagnards took it back from the VC over the next five years. Then the NVA showed up. *Hans Halberstadt*

This sergeant wears the "master-blaster" wings of a master parachutist, a 7th Group flash on his beret, and the Airborne tab on his shoulder; he's a member of the old guard. *Hans Halberstadt*

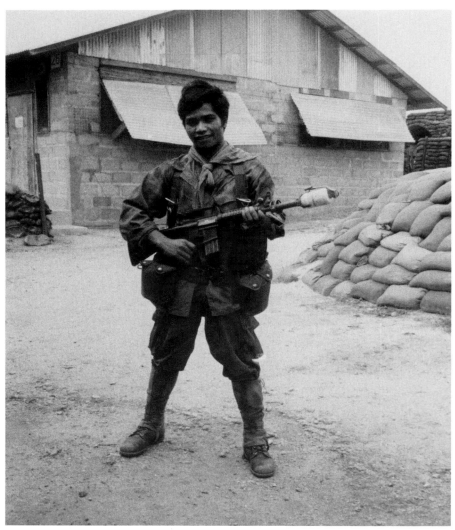

Don't mess with this small, tough man. Americans who knew them almost always admired and respected these tribal soldiers. This one is about to leave on patrol, and that's a white phosphorus (WP) grenade on the muzzle of that M16. He's got spare magazines in those canteen covers, and wears a McGuire rig too. This guy is ready to tear up the town. *Don Green*

A Hatchet Force "mounts up" at FOB-2 in Kontum. Hatchet Forces were early, quick-reaction forces that could reinforce or relieve camps in trouble. *Don Green*

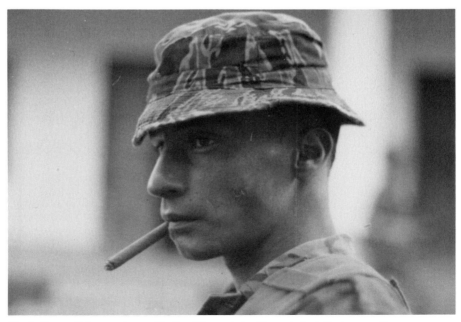

Capt. Gerry Schumacher with the "tiger stripe" boonie hat that was often worn by Special Forces soldiers in the field—to the annoyance of some conventional commanders, who expected a conventional appearance. *Gerry Schumacher*

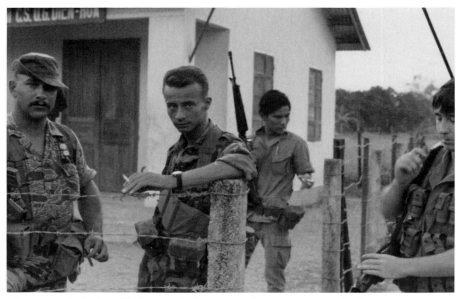

Since everybody is still clean and the pucker factor appears to be low, we will assume that this patrol hasn't left yet. Sergeant Sattamore and Captain Schumacher before a night ambush patrol. *Gerry Schumacher*

The exotic cultural traditions of the Vietnamese, including music and dance, fascinated many Americans. *Anonymous*

Your man in Khe Sanh, young Sgt. Russell Mann, age twenty-three. You can tell he's Special Forces by the Rolex watch, the CAR-15, and the steely look. March 1968, during the Tet offensive. *Russell Mann*

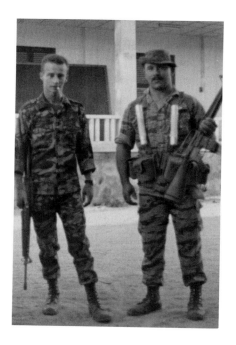

Captain Schumacher and Sergeant Sattamore drop by the district compound. Sergeant Sattamore is carrying about twenty pounds of ammunition in canteen covers on his load-bearing equipment (LBE), just one of many improvisations developed by Special Forces troops in the field. *Gerry Schumacher*

Montagnard houses were simple, well ventilated, and clean—the pigs didn't know how to climb up the pole ladder. *Russell Mann*

104

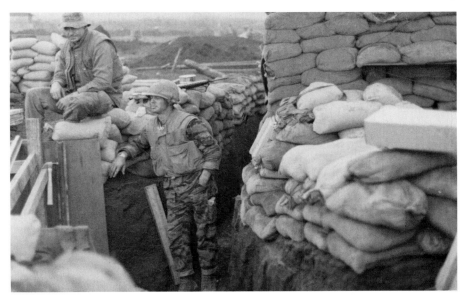

Sergeants Mann (team medic) and Durham (team radio operator) contemplate the new defenses, still under construction at Khe Sanh. *Russell Mann*

The North Vietnamese Army (NVA) was just outside the wire at Khe Sanh. The "zoomies" from the US Air Force could hardly miss because there were so many attackers, and the fly boys kept busy dropping napalm on the unlucky besiegers. *Russell Mann*

Revolutionary Development (RD) cadre move out on patrol. The black pajamas looked confusingly like the uniforms of the VC—a mixed blessing depending on the situation. *Gerry Schumacher*

Robin Moore was a civilian author who went through airborne and Special Forces training, then patrolled with Special Forces teams in Vietnam. Here he is with a Swedish K 9-millimeter in the jungle. *Don Green*

A pause on patrol. These Yards are armed with World War II-vintage US M2 carbines—small, light, reliable weapons that were just the right size for the little tribesmen. *Don Green*

The smiling Montagnard in the center is a converted VC who surrendered and went to work for the opposing team. *Don Green*

A company-size patrol returns to the village after a few days of prowling around the neighborhood. Such patrols were routinely greeted by everybody in the village, lining the road back into camp. *Don Green*

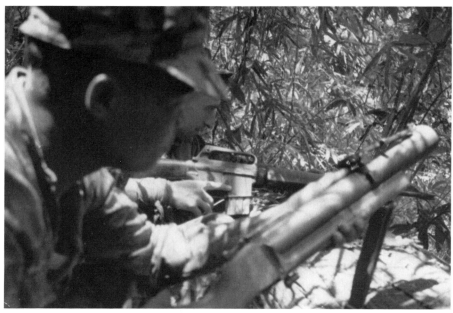

A Yard with an M79 grenade launcher and an American with an M16 wait in ambush for a VC patrol. This cat-and-mouse game was played out for years, nether side quite sure who was the cat and who was the mouse. *Don Green*

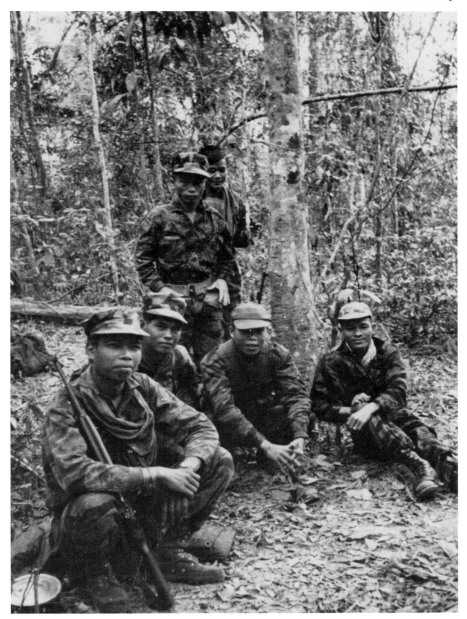

Six sturdy Montagnard tribesmen take a break in the jungle during a patrol.
Don Green

A patrol of two Americans and ten Montagnards in a bamboo thicket. This kind of terrain is characteristic of the Highlands, and could be cool and comfortable.
Don Green

The man coming up the trail with the apprehensive expression is a VC who has just walked in to surrender. He has been watching the patrol, and after seeing that they had treated his family well, decided to swap sides.
Don Green

A Montagnard "striker" and his children. Special Forces soldiers often became very close friends with the tribesmen and their families. *Don Green*

The classic ambush is shaped like an *L,* and with luck the victims walk into it along the long axis—although it doesn't always work that way. This patrol is set up on a well-used VC highway. *Don Green*

The team leader conducts a preliminary field interrogation of the VC captive. Without the intervention of the Special Forces troopers, the Montagnards would kill the VC. *Don Green*

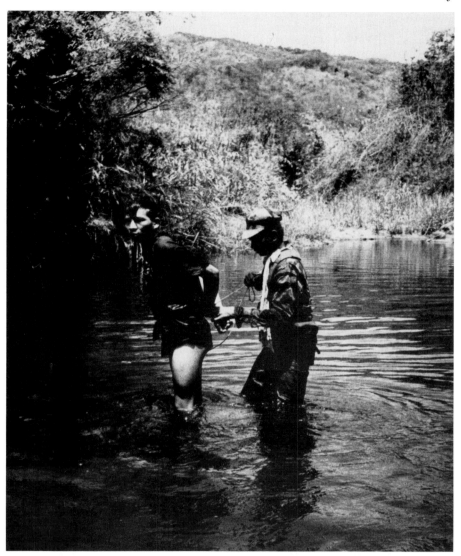

Here's the one survivor of the VC patrol, being collected by one of the Yards. His apprehensive expression is justified; the Yards don't like the idea of prisoners, although the Special Forces troopers tried to change that attitude. *Don Green*

One of the VC was killed trying to escape across a stream. The team sergeant retrieves his body. Unlike most Americans who participated in the war in South East Asia, Special Forces soldiers knew the VC and NVA at close range, sometimes by name. Special Forces soldiers often respected the VC, in life and death, as dedicated fighting men. *Don Green*

Rest break in the jungle. The sergeant has an M16 rather than the more compact CAR-15 version that became standard issue later. *Don Green*

Deep in enemy held territory this Montagnard tribesman stands guard while other members of the patrol take a break. His weapon is a World War II vintage Thompson .45-caliber submachine gun. *Don Green*

Montagnard tribesmen were eager to fight the VC and NVA. Despite their "primitive" Bronze Age culture they made superb soldiers and good friends to the Americans. *Don Green*

Sgt. Don Green in a Montagnard village. *Don Green*

A patrol returns to a fortified village. *Don Green*

The long line of a patrol returning with at least one Viet Cong prisoner in the early sixties. *Don Green*

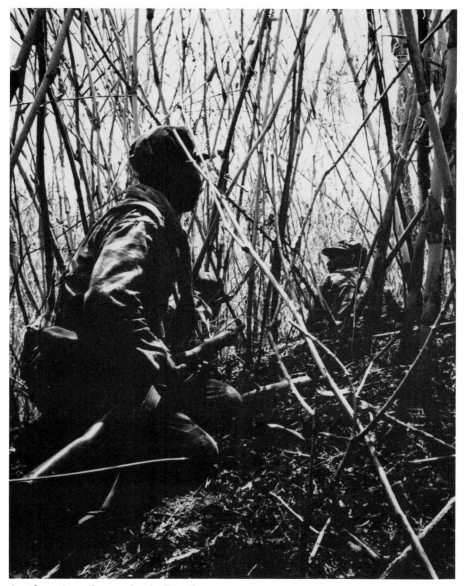

Another view of an ambush. *Don Green*

A patrol is coming back to the village with a VC prisoner. *Don Green*

Inspecting the body of one of the slain VC. Until Special Forces started helping the Montagnards defend themselves from the VC, beginning in 1962 at Boun Enao, the Yards were often preyed upon by the VC who stole their food, killed their livestock, and forced the tribespeople into forced labor as porters. *Don Green*

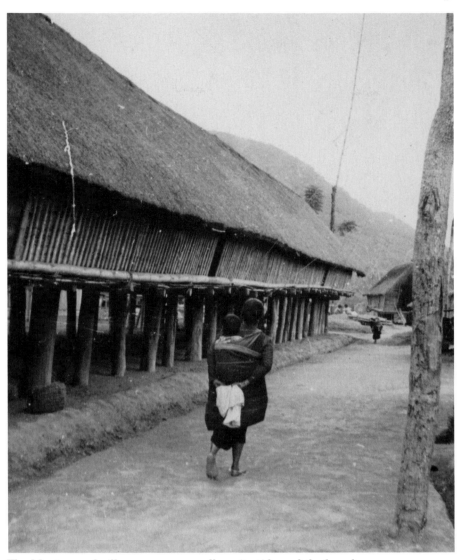

The Montagnard villages were normally quite tidy and the long houses were typically handsome structures, all neatly aligned. *Don Green*

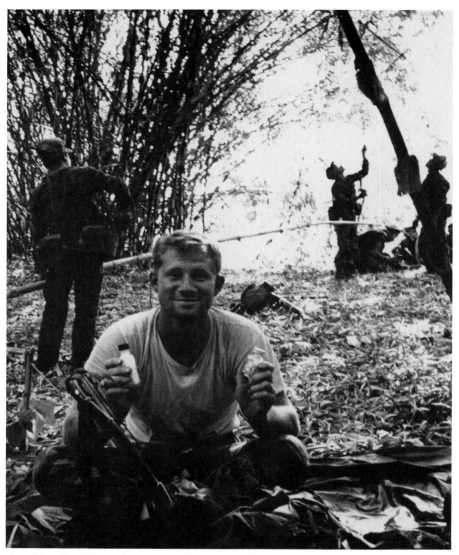

Our friendly, full service team medic is ready for any emergency. *Don Green*

Lt. Col. Martha Raye with three admirers—two of her beloved sergeants and Snoopy, a beagle donated to 5th Group by Conrad "Ben" Baker. *Conrad "Ben" Baker*

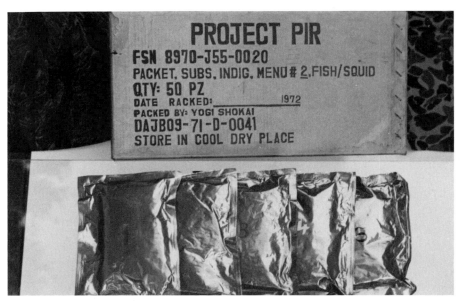

Ben Baker's home-brewed field ration designed for the Montagnards. After the US government told him that it would take years and millions of dollars to develop a suitable ration for the Yards, Ben did it in his Okinawa kitchen with two hundred dollars of his own money—in eight weeks. These packets are Menu #2, Fish and Squid—yum! *Conrad "Ben" Baker*

A Montagnard kid tends a bear cub pet. Bears were one of many such pets that Special Forces soldiers kept, often at great expense. *Don Green*

Ben Baker may have been a civilian, but he traveled a lot, and in some rough neighborhoods. Here he is at a Montagnard grave site; the carving of a pregnant female figure represents the Montagnard concept of reincarnation. The paratrooper model M2 .30-caliber carbine that Ben's holding is Baker's method of putting off the need for reincarnation for as long as possible.
Conrad "Ben" Baker

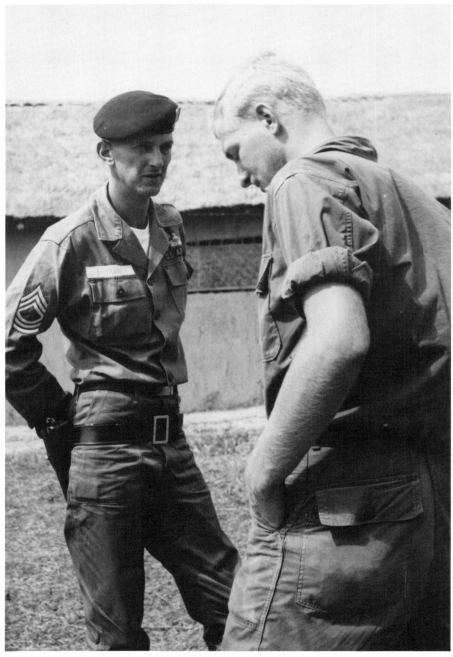

M/Sgt. Arthur "Stretch" Senkewich was one of the early Special Forces trainers who began the process of teaching the Montagnards and Vietnamese the basics of modern military operations. Although he wears his beret here in camp, he would never do so on a combat operation. *Hans Halberstadt*

Special Forces instructors initially served six-month temporary duty (TDY) assignments in Vietnam, rotating in and out from Okinawa.
Harold "Jake" Jacobson

Two scrawny NCOs in front of their palatial, air conditioned quarters. Harold "Jake" Jacobsen, on the left, carries a Swedish K 9-millimeter submachine gun, one of the many odd, exotic, worn-out weapons issued to irregulars in the early years of the war. *Harold "Jake" Jacobson*

continued from page 96

incongruous. Here I was, on a plane to San Diego, with just a meal and one nights' sleep since standing in a remote compound in the wilds of Vietnam, surrounded by smoldering bodies. It seemed like perhaps an hour from the time that I left the battlefield until I landed in San Diego.

First Blood

My first combat operation was a night ambush with a platoon-minus (about twenty PF [Popular Forces] soldiers) plus my interpreter, my American NCO, and myself. The setup was classic: We set up about eight or nine at night, just at twilight. Then we shifted positions about ten into our final ambush location. We were lined up as an inverted L along two trails. Because of the terrain, we were prevented from setting up as well as we might have on one side.

My NCO was a veteran of the Korean War and already had a couple of tours in Vietnam by that time. He was taking me under his wing, teaching me the ropes, trying to keep me out of trouble. He and I were at the corner of the ambush, in the center.

About two in the morning I noticed a figure standing above me. He was dodging side to side, obviously trying to look at me. I thought at first that it was one of the South Vietnamese—the squad or platoon leader—who had come back to talk to us. While I was trying to figure all this out, about the time I realized I might be looking at an NVA, the guy tried to fire on me. But he had a stoppage of some sort, an empty chamber or a jam, because I heard the *click* as he pulled the trigger, and I heard the bolt go back to clear the weapon.

In a split second I concluded that this must be what it is all about, and in my sharp fear and terror I unloaded the entire magazine of my .45-caliber "Grease Gun" into the guy. I hit him with nearly all the thirty .45-caliber rounds. He literally went airborne—he was raised off the ground by the impacts.

The rest of the ambush team then pivoted to their rear and started firing in our direction, right back at me, the NCO, and interpreter. The NVA took up their own fighting positions and started shooting—also in our direction! The three of us were trying to dig holes in the ground with our teeth at this point. There were hand grenades flying over us from our men, the NVA were shooting B-40s back into the position, and there were tracers coming from everywhere. I thought, "This has got to be hell."

Well, the NCO was a big guy, and he happened to be on top of the radio at that moment. I was trying to get to the radio to call for illumination, to make some sense of what was happening, and to call for some artillery. It was the only thing I could think of to do right then. But I could *not* get this guy off the radio! I finally had to brace my feet against him and my back against a tree to push him off the radio so I could get at it!

When the shooting stopped there turned out to be a couple of casualties on each side, far fewer than all the firing had suggested—although it scared the living crap out of me.

But the next day, when we got back to the compound, the NCO was telling everybody what a hero I had been, how I had killed about four of the VC myself, and how I had led the reaction—none of which I had done! I didn't deserve any of this praise. It took me a few minutes to figure out that the NCO was mortified because he had lain across the radio, and I couldn't get him off. Even though almost none of the praise was true, at least it helped establish my credibility with the team.

Ambush

We got intelligence that a large NVA unit was going to come into a village, and we mounted a large operation to ambush the enemy force. We put in six or seven ambush sites around the village. I went out with the RF unit that night. We moved into our designated locations, the preliminary one about nine. Then we started the shift to the final position about eleven. It was a black night; you couldn't see the hand in front of your face.

I was following a Vietnamese soldier. We moved for what seemed like a very long time—far too long. Normally a shift took only about fifteen minutes, but we moved for at least an hour. I began to worry about the six other ambushes set up in this general area, any one of which we might be walking into. So I tapped the little Vietnamese guy on the shoulder and asked why we were still moving. He replied that he had lost sight of the guy in front of him about forty-five minutes earlier and was trying to find the ambush position.

Well, I had no idea where we were now; we'd made all sorts of twists and turns in sugarcane fields, thickets, and underbrush. I said, "We are staying right where we are!" The little Vietnamese guy said he couldn't do that; his squad leader would kill him the next day if he didn't link up with the rest of the squad.

Behind me was the interpreter, my NCO, and three of the RF soldiers. We were the tail end of the ambush force. So we stopped—the NCO, the interpreter, and I—and all the Vietnamese insisted on going ahead. I thought it was pure suicide to proceed, and we sat down right where we were and waited. Not more than five minutes later, the four stumbled into the ambush position set up by the Korean White Horse Division soldiers, and all four were killed.

Meanwhile, though, the NVA battalion that we were after had gotten into the village undetected. When the Korean ambush started shooting, three or four of the others opened up as well, even though they didn't have targets. But the NVA in the village concluded that they had been discovered, and they broke and ran. And guess where this battalion decided to run? Right at the three of us, sitting there in the weeds, trying to stay out of trouble!

Somebody fired some illumination rounds, and now we could see—far too well! Suddenly we saw all these guys in pith helmets, with AKs, charging toward our position. I thought, Well, we have had it now! We lay as flat as we could and watched them stream past. Some of them ran past, then stopped to turn and fire back at the ambush sites.

A couple of the NVA dove into the bushes beside us, got off a few shots, and got back up to run again. As one was departing, he said the Vietnamese equivalent of "Come on, let's get out of here!" to us.

I told my NCO, "Don't shoot anybody!" It would have just drawn attention to our position, from both sides. So we stayed put all night, and at dawn we were still right there, with our eyeballs wide open. There were a few dead NVA around us, all casualties from the ambush. That was quite a feeling, to have a couple of companies of NVA charging all around us.

Pet Monkey

I had a pet monkey that I kept with me in my hooch. Whenever there was an attack, this monkey would quickly climb on me, wrap his arms and legs around my head, and start pissing on my face! I could *not* pry this damn monkey off my head. So here I was, running to the old French bunker that I used for a command post, with this monkey on my head, claws dug into my skull, pissing like hell on my face! Somehow, I just never got used to that.

"What Took You So Long?"

Two of my NCOs were assigned to a Montagnard compound that got hit one night. Most of the Yards broke and ran—and were shot in the back—but these two sergeants stayed in their position and kept fighting, alone, all night long. The NVA overran the entire compound. These guys had an M60 machine gun; during the fight they burned up one machine-gun barrel after another. The NVA dead piled up in front of their hole so deep that they had to go out at intervals and clear away the bodies to maintain their field of fire. They were surrounded by the NVA—dead NVA!

It took us all night to get a reaction force together and to get out there to their compound, fighting some NVA on the way. When we arrived, these two guys were still sitting in their hole, still surrounded by bodies—drinking beer.

"What took you so long?" one of them asked me. They were unscathed. These two guys were just about the only survivors from the entire force. They were quite nonchalant about the whole thing.

"Ruff-Puffs"

I worked with many foreign military, paramilitary, and local militia units in Vietnam. There were the "Ruff-Puffs" [RF-PF, Regional Forces and Popular Forces], the People's Self Defense Force, the Revolutionary Development Cadre, the Provincial Reconnaissance Units, the Montagnards, a Korean army battalion from the White Horse Division, and to a lesser extent, the regular Vietnamese army. I didn't really work with US Army units. In fact, outside of our team members, we rarely saw other Americans.

My first assignment to Vietnam was to MACV, subassigned to MAC Corps, and assigned as a MAT team leader. A MAT team was set up like a Special Forces A-team, only smaller: a heavy weapons specialist, a light weapons specialist, a medic, an assistant team leader, and a team leader (five guys as opposed to twelve on an A-team). We were supposed to do with the Ruff-Puffs what the A-teams were doing with the Montagnards—advising them, training them, taking them on operations. The ops were more militia-type missions, protecting villages and patrolling, than the long-range recons that the Yards were doing.

After I had served as MAT team leader for four or five months, I was assigned to be district senior advisor. That was a pretty good assignment for a young, twenty-one-year-old captain—a job that would normally go to a thirty-eight-year-old major or above. It was the largest district in South Vietnam, and it was in many ways a showcase district, with demonstration hamlets and a lot of attention.

Things started to change in my compound, an old Chinese fort with a moat, a big wall, and big gates at the front and back. You could fire a missile through the front gate, and it would sail right through, out the back gate. The place was indefensible.

Inside were the quarters for the district chief, his headquarters staff, his guards, and the largest Special Forces A-team ever assembled, Detachment A-503, with thirty-five men. Two of my MAT teams came in from time to time, but normally they were always operating outside the camp. Finally, we had a district team in the fort, too, with the intelligence people and the folks who ran the teams on operations.

We supervised thirty-four villages and fourteen hamlets. The villages each had a PF platoon guarding it, plus three Regional Force companies. These RF companies were each set up in classical triangular compounds, with barbed wire and firing pits all in exactly the same place in each one—just as the French had designed them many years ago. Also within the district were twelve CIDG [Civilian Irregular Defense Group] companies who were mostly managed by the SF A-team inside my compound.

The A-team had built themselves a compound within the compound because the Yards didn't trust the Ruff-Puff Vietnamese at all. The whole compound wasn't more than three or four city blocks from one side to the other, only about four hundred meters across.

As part of the defenses of the compound, we had a one hundred-kilowatt generator inside the SF compound to power a series of big spotlights that illuminated the perimeter at night. Well, many of the Vietnamese brought their families into the compound with them, and almost all of them were tapping into the output of this generator. Inevitably, they would overload the generator, and it would go out. We would then be attacked by the VC, and we couldn't turn on the lights! The district chief literally threatened people with execution for tapping into the lines, but they continued to anyway. And you could bet that, just as soon as we had a blackout, the VC would attack.

Training the Regional Forces

We were tasked with training a Regional Force unit for an air mobile assault. Now, normally this was not something they liked to do or were good at. Their specialty was guarding bridges around the hamlets.

There were three of these RF companies. The American helicopter pilots were very concerned that the Vietnamese wouldn't get off the helicopters if they came into a hot LZ, so this became an important part of our training. We worked with them for a couple of months, and finally came the big day: We were off to hit an NVA stronghold. It was a pincer operation, with a Montagnard unit assaulting from one side and these RF companies coming in from the other.

When we came in, the LZ was hot. The gunships came in and prepped the LZ, which happened to be tall elephant grass. The RF troops had been so conditioned to get off the helicopters early that they jumped from ten or twenty feet in the air! None of them got shot, but we had about twenty-five casualties (broken legs) right there in the LZ.

All in the Family

I had a Ruff-Puff soldier who told me that he knew that the VC were going to visit a particular village that night, where they were going to be resupplied. So we took the Popular Force platoon out and set up an ambush. When the VC showed up, we killed about ten of them!

The next morning the district chief flew out to pin medals on this platoon, especially the guy with the information. This was a big deal for them, and three or four got medals for their bravery.

We had killed these VC near a house that they had gone to for supplies. I discovered that one of the PF soldiers in my platoon lived in that house— and that one of the VC we had killed was his brother! While we were decorating this guy, his family was weeping over the body of their other son, his Viet Cong brother, just a few feet away!

Another incongruity: We had an old woman in our district with cancer. Even though her son was a notorious Viet Cong leader and on our Phoenix hit list, we took her into Nha Trang for regular treatments. Sgt Sattamore and I drove her to Nha Trang about fifteen times for radiation treatment to reduce her tumor.

The war was like that for me—much more personal than for other Americans. We knew the enemy, often by name. The enemy knew us by name, too. I found my name on one of their hit lists one time—they had their own Phoenix program, too.

Tet

It is a Vietnamese tradition that the first visitor of the new year brings luck—good luck or bad luck. So it was the district chief's new year routine to visit the village chiefs in each of his fourteen villages on Tet, the Vietnamese new year, and he took me with him.

The problem with this was that you had to have something to eat and drink with each and every one. None of the chiefs would let you leave without drinking some of his special brew and eating some special delicacy. We would eat and drink and visit for maybe half an hour, then leave to go visit the next village.

Some of these villages and hamlets were pretty safe, but many were virtually VC communities. Normally, the district chief was very cautious about moving around and visiting these places, but for some reason, not on Tet. This district chief had been a member of the Viet Minh and had fought against the French. I later learned that he struck deals with the VC, and I believe that he was striking deals that day while we were visiting.

By the end of that day, he and I were so drunk that we couldn't see straight. I have never been more sick, or more drunk, in my life. I ate countless fish heads and chicken eyeballs, and drank more rot-gut booze. I'm surprised that I didn't die of alcohol poisoning! We were staggering into "E" hamlets (the least pacified, virtually enemy controlled), and the VC could have shot me with an RPG [rocket-propelled grenade], and I wouldn't have felt it.

CORDS

The CORDS program was a wide-ranging activity that included everything from bridge-building to Phoenix. It included a lot of unconventional warfare activities and some things that were extremely political: building schools, harvesting rice, organizing elections. John Paul Vann was one of the high-level government officials who were instrumental in the CORDS program. And MAT was the military part of CORDS.

MAT had the mission to train RF and PF soldiers. The American personnel were typically well-qualified light- and heavy-weapons specialists, medics and engineers, drawn from the regular army. All were at least reasonably language-proficient and had a knowledge of culture and customs. It was, in a way, Gen. Creighton Abrams' (who was notorious as a critic of SF) answer to Special Forces.

Phoenix Program

Phoenix was run independently in each province and district. Our mission was to collect information on key VC people, hunt them down, and "neutralize" them [which was normally done with a .22 caliber pistol with a silencer attached, applied to the head at minimum range]. We did that with the help of the Koreans, with covert operations, with guys in black pajamas and AK-47s.

At the beginning of the program, many VC targets were claimed as neutralized, only to turn up again, alive. So we were required to photograph them after they were dealt with. The South Vietnamese were quite aggressive with these guys, and there wasn't usually much to photograph when they got done with them.

I am still not too comfortable about Phoenix. That discomfort has to do with just who was a combatant and who wasn't. You could justify the Phoenix program if you were after a combatant, but when you start targeting people who have political significance, I get uncomfortable about it.

Miles from the Closest Meatball

While the regular SF camps were on the end of some sort of supply line, MACV completely forgot about those of us in the CORDS program. If we wanted a steak or spaghetti and meatballs, we had to go over to the A-team compound and beg a plate. We didn't get anything from the American food supply system except C-rations. When I asked them where our chow was, they replied, "You're on per diem." But what the hell was per diem out in the hamlets, 200 miles from the closest meatball!

The MACV attitude was, "Send them out there, and they will figure out a way to survive." I really resented it. Not once in my entire time out there did I get even one warm American meal sent to us by MACV! So we got them the old-fashioned Green Beret way—we stole them!

Every time we picked up an NVA pistol, an SKS carbine, or any other booty, we took that right into Cam Ranh—and we made sure that we had a real good war story to go along with it! In fact, we had a little mama-san sewing up these VC and NVA flags for us. We shot chickens and let them bleed all over flags; the guys in the rear area were real suckers for that. Actually, the best technique was to pull the chicken's head off and let the blood just squirt out on to the flag; there were fewer incriminating feathers that way.

Our favorite story to go with the flag was that three enemy soldiers came running up the hill and tried to plant this flag in our compound, but that our guys got them all, and that the flag was booby-trapped, and two of our men died taking it down! Well, the mess sergeants would just eat all this up, and we could trade that flag for all the steaks, fruits, and vegetables we could carry. That was, honest to God, how we had to operate. That is exactly how we got American food!

If, for whatever reason, we couldn't get anything and we were out of C-rations, we ate what the Vietnamese ate—rice balls with leaves and stuff mixed in. Now, my wife tells me when we go out to exotic restaurants that I'm not very adventurous because I prefer steaks and hamburgers to things like dolmatis [a Greek dish featuring rice and lamb wrapped in grape leaves]. I have had all the adventurous food I want, thank you.

Throwing the Book at the NVA

When you worked with the Ruff-Puffs, you were at the very bottom of the priority list for air and artillery fire support. The NVA knew this. So when we got into a battle with the NVA, we were not only fighting with a less-skilled force than an American unit, we could expect little or any support from artillery or the Air Force. In a way, though, that gave us an advantage that many American units didn't have—the enemy didn't avoid fighting us.

While some people might say that is a disadvantage, we didn't have the frustrations that the Americal division, for example, did. When they made contact, the NVA broke off and disappeared right away. They would leave large quantities of booby traps behind them, and these American units would take large numbers of casualties from the booby traps, without even the satisfaction of a good firefight. Their frustration levels built accordingly, to the point where their behavior as units was sometimes erratic because they wanted revenge on an enemy who had been hurting them, unseen, for years.

But in my case there was a kind of catharsis in our ability to meet, engage, and defeat the enemy—to shoot them and kill them. We had some fairly long (for Vietnam) engagements with the NVA. It was not uncommon to fight it out with them. These engagements were typically at night; only three or four of my engagements were in daylight.

One of these, though, was rather comical. We had cornered some NVA in a rice paddy. (Well, on second thought, if they were here telling the story, it was they who had cornered us.) I called for close air support, but the available aircraft had already expended their cannon and machine-gun ammunition. They still had some napalm and some five-hundred-pound iron bombs, though, and dropped that for us. The two fast-movers went back to rearm while the FAC stayed overhead.

When the close air support aircraft left, the NVA decided it was a good time to close with us. They started coming across the rice paddies at us. This kind of behavior—a daylight, prolonged engagement—was completely unlike what they would do with an American unit. It was obvious that they thought they could take us.

The FAC could see that we were in trouble, serious trouble, and even though he didn't have any fast-movers to control, he made runs on the NVA, firing his marking rockets among the enemy soldiers in the open. This confounded the enemy. They knew what the marking rounds were, but they didn't see any fast-movers, so they kept coming.

The next thing I knew, the FAC came flying by, a hundred feet off the deck, firing his little .38-caliber revolver out the window! He started throwing anything in the cockpit at them. He made pass after pass at the NVA, dropping smoke grenades next. In fact he threw the book at them—his aircraft log book!

As desperate as the situation was, I will always remember looking up from that attack and watching all that paper fluttering out of the sky. The poor FAC must have been mighty frustrated, because he was taking hits on every pass. After about a half hour of this, while the NVA were closing in and we were trying desperately to break contact, a flight of four F-4 Phantoms arrived on station. They started laying napalm on the NVA and fried a bunch of them. Our goose would have been cooked if they hadn't arrived.

But that behavior shows the kind of love and brotherhood that we had for each other, even between the Army and the Air Force, in Vietnam. You sometimes hear about the "fragging" and the protests and the other problems of the Vietnam era, but incidents like that one are, to me, much more indicative of how we got along with each other. Never before in my life, and never in my life again, will I experience that kind of brotherhood and mutual support. It infuriates me to see Vietnam described so often in a negative way, when so often people really cared for each other.

People's Self-defense Force

We got a call one night that one of our PSDF [People's Self-Defense Force] hamlets had been hit by the NVA. Now, the PSDF was a program I personally thought was stupid. It gave guns to old men and children who didn't know how to use them; they were supposed to be able to defend their own communities, but they just managed to get themselves into trouble.

Anyway, the PSDF in this particular hamlet made the serious mistake of firing on the NVA and were getting their butt kicked as a result. They had a lot of women and children injured, and we had to go try to help them.

Somebody had to go in to mark an LZ so the "dust-off" [medical evacuation] helicopter could come in and get the wounded out. According to the report, the NVA had broken contact, and the engagement was over.

We got airborne from our compound—just myself, one of my NCOs, and my interpreter. But the PSDF were so unskilled that they couldn't even mark the little courtyard where we were supposed to land. We were flying around in the dark trying to identify our LZ. Finally, we spotted what we thought was the right place and came in. Just at treetop height, prior to landing, the pilot turned on his landing light to make sure that we weren't going to hit any wires or obstructions. I could see thirty or forty VC and NVA soldiers with AK-47s, SKSs, and I realized that we were landing in the village school yard, rather than the courtyard where we were supposed to go.

It was obvious to me that this was where the enemy had regrouped after the initial attack. We were only about two feet off the ground when I realized what was happening; I opened up with my M16 on full auto. The VC and NVA were apparently in shock as a result of the helicopter attempting to land directly in their midst. Even so, they recovered quickly, and some started to fire on us.

But the helicopter door gunner didn't understand what was happening. He mistook them for the PSDF villagers and tried to take my M16 away from me, thinking I was trying to kill innocent civilians; we nearly had a firefight between the two of us. Only when he noticed them firing at us did he get his cue and open up with his M60.

We pulled up and out of the school yard. The pilot called that he thought we had taken some hits. He managed to find the right LZ this time, and we settled into the courtyard where the PSDF villagers were.

The villagers rushed the helicopter. Everybody was trying to get aboard: women—some with babies in their arms—children, old men. They were all trying to get on. But they weren't wounded, and we were there to get the casualties out. While we were trying to sort out the wounded from the uninjured, the VC and NVA attacked again. So we were tossing civilians off the helicopter because they weren't wounded, and then, right there in front of us, they were getting hit! I pulled one guy off the helicopter, and right while I was holding him, he got shot in the head. Half of his brains spattered all over my face!

Finally, a couple of gunships came on station and started putting some suppressive fires on the enemy force. The NVA assault petered out, and we were able to effect the dust-off. We were afraid to leave anybody in the village, so all of them were evacuated.

I was on the last chopper out. The flight back to Nha Trang and the hospital was weird. It was a hot night, humid and rainy; everything was wet, sticky, and uncomfortable. Finally, we landed at the hospital helo pad, and Sattamore and I walked into the emergency room. There were lots of wounded everywhere—some missing limbs, some with sucking chest wounds, others with brains leaking out of head wounds, others with less critical injuries, all waiting for attention.

The uninjured villagers were there too, milling around without any guidance from anybody. They had been ejected from the emergency room, and now they were squatting on the tarmac in front of the place, talking and crying. Inside the hospital were babies, old men, children, grandmothers—injured, dead, and dying. It sent chills through me. I thought, How sick this whole war is!

I looked at my interpreter, a South Vietnamese soldier. He looked at me and asked, "What now, *Dai-uy?*"

There was a club nearby for the doctors and nurses (although open to other American personnel), a place called (I think) the Operating Room. So I took the interpreter, and we went down the street for a beer. As we got close to the place, we could hear the music—"I Can't Get No Satisfaction" was playing, as I recall—and we went in. There were lots of American nurses and doctors dancing, everybody in their party clothes, the women in short little mini-skirts, all having a wonderful time. Of course, they had probably been up to their armpits in gore an hour or two before, and other doctors and other nurses were busy up the road.

But the incongruity of it all was devastating. Just a hundred yards away were kids, old folks, babies, a grandfather with his intestines hanging out—and they were in there dancing! Just a little earlier I had been out in that village with the NVA, with the gunships and the dust-offs. I thought about the NVA, too. They were off in the bushes someplace, nursing their wounded, too. We raked them with those Cobra gunships! And here the nurses were, in their tight, abbreviated little tops, dancing and laughing. It was very, very strange.

When we had gone into the village that night, there had been seven serious casualties; by the time we left there were forty-five. I was thinking, I should have just let those seven die, or left them there till morning. Maybe the NVA would have left. Maybe the only reason all those people got hurt was because we showed up, and the NVA responded to an opportunity. Did I make a mistake? I don't know. Of course, the NVA could just as well have finished off the whole village, too. I will never know.

Dumb Stunts, Part I

I watched some Vietnamese do incredibly stupid things. One was on a patrol of our perimeter at night. We were moving down a trail, and, in the light of the illumination flares that the camp mortar team were sending up, you could clearly see a section of trip wire across the trail. I watched this little Vietnamese soldier go up to the trip wire. He looked at one end, he looked at the other, and then he reached out and pulled the wire! The last thing I saw of him was a fireball that enveloped him, blasting his body sky high. Everybody knew what that trip wire meant! Everybody was trained to avoid booby traps! It was so *stupid*!

Dumb Stunts, Part II

We had one guy on the A-team who had just arrived from Fort Bragg and the Q course and was out on a patrol with me. I guess they were pounding out Green Berets faster than normal, and he was one of those people who were run through a little too quickly, because he was not quite up to speed.

We moved down the trail behind the guy on his first real time on "point" [walking first in line in the patrol—the first target for the enemy]. He did all the hand and arm signals with crisp and dramatic precision and flare. Apparently this guy had watched a lot of war movies, because he scowled a lot on patrol.

He encountered a cave that needed to be cleared. With textbook precision, he directed the patrol to spread out in a skirmish line, then to drop down to the ground. He moved to the edge of the cave mouth, produced a hand grenade, and pulled the pin. He deftly chucked the grenade into the cave, just the way they teach at Bragg. Then he stepped to the cave mouth and fired a burst of full-auto into the cave, when the grenade detonated pretty much in his face. He had done everything by the book—except the little part about waiting for the grenade to go off.

The poor guy was not badly hurt; the grenade had rolled fairly far back into the cave before it went off. But when he turned around and came back to us, he had shrapnel sticking out of a cheek, little pieces in his chest, his arm. They were all little fragments, and none were at all serious. Once we determined that his injuries were slight, the whole team just rolled down the hill, laughing.

DOY McPHAIL

Doy McPhail retired from the US Army as a sergeant major after a long career in Special Forces and now lives in North Carolina.

The Late, Great Walt Shumate

Sgt. Walt Shumate died of cancer in 1993, but he became one of Special Forces many living legends while alive, and his legacy will linger for a long time. He asked that his ashes be spread on a drop zone at Fort Bragg. Before he died, Walt pre-paid a substantial bar bill for his friends to get drunk in his honor. Most, but not all, of Walt is now a part of that DZ, but one famous component is still US government property. In fact, Walt is still a visible presence at Fort Bragg if you know where to look (and I am not going to tell you)—because, when he died, his mustache was removed with great ceremony, and is now framed and displayed on the wall of . . . well, if you don't know, it's because you don't need *to know.*

I was a platoon sergeant in the 501st Battalion of the 82d Airborne Division when one of the other NCOs from the 505th told me, "If you're looking for a good soldier, get Walt Shumate. He raises hell, but he's a good trooper. And they're trying to '208' ['undesirable' discharge] him out of the Army."

I started doing some checking, and the more I heard about him, the more I thought he ought to be in my unit. It turned out that he was always studying weapons and that kind of thing, and he worked hard at soldiering. But even so, he was being brought up before a 208 board.

At the conclusion of the hearing before the board, the colonel said, "Private Shumate, is there anything you would like to say to the board before we make our decision about what we'll do with you?"

"Sir," Walt said, "ever since I was a little boy, I always wanted to be a soldier. But it seems to me, ever since basic training, I know more than the sergeants. They resent it . . ." He went on, and he just about had the colonel in tears. The board made its determination, and Walt stayed in the Army. The colonel promoted him to Spec-4 and transferred him out of the unit. That's how I got him.

He and I ultimately went to Special Forces. He made three trips to Vietnam. He was a remarkable person. He had a way with people; they either hated him or loved him.

He retired as an E-9 in Delta [the US Army's elite counterterrorist force, commonly called "Delta Force"], then was a GS-13 safety officer here at Fort Bragg. He died in 1993, of cancer, and he left five hundred dollars in his will for the bar at the Green Beret Sport Parachute Club here, to underwrite a party. He had everything worked out. He was Catholic, so they had a mass for him. After the service, we all went out to the drop zone and spread his ashes, then everybody adjourned to the bar.

VERNON GILLESPIE

The long years of anger and oppression finally boiled over on September 19, 1964, when the Montagnards rebelled against the South Vietnamese. Capt. Vernon Gillespie's camp at Buon Brieng was the only one that didn't participate. That was because he saw it coming and acted to prevent the crisis.

Gillespie and Maj. Edwin Brooks, along with several other SF officers, managed to suppress the rebellion with minimal loss of life. This was accomplished at great personal risk, and was documented by National Geographic's *legendary writer-photographer Howard Sochurek, who happened to be present when the mutiny began. These officers were rewarded for their gallantry by the US Army in the traditional way when politics and integrity collide: They were sacked and censured. Major Brooks, alone, confronted several hundred angry rebels and ordered them out of their positions and back to their compounds—and they went. As a result of this courage and initiative, his military career was destroyed. Vernon Gillespie describes the events.*

Montagnard Mutiny

Maj. Edwin Brooks was a B detachment commander in II Corps and his headquarters was in Pleiku. He commanded a number of A-detachments in the II Corps tactical zone, including the one I commanded, the camp at Buon Brieng. Major Brooks commanded the A-teams, but the actual command of the camps themselves was assigned to the Vietnamese Special Forces, the LLDB.

We recruited and trained strike forces. My camp had about 700 Montagnards under arms at Buon Brieng—a battalion. We trained, armed, and equipped these forces to secure the small portion of South Vietnam that surrounded our camp (primarily jungle), which contained infiltration routes used by the Viet Cong and, later, by the North Vietnamese Army to conduct operations in South Vietnam. The two tribes in the area were the Rhade and Jarai. Our camp at Buon Brieng was right between the two tribal areas, and I had recruits from both tribes. They worked well together and got along well with each other. I didn't have any trouble with them.

Our primary mission at my camp was running reconnaissance missions down toward the Laotian and Cambodian border to interdict the NVA infiltration routes. We also rescued captive Montagnards that the VC were using as laborers and porters at their way-stations. We brought those people back to Buon Brieng to get them away from the VC and deprived the VC of this source of labor.

There's one thing about Montagnards: Once you are accepted by them, they won't lie to you. So if you ask them leading questions, and they don't want to answer, they just won't tell you anything—which provides an answer of its own.

We noticed that something was wrong in the camp at Buon Brieng in late July and early August of 1964. We didn't know what was wrong, but the tension was building among the Montagnards. Sometime about the middle of August, I briefed Major Brooks on the situation, and he believed me. Then I went down to Nha Trang and briefed the group commander. I had a friend in the CIA, and I told him, too. He went to Saigon to brief the J-2 [Joint Services level intelligence officer] at MACV. The essence of the information that I passed to the higher headquarters was that tension was building, and it seemed that something would happen about the middle of September. That information was ignored by everybody except Major Brooks.

On the nineteenth of September, all hell broke loose. The rebellion actually began on the night of the eighteenth in our camp, and we were prepared for it. By the morning of the nineteenth we knew that the rebellion was occurring over a much wider area. The leaders of the Montagnard battalion at Buon Brieng were receiving orders over our regular radio net to take specific actions.

I told the Montagnard battalion commander (a guy named Y Jhon Nie) that I was taking command of the camp and that the Vietnamese Special Forces in the camp were under US protection. Any move against the Vietnamese would be considered a move against the US government, and we would fight. Y Jhon kept the camp pretty much out of the events that followed. Once we put down the rebellion in Buon Brieng, Y Jhon and I got on a helicopter and flew down to Ban Me Thuot to see what we could do about the rebellion in that area.

I ran into Major Brooks there; he had flown down from Pleiku and had put together a rag-tag collection of US Special Forces people from the liaison team at Ban Me Thuot and formed us into a group. We tried to get support from the local US MACV personnel in the town, but they just stayed hunkered down and wouldn't give us any help at all.

On the afternoon of the nineteenth, Major Brooks, completely on his own, took this little force and went to the radio station where the rebel commanders and about a hundred Montagnard soldiers were sending orders to the rebel units around the highlands. I was part of a small force that secured the gate to the compound, and Major Brooks and the rest of the group went into the radio station and dragged the rebels out. Although I didn't see it myself, one of the guys who went in with him reported that he walked in and said, "Okay, get your asses out of here!" And they left!

They came out of the radio station. We tried to get some trucks from MACV to take them back to their compound at Bon Sar Pa just outside of Ban Me Thuot. When it became apparent that MACV wasn't going to furnish any trucks, Major Brooks ordered me to take a few of the other guys and march the rebels down the highway back to Bon Sar Pa, about twenty or thirty miles away.

At several places on the march we encountered Vietnamese army units in blocking positions along the highway. They had orders to prevent the rebels from getting into Ban Me Thuot. I went up to the Vietnamese commanders and told them what I was doing and told them not to fire on us. We were allowed to pass. Nobody really knew what was going on. We finally reached Bon Sar Pa, and Major Brooks arrived in a jeep. He told me to stay the night in the village, which I did, along with Y Jhon Nie, to try to keep track of what was going on.

By that time Special Forces had the rebellion under control throughout the region. The next morning, after everything was finally over, MAAG finally decided to get involved, and "Fritzy" [Col. John] Freund moved in to take over. The Special Forces people were sent back to their camps.

Major Brooks was now in trouble. Out of six Montagnard camps, five rebelled—only mine didn't rebel. There were a lot of questions asked, and a lot of people in MAAG and MACV saying, "It was out of our control. We couldn't do anything about it." But then other people pointed out that Gillespie's camp didn't rebel, that it could have been controlled.

All the Special Forces camp commanders were relieved in the camps except me, although I was relieved two or three times later. And that's when Major Brooks started to fight. He was fighting for his commanders, to keep them from being relieved.

There was also an attempt by Special Forces headquarters down in Nha Trang to whitewash the whole event. Brooks fought the whitewash attempt, too. Brooks went to bat for his A-detachment commanders against Colonel Spears, the commander of 5th Special Forces Group, and to prevent the cover-up. And that's how Major Brooks got relieved, about a month later.

They brought in a new B detachment to run the operation out of Pleiku. Col. John Spears was sent out to Vietnam by Gen. Harold Johnson, then Army Chief of Staff, to bring Special Forces back into the Army. Colonel Spears was a damn good officer, but he was undoubtedly under all kinds of political pressure to get Special Forces under control.

An After-Action Report was written on the event, a document that was about an inch thick when it was finally published, classified secret. They presented the draft to me in late November and asked me to approve the draft. I read the document, and it was so inaccurate that I told them there was no damn' way I could approve it. I insisted that they include a copy of my own After Action Report as an annex to the document. If they were willing to do that, I told them, I wouldn't object to the report's publication.

The report was published and distributed to the Army worldwide as a "lessons-learned" document. Shortly thereafter, a *National Geographic* article was published. There was such a disparity between the official report and the *National Geographic* article that the Inspector General of the US Army conducted an investigation in January. My team and I were back on Okinawa by that time, and the investigation team visited us there. As a result, the original report was withdrawn, worldwide, and all copies were destroyed.

RICK KIERNAN

Rick Kiernan recently retired from the Army as a colonel after several years as public information officer for 18th Airborne Corps at Fort Bragg, parent command for the 82d Airborne Division. He's currently working in public affairs for the 1996 Olympics in Atlanta, Georgia.

The CORDS Program

The CORDS program that I went to in March 1969 had been set up by John Paul Vann; it incorporated teams of specialists from the US State Department, Department of Defense, Central Intelligence Agency, and Department of Agriculture—a kind of small government. These teams were designed to be sent to each of the forty-four provinces.

I arrived in March of 1969. Things were quite tense. Like everybody else, I arrived in Saigon, in-processed at Camp Alpha, received a weapon and field gear, and got my assignment to a subsector. The next morning I was met by a civilian gentleman and put aboard what seemed to be a civilian airliner with Air America painted on the side. I was new to the game and still didn't understand how all of this came together, far above my pay grade.

The guy flew me out to a place called Duc Wa, one of four districts in Hoa Nia Province that also included Duc Wai, Chu Chi, and Trang Bang, about thirty-five miles northwest of Saigon.

We had a small team, only five people: myself, a captain, two sergeants, and a Spec 4 who served as our RTO [radio-telephone operator]. We all lived in a very small hooch right next to the district chief's house. My assignment was to work with the Regional Forces and the Popular Forces—the Ruff-Puffs, as they were called. We also worked closely with the CIDG folks, the Self-Defense Forces, and "Bravo 43" (the Special Forces B detachment located just across the street). So we had a lot of combined operations with troops from the US 25th Division, the ARVN, the Ruff-Puff, and sometimes the CIDG. This made coordination extremely challenging.

Life in these camps was extremely primitive. On the day we put people on the moon for the first time, I was sitting in a bunker on radio watch. We had kerosene lamps for light (no electricity), and we got our water from a well. We were living in conditions reminiscent of the nineteenth century rather than the twentieth. It was if time had stopped.

The CORDS team was really fascinating. There were about thirty of us from the Army. Across the street, in another compound, were the guys from the State Department, supervised by a foreign service officer. Down the street was the compound for the Office of the Special Assistant—the CIA guys. Co-located on our little compound were the District Intelligence Operations Center and the Province Intelligence Operations Center—the local offices for the Phoenix program. Quite a diverse group. My sergeant and I routinely patrolled with the RFs and PFs, going along on operations with a company of soldiers. I had responsibility for sixty-two PF platoons and thirty-one RF companies, assisted by twelve MAT teams.

JOE CHOFFY

Joe Choffy is a certified member of the "Over the Hill Club," the guys who were in SF in the really early days. In his case, that was even before the beret was authorized headgear, and he was at Fort Bragg when President Kennedy visited and bestowed his favor on the little unit—to the disgust of the conventional Army. Choffy's military service actually goes back to the closing days of World War II; he served as a combat engineer in Korea, then went into Special Forces in 1960, as a sergeant. This story is from 1962.

Adventures with Second Lieutenants

One morning at breakfast, Lieutenant Strand told me that I was going on a patrol with him that afternoon. Now, he was a second lieutenant and the team XO. The guy had no combat experience whatsoever, whereas I had experience with both combat and second lieutenants in Korea and neither were very good. As he explained the mission, three patrols were going to operate in the same general area, then meet in a little abandoned village.

Later in the afternoon, well before the time I'd been told we'd depart, I heard a bellow from the lieutenant. "The patrol left without us!" he said. So he, I, and Sergeant Cole took off on our own to try to catch up with the rest of the patrol, which had left about a half hour ahead of us. We crossed the river behind the camp and moved into the jungle.

We moved through the jungle for quite a while, over hill and dale. After an hour or so, the lieutenant (who had the compass and the map) said something to the effect of "Oh, shit!"

This is always a bad sign, especially from lieutenants. "We've been moving on the wrong azimuth," he said. He was ninety degrees off, and we were far from where we were supposed to be.

We made a right angle turn and dove into the bush, off in the direction of where we were supposed to be, miles away through the jungle. I was carrying a .45-caliber Grease Gun with two magazines taped together, plus another eight mags in my ammo pouches. The lieutenant was carrying an old .30-caliber M2 carbine left over from World War II (this was before the days of the M16 for most of us, although the visiting NCOs had the new rifles). We didn't have a lot of ammunition; if we had gotten into a good firefight, we would have been dead meat.

We moved on and finally came to a trail just about twilight. There were no footprints or signs that the patrol had come this way. We decided that we would have to find a RON position for the night. We moved twenty or thirty yards into the jungle, squatted down, opened a C-ration can, and prepared to wait and see what developed. The three of us took turns keeping watch, two hours at a time.

Around one in the morning, we heard heavy gunfire in the distance, off to our right, from the direction we had come. We didn't know who or what it was—if our patrols had run into some VC—but there wasn't anything we could do about it, regardless. At first light we inspected each other for leeches, ate some C-rations, buried our trash, then moved out.

After traveling up this trail for a couple of hours, we crested a hill about eight in the morning and started down into a little valley where the abandoned village was. Through the trees we could see the roof tops of the buildings. "That's it," the lieutenant said. "That's P Sar Dit. We'll meet the rest of the patrol there."

As we descended the hill and got closer, I noticed that there was smoke coming from the "abandoned" village. I pointed this out the lieutenant, and he decided to hold up to think about this for a minute. *Now, is that our guys?* we wondered. *If the smoke means our guys are in the village, we should have bumped into an outpost along the trail. But we didn't. So . . . let's just swing off the trail, and move up carefully to see who's home.*

We got off the trail and swung out a couple of hundred yards to come up on the far end of the village. After working through some tall grass, we finally came pretty close to the edge of the little town. There were no real trees or anything else to provide concealment from here on in. Sergeant Cole volunteered to move up closer to investigate and report back.

It was about forty yards to the edge of the village. Sergeant Cole took off, walking up the main trail just like he belonged there. When he got closer, he squatted down in the weeds, not very well concealed, and we could see him peering into the village. Then he suddenly got up and started running back to where we were. "Jeeze-us Christ, there are VC in there! Fifteen or twenty! They got two dogs with 'em! They got four A6s [light machine guns], two BARs, and the rest have rifles!"

The lieutenant said, "We gotta hit 'em!"

I looked around. There were three of us. We had no cover or concealment, there were no good ambush positions nearby, we had a light ammo load, they out numbered us at least five to one, and they out-gunned us with their machine guns. The lieutenant looked at me and said, "Sergeant Choffy, what do you think?"

"I think we ought to get our asses out of here," I told him. "If we get in a firefight and somebody gets hurt, we are in deep shit. We don't know where the hell the rest of the troops are."

The lieutenant said, "You're right." So we ran back to the heavy grass, worked back into the grass about ten feet from the trail, and hid out for maybe a minute. Then we heard them coming down the trail: *slap, slap, slap, jingle, jingle, jingle,* as the VC unit trotted by. We could see them through the grass—and they weren't wearing VC black pajamas; they were wearing NVA khaki and pith helmets! This was a hard-core unit!

We waited in the grass for about five minutes, then took off, down the trail, well behind the NVA patrol. After we had moved like this for an hour or two, I asked the lieutenant how long he intended to keep up this nonsense. We hadn't seen a sign of the main body of our patrol—the guys we were supposed to link up with.

"Let's give it another hour. If we don't find them by then, we'll go back to camp."

Then, sure enough, an hour later we bumped into the patrol, turned around, and went back to the village with them where we set up to stay the night. During the night we got indications that the enemy was prowling around the vicinity, but they didn't attack us and we didn't ambush them. And the next day we went back to camp without firing a shot.

OTIS HEDGES "BANE" ASHLEY III

Otis Hedges Ashley III, nicknamed "Bane" by his mother ("You are the bane of my existence!" she is reported to have said) retired from the Army as a lieutenant colonel, then trained to be a veterinarian. He and his wife (also a former Army officer) spend a lot of time training for and competing in triathalons. Bane is working on a book about his many adventures.

"We Need Men, Not Wussies!"

If you were born a redneck, with a name like mine, you had to be ready to whip every single kid on the school bus every morning! I come from a long line of rednecks and criminals, moonshiners and gunrunners. I was abandoned when I was fourteen. I came home from school one day, and my parents weren't there. They never came back! I raised myself from then on, and life actually improved once I got in Special Forces. Combat was no big deal after my childhood! I lived out of an old car for a while, got out of school a bit early, and went to a scumbag recruiter and told him, "I'm 18. I need to be in the Army."

He said, "Right!"

I was five foot three and a half, one hundred seventeen pounds, and sixteen years old. The recruiter showed me how to juggle my birth certificate, and I went in the Army in January of 1962. While I was in basic training, the recruiting team from the Airborne school came swinging through the windows during the sixth week, doing chin-ups and being manly. They pointed at me—the little "wussie" in the front row—and said, "We need men, not wussies like Ashley here!" Naturally, I immediately signed up. The same thing happened during advanced individual training, but with guys wearing berets. It was during the time when it was possible to sign up [for Special Forces] right out of basic, as a private, unlike later.

I am terrified of heights—still am, always will be. But I was very fortunate. I was the first third-generation military parachutist to go through the program at Fort Benning. Then it was on to "Special Farces" and Training Group, where I arrived as a wide-eyed sixteen-year-old. I was impressed with everything that moved or hopped or crawled. I fell in love with the whole military experience.

I was trained as an engineer and attended the HALO [high-altitude low-opening, the military free-fall parachute technique that involves jumping from a high altitude and waiting until you are about three feet above the ground to deploy your canopy] course. Shortly thereafter, I attended the Ranger school as a private first class. I made honor graduate at Ranger school, something of an accomplishment when you consider that we started with one hundred fifty-six people and fifty-nine graduated. I think I was very fortunate to have served in combat in Vietnam with both the Rangers and with the Green Berets.

I went to OCS as an E-5 and was fortunate enough to make distinguished graduate there. Then I was sent back to Bragg and Smoke Bomb Hill to the newly formed 6th Group.

Hill 875

Shortly after I arrived in Vietnam as a nineteen-year-old freshly qualified Special Forces second lieutenant I was assigned to Detachment A-245, a team that was supposed to set up a camp at Dak Seang. The monsoon season made that momentarily difficult, so half of us were sent to Dak Pek, and half (including me) to Dak To. We staged out of these two camps with the teams assigned to those camps. While waiting for the rain to let up, we went on operations with the teams from these other two camps, A-244 and A-243.

My first real operation was a seven-day patrol that ended up putting us right on top of an element of the 304th NVA Division. We took out three platoons of Yards, the local guys we were training to go into Dak Seang with us. The other platoons got more experienced Americans, but the guy who went with me was a guy named Dunn [Sp4c. Creighton Dunn, killed in action October 29, 1966 at Dak To].We were both nineteen, but he looked twelve, with blond hair and glasses, a nice guy but TDY from Okinawa. Neither of us had a lot of experience, although I had been to OCS and Ranger School by that time (having already been in the Army for three years).

The Yards in my platoon came from four different tribes; Banar, Sedang, Rhade, and Jerai. It was very fortunate that among them was an old recruit who showed up with bits of his old French army uniform, complete with decorations and a kepi; he became the assistant platoon sergeant. The presence of this old colonial soldier just added to what was a very surreal climate on the patrol. The Yards were having a swell time for the first few days, sliding down hills, falling in the streams, laughing and enjoying themselves.

On the fourth day out, though, that changed. I was called up to the point, at the edge of a narrow and deep stream. The point man indicated a flat rock on the far side; on this sun-baked rock was the clear, dripping imprint of an NVA sandal.

That was the very first time that I realized that this was war, for real; it wasn't Camp Darby at Benning. I remember the feeling vividly: I realized that, until now, I had just been playing soldier. I was a teenager, dumber than a sack of hammers, and until then, I had felt indestructible. It never really occurred to me, until that moment, that someday I might really have to engage in combat. When you play those games in the Army schools, it's just like being back on the old playground—you just know that the referees will be along sooner or later, the "dead" guys will get back up, you're going to be critiqued. I had boxed, and you could get hurt. I had gone to jump school, and you can get killed there. But this was the real thing in a way that nothing else before ever was.

We started across the stream, and now the Yards were really quiet and serious. Everybody "locked and loaded" [chambered rounds]. Then, just at dark, we made contact.

The point man was no more than thirty meters ahead of me; first one, then two, and then three AKs opened up on us. Then some SKS semi-automatic rifles started firing, too, and I heard some of our .30-caliber carbines firing. My blood absolutely ran cold, it frightened me so badly! Later I was in worse situations, but I have never been so scared as I was that day.

I could feel the muzzle blast of those weapons, they were so close. I thought I could feel the ground shake from their concussion.

Several grenades detonated; I could tell from the sound that some were ours and some were theirs. Then from out of nowhere, some clown fired an RPG-7V into our midst; it detonated in a tree about fifteen meters behind me. The guy who fired it was so close that I heard it launched, then the impact almost immediately. Fortunately, the shrapnel sprayed away from me, but the detonation was just deafening!

Everybody was yelling now. Then I saw something pretty incredible: The Montagnard next to me actually used his teeth to pull the pin on a grenade! It was odd enough that I thought, *Man, does his dentist have any idea what he's doing with those molars?* But he threw the grenade only a short distance to our front. I crawled over and tried to tell him in Vietnamese, "Don't throw that thing unless you can actually see people to throw it at!" Then I looked up and realized that, in fact, he could see somebody out there. The NVA were right there in front of us. That was the second big jolt; I could actually see them, about thirty meters away in the jungle! The Yard didn't come close to them, but he had the right idea.

It became one of those slow-motion things. They knew where we were, we knew where they were, and they knew that we knew! I couldn't function. I was completely confused and disoriented. I was ducking and trying to save my own hide. It was really disappointing, later on, for me to consider how badly I performed in those first minutes.

We started to take fire from the rear and from the right, as well as from the front. We were just about surrounded. The bullets were whistling through the trees, ricocheting off things, and it was almost impossible to find a target. I was basically trying to hide.

Then, very shortly after all this started, two Montagnards were hit to my right. It wasn't like in the movies. They dropped their weapons and were writhing on the ground, within ten feet of me. One was shot just below the nose, and the bullet took off part of his upper lip. In the cowboy movies I used to watch, that never happened. You never saw any blood. This was Attention Getter Number Three, and the day was just rocketing downhill, getting out of control.

I started crawling around. It finally dawned on me that the *cracks* I was hearing were bullets going right by me; I had heard about the sound from the old-timers, but this was the first time I experienced it for myself, and it was very frightening.

There was a little lull in the firing, so I tried to tell the Yards to calm down and be quiet for a moment, trying to get them to not draw any more NVA fire. Unfortunately, I said that rather loudly—and the whole world came apart as the NVA opened up on me! I remember looking down at that old Montagnard who served with the French; he looked up at me and just shook his head in disbelief at what I had just done.

Now we could hear the NVA talking, yelling commands, firing and maneuvering. My teeth were chattering from excitement and fear. It was very surreal, and then I realized that the whole platoon was looking in my direction. They were looking at me to lead them. I was an officer in the United States Army, an Airborne Ranger, a fully qualified Green Beret—and they were looking at me because I was in charge. It was the darndest thing for a child to figure that out—and to be factual, that's what I was at the time, a teenager.

I had a flashback to an incident a few days before. Brigadier General Joe Stillwell came out to see my team leave Fort Bragg when we left, and he shook hands with the A-teams as we boarded the aircraft. When he got to me he noticed a black eye I had acquired while intervening in a squabble the night before; he said, "Ashley, I was going to tell you to take care of these men, but obviously you can't even take care of yourself!" The whole thing, at the time, was a game, but it occurred to me then that Stillwell's words came true at that moment.

The old Yard started crawling around, organizing the platoon, indicating fields-of-fire for the soldiers, something I should have been doing.

All this transpired over an extended period of time—maybe thirty seconds or so—and although the point men had returned fire, I hadn't done anything. People started returning fire and throwing a few hand grenades. Finally, I started crawling around to the men, directing their fire, but I was very confused about where the enemy actually was; were they in the trees, were we surrounded, what was going on?

After crawling only five meters or so, a bullet hit the stock of my M16 right at the hand-grip, splattering bits of fiberglass into my face and left hand. Another round in the same burst of fire hit my rucksack, striking a little camera I carried, and chunks of that went into the back of my neck. That was a severe attention-getter. Then, everything went silent for a moment, but when I started crawling again I drew fire again.

My radio operator crawled over, and I reported, "We are in contact. We have casualties!"

The guy on the radio responded that the other two platoons had already reported that they could hear the firefight. He said, "Are you sure you aren't engaging friendlies? Monkeys? Gibbons?"

"No," I told him, "I am hit, Dunn is hit, and at least two of the Yards are hit—and not by Gibbons. I need artillery, and I need it right now!"

He passed me off to the fire support battery co-located at our base camp. "Fire mission!" I called. ["Fire mission" is the first phrase of the "call for fire" or a request for artillery, a very ritualized procedure learned by all young combat-arms officers in the Army.]

After a pause, he responded, "Great, glad to oblige; what's your location?" I couldn't tell him—I didn't know! I had not been paying attention, I had been *playing* army. It was the sort of behavior that makes dead people in wholesale quantities. This was just another little lesson in my professional development course, a program that was evolving at what seemed to be light-speed.

Some A-1E Skyraiders appeared over head, and we finally established where we were when I could tell them exactly when they flew over our position. They radioed that back, and it turned out later to be about 4,000 meters from where I thought we were; I wasn't even in the ballpark. But now I at least knew where we were, and that was a start. And we got some help from the Air Force, too, who brought in an FAC to coordinate things. I asked him, in essence, "Get us out of here!" I was thinking, but didn't mention, that I had decided that I had seen just about enough combat for the next thirteen lifetimes, and they could skip the decorations if they'd just get me out of there alive.

"Okay," the FAC called, "I'm going to direct you to an LZ so we can try to get out your wounded."

About then I started getting control of myself and started moving around the platoon, directing people, and it seemed to be working. We moved off, with me in the number four position from the point; we had gone only about one hundred and fifty meters when the whole world seemed to open up on us. We had gone from what might have been just a squad outpost of NVA, then turned around and bumped into what was probably a company of NVA in bunkers on Hill 875.

Relatively speaking, the first engagement of thirty minutes before had been child's play. RPGs fired into us, and then new sounds of the little NVA "burp-guns" but the Yards reacted well this time and fired back effectively, even though all we had were old Grease Guns and M1 carbines from World War II and the NVA had modern weapons. One of the Yards took a round right below the eye and dropped to the ground, dead.

It was dark now, and the FAC overhead called with some cheery news: "By the color of the tracers [NVA weapons usually fired green tracers while US weapons fired red tracers], I can see that you've really stepped into something ugly." We were in a three-sided crossfire at the time, and I had already reached the same conclusion, even without the intervention of the referees for the war-games I was accustomed to at OCS and Ranger School.

I tried to break contact; we had moved about forty more meters when mortars started dropping in on us, my baptism of indirect fire. Now, since we're discussing what a wimp I am, my fear of indirect fire and of heights are ones I have never fully mastered. They can get you anywhere! But fortunately we were under some triple canopy jungle and some of the mortar rounds were detonating in the treetops.

The FAC called to report that a battalion of ARVN infantry was moving toward us, but they were nine kilometers away, and advising us to hold tight. I told him we'd try, but we needed some relief. Since he didn't know precisely where we were in the dark, I told him I'd fire up a flare.

"Do you really want to do that? Then everybody will know where you are," he said.

"The NVA already know where we are," I told him, and so I put up the flare—mistake fifty-three for the day. A world of fire rained down on us— *but,* the A-1Es came in and started dropping some pretty heavy fire all around us, and that slowed the NVA fire from around us. The FAC reported that a lot of fire was also coming from hills nearby. We were being engaged from about fifteen hundred klicks by NVA heavy machine gun fire, .51-caliber stuff.

We hunkered down and, after taking a lot of rockets, mortars, and heavy machine gun fire for a while, it all slacked off and things quieted down. There were F-105s and F-4s overhead and our engagement was turning into something significant. I managed to fall asleep somehow. When I awoke, it was light. I set a new leech record—there were thirteen of them attached to me. We spent the whole day just hunkered down, waiting for relief.

The sounds of a tremendous firefight could be heard in the distance late in the afternoon. The FAC reported that the ARVN battalion trying to reach us stepped into something nasty and was apparently wiped out. "But, no problem," the FAC called. "The Screaming Eagles [troopers from the 101st Airborne Division] are coming to get you!"

We had been out six days now, and we were getting very hungry and thirsty. But I had calmed down, and I started to feel more competent and confident that I knew what I was doing. I started to believe that we would make it out of there alive, for the first time.

We heard helicopters in the distance, putting the 101st into LZs a couple of hills away. Firing picked up in the distance as the NVA engaged the 101st. We took some mortar fire, too, from so nearby that we could hear the rounds drop in the tubes before they fired. We could hear the NVA moving around in the undergrowth, maneuvering on us.

We crawled about one hundred and fifty meters to the edge of a little clearing where we hoped the helicopters might come to pick us up, but the heavy machine guns on Hill 875 picked us up first and started firing on our position. This was an entirely new experience because you just can't get away from those big bullets by ducking behind some bamboo. Those .51-caliber armor-piercing rounds are just horrific, and they were hitting all around us, sending up geysers of dirt. Several hit in front of me and my first thought were that they were dud RPGs from all the dirt they kicked up. Other rounds ricocheted into our position, and you could watch them coming at you. I saw two of them, tracers, that tumbled slowly right toward me—and I actually started to put my hand out, to catch one! If OCS actually knew how one of its graduates was doing out here I think the place would have been shut down, the curriculum revised, or the entrance requirements tightened.

The FAC was reporting that the 101st platoons were getting closer, warning us to avoid firing on them. The A-1Es dropped some napalm nearby, and that was impressive. On the radio, I could hear by the call-signs that every colonel in southeast Asia was overhead, trying for an Air Medal and the Good Housekeeping Seal of Approval. They were all circling overhead, putting each other in for awards. The sky was black with helicopters, and I desperately wanted them to put one or two of them down so we could get out of Dodge.

By now we had three dead and thirteen wounded Yards, and both of us Americans were wounded—over fifty percent casualties. We could hear M16s firing now, though, and that was nice, although they sounded wimpy compared to the sound of the AKs. Finally, the 101st's lead element crawled over to us and we effected a link-up.

The first American guy I spoke to was a big black soldier. He looked at the two Montagnard soldiers beside me and said angrily, "Who are the fucking gooks?"

I hadn't realized till then how attached I had become to the little guys, and I contemplated jamming the muzzle of my rifle up his nose.

"Do you have Americans here?" he said.

"Yes," I told him, "there are two of us."

"Everybody else is a fucking *gook*?"

I tried to briefly explain to them that these weren't ethnic Vietnamese, but Hmong-Khmer tribesmen. He said, "What's the difference? A fucking gook is a fucking gook!" I pointed out to him that they were the only reason I was still alive, that they had fought for days, and that they were still fighting and were at that moment holding the flank of his position, keeping his platoon from being overrun. I also told him that most of us were wounded, and that seemed to adjust his attitude a bit.

One of the 101st soldiers crawled over and asked me, "Do you have a medic with you? Our platoon leader's been hit."

"Yes, I'm one," I told him. I wasn't a Special Forces trained medic, but I had been cross trained and was qualified.

We started crawling over to their position. The soldier asked, "Do you guys have an officer with you?"

"Yes, as a matter of fact we do," I told him. "Why do you ask?"

"Well, he must be a fucking idiot. Do you know how many NVA are out here? Do you know what he got you into?"

"He didn't mean to," I said, "and besides he's good looking and a really nice guy. And, I'm him." The soldier looked at me—I was, remember, only nineteen and wearing the shreds of a uniform with no insignia on it.

"No, I don't have time to fuck with you, I need to talk to your officer!"

"Trust me on this," I told him, "I am the officer!"

We finally got to the wounded platoon leader, and I got a good look at him; good God, it was a guy named Bob, one of my OCS classmates! It was awful. He looked at me—a ten-day growth of beard, an eye swollen shut, a hand that wasn't working too well, and a mouth that was messed up; not quite the way I looked in OCS.

I looked at Bob's fatigues in the area where he was wounded; the blood was pumping out of his hip so fast that the fabric moved with every pulse. We cut the pants away — the wound was horrific. The femur was broken. The wound was too high on the leg to put a tourniquet on so we tried direct pressure; I ended up standing on the wound, trying to put enough pressure on it to stop the flow of blood. The pain must have been incredible, but Bob never made a sound.

"I need a cigarette," Bob said."

"I didn't know you smoked," I told him.

"I just started."

The wound was fatal, and he knew it. I remember just how he looked: a cigarette in his right hand, his arm draped across his knee. He never took a puff from that cigarette, and I remember standing on him, with my bare heel pressed against the exit wound. I was dead tired, almost to the point of hallucinating, and I was watching that cigarette because I didn't want to look at his face. The cigarette slowly turned red; blood was trickling from somewhere down his arm, soaking into the cigarette. It went out with a *hiss*. Then it dropped from his hand. Bob was dead.

I crawled back to my platoon. We got some LAWs from the 101st to use against some bunkers we'd found. I had three of these things. I cocked one, put some stuff in my ears to protect against the noise, and crawled forward to try to fire into the bunkers. I pushed the button, but it was a dud. I went back for the second, and dashed out, John Wayne style, and tried it—but it was a dud, too! But I guess the entire NVA division had been waiting for this target, and they all opened up with a mass of green tracers. I managed to get back, and this time decided to just shoot the third one from behind a log we had as part of our perimeter; that one was a dud, too! I was zero-for-three at bats with the LAW.

Finally, we got the word to pull back to the clearing. The NVA must have pulled back by then because the firing had stopped and several CH-47s helicopters were already on the ground. We brought out the dead Yards in ponchos, slung on poles and placed them on the ground next to the body bags of the dead ARVN and 101st already in the landing zone. Someone from the 101st came over and told me to move my dead. They didn't want our dead soldiers alongside their own. That was very upsetting to me. There were three rows of body bags—it was the most dead Americans I had ever seen, or ever would see in one place.

Finally, they were ready to put us on a helicopter; the wounded boarded first, Dunn with them, then the unwounded, and I stayed with the bodies, intending to return with them. They put me and the bodies aboard a helicopter, and I still wasn't getting much respect. Of course, I was burned black, I was in tiger-stripes, and was otherwise pretty much a mess. Some ARVN soldiers, very badly wounded, were also loaded on the helicopter, and they weren't getting any respect, either. I went over to one and asked in Vietnamese what was going on—only to discover that they were all NVA prisoners!

"Do you realize these are enemy soldiers?" I asked the flight crew.

"No, how can you tell?" one answered.

"I asked them."

"Do you speak gook?" the crewman replied.

"After thirty-seven weeks in gook language school, I should hope so," I said, trying to imply that I thought he was a screaming asshole of a jerk. But I was able to talk to these enemy soldiers, and that seemed to make an impression.

At last, as I was about to depart, one of the 101st guys grabbed me by the back of the shirt and tried to pull me off the helicopter. "This helicopter is just taking dead, wounded, and officers!" the guy said.

"As I have been trying to explain, I are one!"

But they let me on, and put me in the last seat, right by the ramp. Then they put on thirteen dead in body bags. The bodies were stacked like cordwood, with heads and feet alternating. Then they brought aboard a wounded American; he looked like Dunn, apparently about twelve years old, in a 101st uniform. It was obvious that he was pretty badly wounded, and it took two people to support him as they carried him aboard. They sat him down among the body bags, with his legs over some of the bodies. I thought, "Man, that's weird; they ought to at least strap him in."

We lifted off and headed back to Dak To, jiggling along through the sky. This guy just sat there, no more than three feet in front of me, staring down at the body bags. He looked very, very tired. I asked him, "Are you hit?" He didn't respond but just kept staring down at the body bag on the deck. I asked him some other questions over the noise of the helicopter: Was he part of the unit that went up Hill 875? Still no response. Then, as we banked to make the approach to Dak To, he fell over, right on my feet. Only then did I realize that he was dead—and had been dead for a long time. He must have died in that seated position and stiffened up before he could be put in a body bag.

When he fell over, his arm fell across my boots and I noticed he was wearing a Mickey Mouse watch and a wedding ring—I still remember just what it looked like. I thought, *Man, he doesn't look old enough to be married.*

We landed and when the medics came out, I tried to help pick him up and carry him out of the helicopter. But my left hand wasn't working very well, and I dropped him and his head hit the deck of the helicopter. "Oh, gosh, I'm sorry!" I told him, but he was about as dead as anybody ever gets. His eyes were still open, though, and he still just looked very, very tired.

Some other people came out and helped get him out of the aircraft; they placed him on the helipad in a sitting position. I went over to check the name tape on his uniform, just to see who he was—and the Mickey Mouse watch was already been stolen by someone.

I got shipped off to the hospital for a while, then came back. Dunn was later killed in action [on September 23, 1966], right there at Dak To. Two of the other Americans with me on the operation but with the second platoon, Drummond [S/Sgt. Emanuel F. Drummond] and [Sgt. First Class] Warren Cobley were also killed [on July 8, 1966] there at Dak To, even before we could get to our camp at Dak Seang. A third American, who had been with the third platoon on this operation, a guy named Welsh [Sgt. First Class Thomas Welsh] also was killed [on May 16, 1966] before we left Dak To. The place started out ugly and went downhill from there.

I thought I had experienced the worst that was possible, but later on [see the next story] things, in fact, got much worse. It took about three days for my heart rate to return to normal, but I discovered that many people senior to me in rank and experience who participated in the operation simply failed to function. After a week or so, I realized that this was something that I could, in fact, do. I reached the conclusion that I could not be killed—everybody else might be, but I knew that I would live. I got a lot of pats on the back, and a lot of people seemed to be impressed with what I had done. My teenage ego just sucked that up. I am very nearly ashamed to admit that—I wouldn't have admitted it a few years ago—but that was the way I felt at the time. I had seen some of the bodies of 101st soldiers that had been mutilated, and I started to have a purpose in life. I couldn't *wait* to strap all that back on and go out again.

When I went out on other operations I clearly felt an invisible protective shield come down around me. I was put in for the Silver Star, but was awarded the Bronze Star for the operation. I was later nominated for the Medal of Honor, but didn't get it—perhaps because my team leader, Capt. Billy G. Chandler, beat up the guy who later was supposed to endorse the nomination, which somehow got "lost." Chandler beat the guy up again, when he found out what happened to the nomination. I got three Silver Stars.

One of the pilots who provided air cover near Hill 875 was awarded the Distinguished Service Cross by the Air Force just for flying over the place! This same guy later got another DSC, one as a lieutenant colonel, the other as a colonel; this guy got five Silver Stars and two DSCs. When I compare that to the kinds of things my Montagnards did, it just about reduces me to tears because of the lack of credit, recognition, and respect those guys received. If an American did the same things those little guys did, he'd have to carry his Medals of Honor around in a wheelbarrow.

Dak Seang was a place where the tussling just never stopped. On September 28, 1966, I was trying to put out some Montagnards one morning and triggered an ambush that turned out to be rather messy for everyone involved.

Aw, Bummer—Wrong Army!

We were trying to get the camp at Dak Seang together, but it was very difficult to get anything done because we were in contact so much. We were outside the artillery fire support fan, and the NVA were so close that they would pin messages to sticks and prop them up inside the camp, listing by name the people they were going to kill. It was a little hairy.

The old Highway 1 ran past the camp. It hadn't been usable for years; it was just a trail with a little macadam on it in places, except for about a half mile on either side of our camp. We had jeeps and trucks in the camp, though, and we could travel a short distance outside the gate on the remains of this road.

We were putting out a river crossing nearby on the Dak Poko River, the large, swift river that was just south of the camp. The bad guys had put in a substantial *L*-shaped ambush along that little stretch of road. Two truck loads of Montagnards had been taken down to the river. The bad guys knew we didn't have very many people available—only about two hundred and fifty total—and apparently they decided to try to divide our forces with this ambush. While the two trucks were unloading the troops at the river, the VC ambush team moved into position.

About this time I got a call on the radio that a helicopter was inbound to pick up one of the NCOs who was going off to recon school, and he was one of the guys driving the trucks. I hopped in a jeep and went down to collect him. Five Montagnards hopped in the jeep with me, more for the novelty of riding in the vehicle than anything else.

The NVA were still getting in their holes when I rumbled up at two or three miles per hour. I saw a couple of people on the road. They looked like Yards to me, so I thought they were ours and drove right past them. But I didn't find the trucks and came back up the same stretch of road. As I came back, they must have assumed that the ambush was compromised. They let me drive up very close to them, and then one of them turned around and fired across the hood of the jeep, hitting me above the left eye.

What followed was something like the shoot-out at the OK Corral. They knew what they were doing, but we didn't figure it all out right away. I got a skull fracture and was blind in my left eye. They shot the jeep to pieces. The guys in the back, who were just along for the ride, took most of the fire. It was really weird . . . I saw everything in slow motion. Nothing was working right. There was blood on the floor, but I couldn't figure out if it was mine or somebody else's. I watched the gauges as they were shot out. I was stunned and couldn't really figure out what was going on.

Then a guy ran over and chucked a couple of hand grenades in the jeep, one in the front and one in the back. I knew what that was! It was right between my feet. I tried to get it, then discovered that I was paralyzed on one side. But I was finally able to get a hold of it and drop it to my left, where it detonated. I was blown out, over on the passenger side, and lay on the ground for a while with twenty-nine pieces of shrapnel in me. Then the one in back detonated and really messed the Montagnards up, badly.

While I was lying there, taking all this in, the guy that shot me came over and tried to shoot me again with his Thompson submachine gun. He was pulling the bolt back, but every time he tried to shoot it just went *klunk*. My M16 had ended up alongside me. I was able to retrieve it with my right hand and arm, and I was able to get it to talking—I "wasted" him. He was standing right beside me. I don't think he believed I was capable of doing much of anything—a fatal error on his part.

People were dancing around on the road. Then everybody scattered, and I crawled over to the jeep. I got up, but in the process another NVA fired and hit me in the back of the thigh. I turned and—with one round left in my magazine—hit him in the spine as he turned to run. I thought my leg was broken, but it wasn't. It was very wobbly, and I could see where the bullet had exited the front of my leg. So I stood there, hanging on to the jeep, when some fool of an NVA came over and tried to collect the weapon from the guy I had just shot. It was laying right in front of me, and he tried to pick it up. I was out of ammo, so I whopped him with the M16, and then he and I got into one of those "let's roll around on the ground; I'll beat you to death with my rifle" tricks. I broke the stock off my rifle, but that was okay, because I was on my knees at this point, and it was easier to swing. After that I passed out.

When I woke up I was looking at the dirt. I rolled over and looked around. There were dead and dying folks everywhere. The guy I had shot in the spine was being unhappy, and so was the guy I had shot first. So I got out my old K-Bar knife, crawled around, and cut everybody's throats. None of them could take a joke about that, either, so it wasn't all that easy. I passed out again. When I woke up, I was now a member of the 304th North Vietnamese Army Infantry Division; I was being dragged by a guy who was pulling me along by the armpits.

I said to him in Vietnamese, "You've got to stop; I'm bleeding to death." The guy freaked out, but he kept dragging me. I still had the knife in my right hand because they hadn't been able to pry it out. I managed to reach over and get this guy by the belt, and he went nuts-a-mundo. Then he and I got into another wrestling match. I got over on my knees. I wasn't going to let this guy get away; I thought he was one of my Montagnards. It had already been a real bad morning for me, and I didn't want to get left. He started kicking my head completely off my shoulders, and then I finally got a good look at him and realized who he was. *Aw, bummer—wrong army!* I thought. This thing just keeps going downhill! I tried to stab him with the knife, and I couldn't do it. Finally, he kicked me as I had the butt of the knife against my chest, and he stabbed his leg on the knife. That got him to turn me loose! He grabbed his leg, we rolled around some more, and I killed him.

I crawled around for a while. I couldn't get up, and I couldn't walk. I kept dodging NVA folks, and finally I got back to the road. I was trying to crawl back to camp when the NVA reaction force arrived and (as luck would have it) spotted me on the road. They were really bad shots, because they were within one hundred meters of me and they absolutely shot the road away. But I only took one more round, this one across the left side of my head (I now have a kind of permanent part in my hair).

The Yards heard all this, of course, and came running up. They found me there and looked at me. Their expressions seemed to say, These lieutenants will do just about *anything* to get attention! It was a bad day.

By this time I was having a hard time telling who were the good guys and who were the bad guys, and according to the Medal of Honor statements that were prepared later, I was trying to kill everybody. They wrapped me and the knife in a blanket, strapped me to a litter, put me in a helicopter, and shot me out of there to Dak To. Apparently I tried to carve up the medic when he tried to put in an IV, and I'm a little surprised they didn't just dump me out the door somewhere between Kontum and Pleiku.

STEPHEN LEOPOLD

Stephen Leopold is an attorney now, still in the Army serving as a lieutenant colonel in the reserves. In 1968, while a fresh lieutenant recently arrived in Vietnam, he was captured and held until 1973, first in Cambodia, then in North Vietnam, including a couple of all-expense-paid years at the Hanoi Hilton.

Captured by the NVA

I was captured near the town of Ben Het, a small town near the Thai border. Our camp was about ten "clicks" [kilometers] from where Laos, Vietnam, and Cambodia intersect. I was just plain lucky to be captured there because if it had been anywhere else they wouldn't have had any way of getting me out and would have just shot me right there. After I was captured and wounded, I was held in northeast Cambodia for about a year and a half and then marched north and held just outside Hanoi for about a year. After the Son Tay raid [during which helicopter-borne American commandos attacked the Son Tay prison in North Vietnam in an attempt to release American prisoners; unfortunately, the prisoners had been moved], very near the camp where I was held, we were moved into Hanoi itself for the last two years of the war. During the last two months they moved us into the Hanoi "Hilton"—we'd finally hit the big time!

Before I was captured, I had been in country all of a month, at the camp for all of ten days. At that time there were three officers on an SF A-team: the commander, the XO, and the civil affairs/psy-ops officer. I was assigned to be the civil affairs/psy-ops officer, then was kicked upstairs to be the XO when the number two guy had to go someplace else.

I led a patrol mission . . . to a hilltop about four clicks west of our camp overlooking an old French road that went around a bend, past the remains of an old French fort at the bottom of the hill and into Laos. The Ho Chi Minh Trail was three clicks across the valley. We needed to occupy the hill to keep the NVA from using it to rocket our camp—which they did every time we abandoned the place!

S/Sgt. Michael McCain and I and a hundred Montagnards, plus one or two Vietnamese ARVN special forces, set up on this hilltop. Mac had been in country for four tours, as early as 1962. He really liked it over there.

We were overwhelmed the next morning by about two companies of NVA. It was no contest, really. The Montagnards had old, World War II weapons because the Vietnamese wouldn't let them have anything better. So when the NVA attacked, the Yards ran off. I couldn't blame them; they didn't have anything to fight with. I've never been bitter about it. It was like the Italians attacking the Ethiopians.

Combat happens relatively quickly. I'd been in places where mortar and rifle fire came in; you can accept that pretty dispassionately when it's just a stray round. It's different when you're asleep and wake up to a firefight outside the window. . . .

It was one of those things . . . we had talked a lot that day, Mac and I. He'd been through a lot. If I had been on the other side of the hooch, he'd have lived through it; I would've been just another of his lieutenants that got killed. But this time, he was in the wrong place at the wrong time. It teaches you some of life's lessons. He'd been over there for four and a half tours, and if he'd wanted to stay back in Nha Trang and run the NCO club they would have let him. But he insisted on being in the combat zone. So two grenades came into the hooch, and Mac caught most of both of them. He was dead very quickly.

I was blown out of the hooch. It was funny, in some respects. It happened very quickly. I was lying there thinking, *Am I dead or am I alive? Well, I'm alive. Where am I hurt? Well, I'm hurt here and here, but nothing in the gut, no massive bleeding. I guess I'm not going to die right away.* The NVA stuck AKs in my face when I came to. They bound me and then took me off the hill. I could hobble—this was before they were carrying me. We were just two miles from Cambodia and the huge concentration of NVA staging and R&R area, hospitals, and camps, so it wasn't much of a problem for them to haul me around for a week.

Your training kicks in. I was thinking, *Well, they didn't kill me up there.* There wasn't anything I could have done about it if they had wanted to. So I was wondering if I was going to live there or die there. Well, they collected me and took me off the hill, and I was wondering what they were planning to do. By that time I figured that they had orders to take prisoners, rather than shoot them, so everything started to make some sense.

It's really amazing, looking back on it. I wasn't terrified because I was in a state of shock—but I should have been. After a while I figured that if they had been going to shoot me they would have done it two hours ago, and they didn't. Since I was alive, I was going to stay alive unless my wounds went sour or we got bombed or something.

Within two hours of capture, they had me miles away, talking to some NVA division commander and his intelligence officer. The commander, a general, was actually a very nice guy. But they knew more about that camp than I did! I spent my time trying to give them disinformation, but their map was better than the one I could have drawn! They had been watching it for months, and they had infiltrated it, one way or another, through the Montagnard force.

I spent a lot of time in the jungle and was sick a lot. I got malaria. When they finally took us north, they weighed us. I was 112 pounds. The irony was that I was listed as missing in action for five years. The pilots, who were really very grossly mistreated until about 1969, at least were identified and acknowledged. They received at least one Christmas package and letter, unless they were cooperators, in which case they got more. Those of us captured in the south were also in Hanoi, but as far as anyone knew, we didn't exist! Unless you made tapes, nobody knew you were alive. So I spent five years as missing in action.

We called the food they gave us "Uncle Ho's No-Cal Diet." It couldn't have been more than 400 calories a day: a little bowl of pea soup (two chick peas with some broth), or peanut soup (with literally one or two peanuts in some liquid). We had that, plus two small cups of rice each day. The only meat I had in the first eighteen months was from a monkey once, and we had some pork fat once. That was it for a year and a half.

It seemed to be a general rule that the further you were from the front-line combat troops, the worse the treatment was. Front-line troops respected their adversaries. The NVA guarding me in Cambodia were not bad people. And I wasn't in love with their commander, but he was better than anybody we had up in North Vietnam! He'd been a front-line commander. He could be funny about some things; he got mad at me because I was the ranking officer and I didn't take their indoctrination course too seriously. We had three days of lectures informing us that we were the "running dogs of the odious Nixon clique and the US imperialist war." Then we had a goddamm exam! They handed out these lined blue books, just like in college, and said, "Write for me what you think of the US war." Well, what I wrote him was not what he wanted to hear. He was so upset that I was sent back into solitary confinement. He used to tell me, "You know much more than the others, so you must think more carefully about your crimes!"

As we moved deeper into Cambodia, the NVA I was with seemed fairly happy. They had an easy enough mission, although they had to carry me at times. But they were away from the B-52 strikes—it was like an R&R mission for them. They weren't upset with me and didn't treat me badly at all. But when we got to the camp it was different.

The camp in Cambodia was deep in the jungle, under triple-canopy jungle. They kept us in bamboo cages at night. They saw I was kind of hardcore and not cooperating, so they put me in solitary.

I spent the first six months on a hilltop by myself. I didn't see another American for another four and a half months. Then a guy named Pete Dravic came in. Then Mike Benge, a civilian missionary, then Perecone and Dave Suitor. There were three officers, about ten enlisted guys, and the civilian.

We had one guy die of malaria, over on the other side of the camp, and another guy died in an escape attempt. You could get sick and die in the camp, in Cambodia, although that wasn't true in the north because they did have medical facilities.

My directive to the guys, as the senior officer in the camp, was, "I don't care what you tell those guys here . . . but I better not hear anybody on the radio!" You've got to make some effort to make a tape for the NVA. They were good troops. They gave the NVA nothing important, and they survived. But boy, it was boring! The boredom in that camp was incredible! They were trying to bore us to death. We were lucky they decided to move us in 1969 up to North Vietnam, where the physical conditions were a lot better but the psychological conditions were a lot worse.

We were marching north and passed a group of Montagnard laborers on the trail. There were a couple of ancient (maybe forty-year-old) women, with black teeth, all bent over, in the group. Black Jack turned to me and said, "Zorro, it's been two and a half years since I've seen a woman, but that's still *ugly!*"

Conditions in the north were totally different. The war was strictly us against them, and communism had nothing to do with it. It had nothing to do with capitalism or America or any of that. It was strictly personal. It was that group of guards and their commander vs. us—and who's going to retain their sanity. We discovered how alone we were, and we reduced the war down to its simplest terms—us against them.

POW Humor

I found that humor helped get me through. The Vietnamese are a lot of fun. They were awfully xenophobic, but also funny. The camp commander called me up for what we called an "attitude check." They trolled all the time to see if any of us were coming around to their point of view and wanted to start making propaganda tapes.

Funny things happened every day. The Vietnamese just didn't understand American culture. And we learned how to use this to our advantage. For example, the Vietnamese just couldn't understand how we could communicate around the whole camp, between these warehouses that were separated from each other. It was incredibly easy. They happen to be extremely prudish, particularly when it comes to non-Vietnamese. They all refused to come within a hundred yards of our latrine—which made it the ideal place to use for a message drop. The whole camp used it. It was easy to leave a little piece of paper there, under a rock or even out in the open. The guards sure weren't going to investigate.

We had a lot of fun in that camp. We were really lucky. I was in with guys from all over. Some are still friends—the best friends anybody could have. We had a motto: You can either laugh or cry, and we are going to laugh! If you start crying, getting into self-pity, that will destroy you in a hurry. So we tried to laugh.

For example, Zigler was a dirty old man, and the Vietnamese are prudish and puritanical. Well, we were only allowed to speak English, to control who we talked to, but there were a number of guards who spoke English and used us to practice. But it wasn't like having a real conversation. You got tired of being somebody's language punching bag. So Zigler would insist on talking about sex! At first, they didn't understand what he was talking about—so he explained it in greater detail! God, he could get rid of the North Vietnamese cadre in a hurry! When they realized what he was talking about, they just disappeared!

Communication Skills

The other guys were real good. After the NVA put me back in solitary, we still had a way of communicating. The nearest prisoner hut was just about twenty yards up the hill. I could hear them talking. Then we worked out a way for me to participate in the conversation. They'd be chatting away, and one would say, "Ain't that right, Zorro?" If I coughed twice, that was "yes." One cough meant "no."

And I could write notes sometimes, with tobacco ash and any spare paper I could find. I left the notes down by the latrine. So, even though I was supposed to be in solitary, I could still communicate with the other guys.

The compound was laid out in a semicircle, with an inner fence and an outer fence, and ten huts that could hold up to ten people each. The latrine was down at the bottom of the little hill, and the guard shack was in the middle. There was always a guard on duty, at least one. Before the escape attempt, they let people wander around and visit, but after that we were pretty much confined to quarters.

The camp doctor was a real nice guy, although I don't know how much of a doctor he was. They gave us quinine for malaria, but that was about it. I got a humungous abscess, and they didn't do anything. They weren't about to waste much of their medicine on the likes of us.

I don't remember it as a time when I was brutalized as much as warehoused. They put me in solitary and tried to break my will through isolation techniques—and it didn't work. It didn't work because the other guys were supportive. I encountered very few guys who had a "me first" attitude.

The latrine was only used to dump and clean the big buckets we kept in our cells for sanitation. They were emptied once a day. Messages were consolidated, written with spit and charcoal on the stuff they gave us for toilet paper, then rolled up tight and tucked between the lid and the rim of this bucket. There was no way any Vietnamese was going to look in there, believe me! It was fairly easy to let the other guys know which bucket they were to retrieve. Once they were all cleaned and back in their cells, with the doors closed, the notes could be removed and read. The guards never caught on because they refused to come close to the latrine.

I started a food fight once (and got decorated for it later, after we got home) so I could be put in solitary so I could communicate with some other guys there who were out of the "loop." The guards got furious and beat the shit out of me and tossed me in solitary for thirty days. But communicating with the other guys was real simple. Unfortunately, at first, the other guys didn't know about our message system. At first I left them a message in my shit-can, but it came back—they didn't notice it. So I took some old, stale bread that they gave us, wrote a note, and stuck it into the bread with a little sliver of bamboo. It said, "I am Lieutenant Leopold. Look for message under rim of bucket."

I put this inside an empty bucket where they were sure to see it. And sure enough, my bucket came back, empty. Now these guys were into the loop.

Until the Son Tay raid, Dave Suitor and I were kept in an awful prison outside Hanoi. God, it was bad! The walls were black. We were only let outside for maybe five minutes a day. It was terrible. Suitor could hear the attack on Son Tay in the middle of the night, although I slept through it. We didn't know what happened, but the next morning there were 400 Vietnamese at our camp, in the rain, digging.

The Shit-Can Express

We developed what we called the "shit-can express." I got put in charge of commo for the camp by Colonel Guy. Some new guys showed up in the camp, so we sent them a message in the shit-can express. The first message was along the lines of, "Hi, how are you?" just to make sure that they were getting the message. Then we sent them a message saying, "Pay attention down at the cistern." That's because the bath house, down by the camp cistern, was another place the guards kept far away from. Their prudery kept them as far as they could get from a naked American body!

Well, everybody came to the bath house on a regular basis, and we had a hole through the wall so we could talk to them. The guards stayed outside, smoking and chatting, and the door was closed. While two guys kept an eye on the guards and four guys made a lot of noise yelling and splashing, one guy could use the hole to listen to whatever the current information was. The messages came down from Colonel Guy, to us, and we passed it on to all of them.

This way, although we were segregated from the enlisted guys, we could still pass the word to this group. They went back to spread it around the enlisted cells. So, everybody knew everything! Everybody, that is, except the people who were cooperating. Colonel Guy didn't want to expose the communications network to these guys, eight enlisted guys.

The Plantation

Three nights after that they moved us. At two o'clock in the morning, the trucks showed up inside the camp and they told us to get our stuff and get on the trucks. I thought we were going to China. But we went to downtown Hanoi. We called it the Plantation, right in the middle of Hanoi. It's where we think Jane Fonda came to visit in 1971. My cell had "black-washed" walls, and I spent the next year in almost total darkness. Then they moved me to a cell with white walls and a light bulb that was on all the time! But it was a better camp; they fed us better, and there was more of it. There were more people, and less room, so they put more of us together. They even gave us a deck of cards. I knew how to play bridge, so I taught the other guys in the cell how to play, and we played bridge for three hours every night! I haven't played bridge since. Three hours a night, every night for months and months—you tend to "bridge" yourself out!

They had a cook Zigler called "Mama Yang," and to us she looked like Mona Lisa and Marilyn Monroe—but, God, she was ugly.

Officers and enlisted men were kept apart, as were the prisoners who were cooperating. We had names for the buildings—the Corn Crib, the Hog House—and we weren't supposed to be able to communicate. But when Colonel Guy took over the camp, he started tap codes, which we used at first to communicate between rooms. We started out by talking through the walls. If one of the guys lay on the floor, he could see under the crack, outside, and watch for the guards. Then, with a blanket over your head to muffle the sound, you could talk through the wall to the guys on the other side. Even though the walls were two bricks thick, if the other guy had his ear to the wall at the point where I was talking, he could hear me. Then we came up with something better.

We took the wire bail off the buckets and used it as a drill. We drilled holes through the walls, two bricks thick.

Life in the Hanoi Hilton

We got half a loaf of old French bread twice a day. For six months we got cabbage soup (which was okay; I still like cabbage) and for another six months we got squash soup. You can't get me near squash! I *hate* squash! You have to eat it because it has fiber, but their idea of a treat was on Sunday we had sugar squash soup! I ate because I needed what was in it, but God, it was bad! I still like rice, too.

We ended up with about a hundred people in this camp. It was a good camp, in a way. We were able to communicate with each other. When a new prisoner was brought in, we caught up on what was going on in the outside world. For example, when one guy showed up in the camp, the first thing that made the rounds was that *Playboy* magazine was now showing "muff" shots! That was what was important back in the US! I didn't know about the moon landing until years after it happened, until I was in the north. Once we got to this camp in the north, we were getting caught up on all kinds of things. It was like we had died, in a way; we were completely out of contact with our society, in my case from 1968 to 1971.

I took the opportunity to learn Spanish. One of the guys and I spoke nothing but Spanish in the room for about two months. There were very few books in the north, and none in the south. In Hanoi we got a few Russian novels and the *Pentagon Papers* and that's it.

There were two types of guards, the English-speakers and the others. If any were particularly friendly to us Americans, they had a tendency to disappear in the direction of the front. If they were more than formally correct, they generally disappeared. The guards had a great assignment, right in the middle of Hanoi. The bombing raids avoided the compound, and they were far from combat—they were happy. This was as good as it got for the NVA, and they followed orders.

It was different with the cadre. They had learned English, and we could indoctrinate them. There was one guy—most of us really liked him, he was really nice—who always let us out for extra time in the rec room. He always had a light for your cigarette. You could talk to him. He'd tell you about his family, about what he was interested in. He liked to practice his English. He was a good enough communist to think that the Americans should lose, and if they sent him to fight in the south, he'd pick up his AK and go. But he had no particular interest in the war. His attitude seemed to be, "Life's short enough. We don't have to rush things, do we?"

Most of the cadre, though, were rigid, cautious, and no fun at all. Some, like a guy named Phong, were either exceptionally dumb, or they actually believed that stuff their government was handing out. When you saw them coming over to practice their English, you knew you were in for a very boring ten minutes or so. The best way to get rid of them was to turn the conversation around to sex somehow. It worked on all of them except one guy, who was married. If we tried that on him, he didn't care; all he said was something like, "Well, I'm getting some and you're not!"

They dealt with us by keeping the hard-core officers separate from the others as much as possible. Then there were the guys they thought they might convert someday, and they were kept together. Then there was the so-called Peace Committee, the collaborating officers who were recording broadcasts. The newly captured officers were housed next to them. Finally, there were the great unwashed numbers of enlisted men—and the NVA didn't want to have anything to do with them.

We called the collaborators "green socks" guys. They were recording the same kind of drivel that came from Tokyo Rose during World War II—utter nonsense. Well, the guards handed out socks to these guys during the winter, when it was cold, to wear with their sandals. I figured it was just standard Uncle Ho issue that everybody was supposed to wear, but the stories that went around the camp about this development were incredible! Somebody thought the socks came from the British, who had entered the war on the side of North Vietnam! Other people thought the socks had some relationship to how the peace talks were going—the war was going to be over in two months!

That was the kind of thing that kept people going for a while, kept them revved up for a while. But then, two months later, when the war didn't end, there was a tremendous depression. That's when people needed their friends to keep them going, to keep them on the straight and narrow, because the NVA were trolling all the time for the weakest, then putting them in groups to reinforce each other.

Even the hardest core got attitude checks, even Major Montgeau (the Vietnamese didn't like him and he liked them even less. Monte decided one time that he wasn't going to bow to them anymore. Well, this was sometime in 1972. He decided that he was a major and this kow-towing to the enlisted NVA guards was bullshit. Well, the guards solved that! They took Monte to a camp outside Hanoi and didn't bother to give him any water. Forget the food, he didn't get any water at all! After six days of this, Montgeau decided he'd bow after all.

So, if you kept your head, you could deal with the situation. We tried to be reasonable about everything, and the guards (we figured) just wanted to survive the war.

I got to that camp outside Hanoi on Christmas day, "Black Christmas," 1969. Until about that time pilots shot down over the north were brutalized—not as punishment, but for propaganda value. They were trying to get them to break, make statements over the radio that would then destroy the morale of the US troops in the field. It was stupid, but that's what they did.

But after that they just pretty much warehoused us. The only times I got brutalized were when I broke their rules. As far as they were concerned, there was no Geneva Convention, no camp commander within the prisoners. We were all treated as individual war criminals whom they might or might not let go home after this thing was over. But Colonel Guy put us together and kept us together as a military organization—a half-assed group—but a military organization just the same.

The way some people survived it was through hate. Hate is powerful. Hate works. Montgeau used it every day. The problem with that is that, when the war is over, it still isn't over for you. Then there were the Bible-pounders; it worked for them. But I was in it for my friends. They kept me alive, and I kept them alive. It was us against them. I reduced the war to those of us in the Plantation against these other guys, the guards, in the compound. When you do it that way—us against them—and you keep faith with the "us," you are in fairly good shape.

The other thing I found is that self-pity will destroy you. The opposite of self-pity is the ability to laugh at what is tormenting you. You either laugh about this stuff or you cry about it, and I found that once you start feeling sorry for yourself, you are in real trouble. I've seen it happen, and you can't talk them out of it. It's pretty frightening. What I learned was that, if you wanted to disarm some Vietnamese trying to propagandize you, just start talking to him about eating pussy. We stopped more interrogations this way than you could believe!

My mother believed I was alive, although she had no reason to. My father, with no better reason, believed I was dead. I was missing in action for five years. It was a long time.

ANONYMOUS

Happy New Year, SF style!

Our Christmas had been pretty badly interrupted by a group of uninvited guests, an NVA unit that attacked on our holiday. So we spent pretty much all the day in action, without any of the usual festivities.

Life in this camp was extremely austere. We certainly never got any USO shows or any other form of entertainment that we didn't manufacture ourselves. Since we hadn't really had a Christmas, I decided that we were definitely going to have a New Years! So I went into Nha Trang, about fifty miles to the east of our camp in the highlands, with our duce-and-a-half truck to collect a band and whatever girls I could find.

We found a band and told them we were having a party on the other side of town. We offered them some money to come along and play for us, and they agreed. They loaded their drums and guitars in the back of the truck, and the musicians and their three dancing girls all piled in. We also bought up most of the beer and booze in Nha Trang, the best stuff we could find (Johnny Walker and Jack Daniels) and that went into the truck with the girls, the band, and the instruments.

Now, the women were "go-go" girls, and they were dressed in little outfits with lots of string and tassels. We decided that three girls just would not go far enough around. We had two MAT teams, an A-team, and a district team, all of whom were going to attend our party. So we started looking around Nha Trang for more girls. We told them we were having a party, and all the ones that wanted to go climbed into the back of the duce-and-a-half. After we had eight or nine girls and the three musicians in the back, we figured we had enough and started back for camp.

It was starting to get dark as we left town, and the MPs at the exit point looked at us with a rather funny expression as we rolled out the gate. At night every bridge was guarded and had concertina wire across it, and as darkness fell the VC started roaming the countryside. The NVA started coming into the hamlets. The night was completely unlike the daytime in Vietnam, and those MPs must have thought we were out of our minds to be going out into the countryside at night.

But as we left the city, there was a long, blood-curdling scream from the girls as they realized that they were not going to any party within the city of Nha Trang. And they kept screaming for about fifteen kilometers! Finally, I stopped the duce-and-a-half, got out, and walked back to the girls. They were calling me every swear word they knew in Vietnamese and in English. I told them, "I am going to my compound where we are going to have a big party tonight. You have a choice: You can come along and go to the party, or you can walk back to town. If you keep screaming, we will be hit by the NVA, and nobody will get to party."

There was a lot of anguished debate. I said, "Okay, what is it going to be?" I was serious; it was just me and Sergeant "Smith" out there with a band and about nine girls in the back of a duce-and-a-half, and by now it was fully dark.

They decided to keep going. We drove the rest of the way up into the mountains as fast as that truck would go, right through concertina wire and the occasional shots from the PF guards. At least the guards were bad shots, and since the NVA didn't usually drive up in American trucks, most didn't

165

fire at us. But we didn't have time to mess around and stop to explain to them what we were doing out driving after dark.

Finally, we got to the camp. And did we party! The band set up and started to play. The go-go girls danced, and the other girls partied with our guys, sat on their laps. Everybody was there: the A-team, the MAT teams, the district team. Even the local Montagnards showed up and joined in. It was just one hell of a party!

We planned to truck them back the next day, but there were some missions that needed to be run, some other things that had to be accomplished, and our vehicles were all unavailable. So we told them that they'd have to stay one more night.

So the festivities began again the next night, with more wine, more song, and more of the same women. A good time was had by all until about 2300 when, over the sound of the music, we all heard a distant sound: *Whump! Whump! Whump! Whump! Whump!* We all recognized the sound of mortar rounds coming out of the tubes. All of us were suddenly running everywhere. But the band and the girls didn't have a clue that anything was wrong. They kept playing and dancing while the rest of us were scurrying around. The girls kept dancing and the band kept playing. But when I looked over at them, the expression on their faces had changed. They knew something was seriously wrong because we were all suddenly running around like maniacs. That party was over in a heartbeat!

We all recognized the sound of incoming mortar rounds and I knew we all had ten to twenty seconds before the impacts. We all had a plan for what we would do. This was not the first time this sort of thing had happened, believe me. But we didn't have a plan that accommodated the band and the girls!

It didn't take very long for us to be in our bunkers and set up our fighting positions, but the girls were still running around the compound in their cute little micro-mini skirts, with the fringe and the tassels, squealing. Mortar rounds were already impacting. We were busy trying to check our wire to see if there had already been a breach, preparing to fight, while the girls and the band members were running all over the compound. We had to climb out of the bunkers, go out and collect these people, and find a bunker for them.

The attack didn't turn out to be much of a threat and didn't last too long. The next day we decided that the party was over and it was time to get the girls and the band back home. But rather than take them back in the truck, we called up some friendly helicopter pilots to come and get them for us— without telling them the whole story before they arrived.

When the Hueys landed to pick up the girls and the band, one of the pilots asked me, "So, just how do you suggest we explain *this* mission?"

I told him, "All you have to say is that you were taking out indigenous personnel."

COL. ANDY DULINA

Andrew Dulina III spent two tours in Southeast Asia, the first in 1967-68 as the executive officer of an A-detachment in III Corps, north of Tay Ninh. His second tour was split between training Thai soldiers preparing to go to Vietnam and as the commander of an A-detachment involved in long-range recon patrols (the LRRPs, usually called "Lurps") up north.

LBJ

We captured a particularly large monkey on one of our patrols and dragged it along with us, trying to keep the Vietnamese from killing and eating it. We brought it back to the camp and turned it into a team mascot—although we certainly didn't need anything else to keep us busy.

The critter became somewhat friendly—not tame, exactly, but manageable—and we named him LBJ. This monkey lived with us for a month or so while we tried to keep the Vietnamese troops in the camp from absconding with LBJ for dinner. He was taught all sorts of nasty tricks and was a source of amusement. When we deployed north to a new camp, the monkey came with us in the helicopter—a memorable experience!

We were in the new camp for a couple of weeks when the NVA started firing mortars at the camp occasionally. The rounds mostly landed outside the perimeter. We didn't think much of it—they were probably just registering their weapons.

We had a daily "mad minute" at this camp while we were getting everything together and planning some tactical operations. Every evening, just about dark, we all lined up around the perimeter and fired our weapons into the jungle for about sixty seconds. I don't know that we ever hit anything.

After about a month we received a particularly fierce mortar attack. Usually mortar attacks only lasted fifteen or twenty minutes; twenty-five or thirty shells would be thrown at us every night about eight thirty. We got our mortar pits in and started to do some counter-mortar fire missions and threw a few back at them. Then, after at least a hundred rounds landed on the camp, a ground attack followed. We estimated that at least a couple of battalions were involved.

But we had just gotten all our wire out, and the Claymores were installed, so we felt pretty strong defensively. We hadn't had a chance to rehearse all our contingency plans, though, and all hell broke loose. We started taking casualties, mostly among the CIDG who were running around, basically out of control. It took a little while, but we finally got our Vietnamese Special Forces counterparts together with us, got a plan together, called in some air strikes and some artillery support from the fire base a couple of clicks to the south of us. The NVA broke through the wire in a couple of places, but not in strength. Things stabilized. We fought them all night, and about daylight, the attack petered out and the shooting stopped. We counted our casualties and went out and picked the bodies out of the wire and cleaned the place up.

This damned monkey had managed to get loose during the battle and had gotten wounded. The medics patched him up, though, and he was fine.

We got a lot of publicity for the attack, maybe because we were a new camp, or maybe because the command was using us to "bait the hook" for the NVA, to get the bad guys to come after us so they could then put a large American unit on the ground. So the day after the attack, Gen. William

Westmoreland came into the camp for an inspection and a pat on the back. He flew in with his normal entourage—five or six helicopters of aides and assorted hangers-on.

The team leader, team sergeant, and I all went out to meet him. Westmoreland noticed the monkey and asked, "I see you've got a team mascot; what's his name?" When the team leader replied, "LBJ, sir," you could see a lot of eyebrows rise. Special Forces were known to be disrespectful of just about anything, and nothing was said about it. But all of his aides looked at us like were entirely out of control.

We took him back to the team room for a quick, informal briefing on what we were trying to do. While we were giving the briefing, LBJ decided to climb up on Westmoreland's shoulder . . . and he starts to attack the supreme commander of the whole world! He started beating him on the head, biting his ears, and generally abusing him! At first the general just tried to ignore the attack and stay focused on the briefing, but then the two of them became involved in hand-to-hand combat.

Of course Westmoreland's whole entourage went completely "bat-shit." About fourteen aides were going for their pistols and were about to shoot our monkey. But we went over and pried LBJ off the general, and the general tried to pretty much ignore the incident. No real damage was done, no blood was shed; but the festivities went downhill from there. Afterwards the team leader, Capt. Joe Lucas, turned to the team sergeant and said, "This monkey had better be out of Dodge by sunset!" Within twenty-four hours the monkey was nowhere to be seen, but the Vietnamese all looked happy and well fed.

The Special Forces A-Team

The SF *A-team* of legend and lore is properly called an *A-detachment*. It is a unit of twelve men—two officers and ten sergeants. This team can be deployed as a complete unit or as two six-man "split" teams, or even as two or three man sub detachments.

The basic team's officers are the commander (a captain) and the executive officer, a first lieutenant. When the team is split, each will command a sub detachment. The classic team includes medics (one senior and one assistant), two engineers, two heavy weapons specialists (mortars, mostly), two light weapons specialists (rifles and machine guns), and two communications specialists. This twelve man unit is designed to train, equip, and lead a five-hundred-man battalion of partisans, guerrillas, or irregulars in operations behind enemy lines.

All team members are supposed to be proficient in the language of the operational area, although real language proficiency has been a problem for SF through the years. But each member of the team is expected to work comfortably with people of very alien cultures; it is an idea that worked in France and Burma half a century ago; it worked in the Vietnamese highlands, and it is still working today in about fifty nations around the globe, some of which you've never heard of.

—Hans Halberstadt

FRED FULLER

Fred Fuller, a civilian, is the librarian of the Marquat Memorial Library at the Special Forces Headquarters at Fort Bragg, North Carolina.

"I'm Sgt. Walt Shumate"

When SF people neglect to pay their bar bills, get thrown out of whorehouses, or get arrested—anywhere in the world—and someone asks their name, the answer is invariably "I'm Sgt. Walt Shumate." Walt Shumate has been blamed for as many as eight separate events occurring simultaneously, thousands of miles apart, in all corners of the globe. He is probably still being identified with all sorts of imaginative petty crimes and joyful misdemeanors.

"This Was Done by Ho Chi Minh!"

Walt Shumate and another NCO had to take a large number of Montagnard strikers down from their ancestral mountains to Nha Trang for a medical checkup. These tribesmen had never been away from their mountains and had never seen the ocean. So it was natural that Walt and (maybe) Doy McPhail herded their little buddies down to the beach to acquaint them with the South China Sea. The Montagnards were predictably amazed and impressed; none had ever seen or imagined so much water in one place.

The small soldiers huddled together in conference, then asked Walt if it was okay for them to take off their clothes and get in the water. It was, as long as they refrained from drowning. In they went, with much splashing and laughing. Then, as might be predicted, somebody got a mouthful of salt water.

A tremendous uproar ensued, and all the Montagnards had to taste the water. It was immediately and universally agreed that this was terrible—a vast, limitless lake of water, all of it bad! It was undrinkable, unusable for livestock, impossible to use on crops. When the uproar finally subsided, Walt Shumate explained to the Yards, "This was done by Ho Chi Minh!"

JIM MORRIS and GREEN BERET MAGAZINE

Special Forces had its own magazine in Southeast Asia for five years, a fizzy little journal that contained a lot less of the "eyewash" that most command-sponsored rags exhibit. During Capt. Jim Morris's tenure as editor, Green Beret *magazine was often a very solid and entertaining periodical. The following story is the product of an unknown author—but Morris recognized the humor in its parody of the format required for writers of military reports (then and now).*

Hood, Riding, Red, Little

Once upon a time there was a female personnel whose nomenclature was Hood, Riding, Red, Little (one each). She was a girl, little, happy. Her duty uniform consisted of the following named items: (1) Dress, red, cotton, shade 76, one each; (2) Cape, HBT, red w/hood, (one each). Her MOS was 94B4S, food handler.

One day Hood, Riding, Red, Little received a TWX from her Mother, Grand, Old, who was billeted off-post in a cottage, brick, red, Capehart type, w/chimney, w/o TV, initial A/DPEN issue (one each). The TWX read as follows:

"Dear Hood. This is to advise you that morning report should read: DY to SK conf to qrts as of 0100 hrs, 1 Jan 68. Went on sick call yesterday (LD: yes), conf for indef pd. However, I am feeling somewhat better. Love, related-type Mother, Grand, Your. Added: Pls see about Sep Rat for me. MGY."

Hood took the TWX to the message center with the following 1st endorsement: "Basic communication complied with. ETA your station approx 1600 hrs this day."

While en route to the TDY destination, personnel concerned came to a forest, thick, primeval. Suddenly, out of the thicket, briar, emerged a wolf, brown, bad, big (one each). Wolf said, "Halt, who goes there, and what are your last four?"

Hood answered, "Hood, Riding, Red, Little, 4032. I am en route to my TDY point and am looking for the house of my Mother, Grand, Old."

"It is two klicks down the road; turn left at Building 2355," instructed the wolf.

"How do you know where she lives?" questioned Hood.

"I've pulled guard duty in those parts," said Wolf, who then caught a bus to the Granny's. Upon arrival, wolf, bad, swallowed Granny with a gulp, single (one each). Wolf then policed up the area, including butt cans, and jumped into bed, initial A/DPEN issue type, and pulled on Granny's AC 146-92's.

Hood, entering: "Hello, Mother, Grand."

"The fool, little, stupid, does not know that it is really me, the wolf, bad, big," chuckled the wolf.

"My, what big EENT you have," exclaimed Hood, Riding, Red, Little.

"All the better to maintain maximum efficiency at minimum cost with Zero Defects," replied the wolf.

Then, entered the chopper, wood type, handsome. Chopper killed wolf with a blow (one each) and performed necessary surgical procedures to remove Mother, Grand, from stomach of wolf, bad, big, dead. With allowance for quarters and rations, they all lived after, ever, happily.

DAN PITZER

Dan Pitzer is retired from the Army but still works with Special Forces trainees as a civilian instructor in the SERE (Survival, Evasion, Resistance, Escape) program, passing along some lessons learned during his years as a prisoner of war.

Christmas with the Cong

I was the senior medic on a Special Forces A-team. We were out on a patrol, got overrun by two battalions of hard-core VC, and I was captured on October 29, 1963. My first year of captivity was spent in isolation. They were trying to break us down and trying to indoctrinate us.

My upbringing had been fairly religious. During that first year, I kept asking God, "Why are You doing this to me? Why am I being put through this kind of torture?" It was "fist-shaking" time, and I was angry.

Then, on December 24, a FAC appeared over the camp and dropped red smoke in the prison camp. I didn't know it until later, but it was a rescue attempt. It was frightening and profoundly exasperating. I was running and hiding from my own country's aircraft (I was dressed in black pajamas and looked like Viet Cong), and I looked up through the trees to see a Huey over-head. It was so close that I could see the gunner, behind his M60, and read the "US Army" on his jacket—that close! But I was afraid to get out in the open, to signal them to come and rescue me.

We had been working outside the camp, and when we returned the place was all shot up. We were told to collect our meager belongings and were given some cold rice. Then the Viet Cong started moving us. We marched for several hours, into the night, and moved along a river, toward a new prison camp.

As we came around a bend in the river, we saw a huge evergreen tree—a Christmas tree—thirty or forty feet tall, standing alone by the water. Something on the tree was attracting fireflies, thousands and thousands of them, and they were twinkling like strands of lights. A brilliant light was moving directly over the top of the tree; it was a satellite, but it looked like a very bright star.

As we moved closer, even the Viet Cong guards were impressed. "*Choi-hoi!*" one said (which means "My heavens!"). A peaceful feeling came over me. We were taken to a new prison camp, and while I was there I had a chance to think about the event quite a bit. I decided that God didn't have to use lightning bolts or burning bushes to talk to me; he had chosen to use something we recognize every Christmas.

From then on, when I spoke to God there in my little bamboo cage, all by myself, and the guards would come by to ask who I was talking to, I always replied, "Someone you will never know."

CLAY SCOTT

Clay Scott retired from the Army in 1983 as a lieutenant colonel with twenty years of service. He is the recent past president of both the Special Operations Association and Chapter 23 of the Special Forces Association. He now works as an administrator for a large airport. His stories come from the central highlands during the late 1960s.

Number One Chop-Chop

I commanded Camp Polei Kleng (Detachment A-241) outside Kontum. One of our tasks was to patrol out to the Plei Trap Valley and to the border, a distance of about forty kilometers. My C-team commander was always leaning on me to get patrols out, all the way to the border. But my camp was already at the extreme limit for artillery supporting fires from the batteries at Kontum, which meant that any patrol west of Polei Kleng could forget about calling for help in an emergency.

Well, I wasn't about to send a company out there just to have them massacred. Nobody would come and support us. We couldn't even make radio communications from out there. If we sent a patrol in, and if we ran into a North Vietnamese battalion, we'd be in deep shit.

To help deal with the communications problem and still get the kind of information my boss wanted, we came up with an alternative plan. It was my intel sergeant's idea: carrier pigeons. Now, there was really something to be said for this idea, so we put in a request for some. Well, lo and to say nothing of behold, a C-130 showed up on our runway with a whole shit-pot full of carrier pigeons. We had cages of these things!

My intel sergeant was as happy as a pig in mud. He trained those carrier pigeons for a month. First, he'd take them to the edge of the perimeter, and they came back. Then he took them out to the runway, and they came back from there. Then he started taking them on operations, and they still found their way back to our camp.

We developed a plan to use them to report on NVA activity out at the border. We recruited one old Montagnard guy and prepared him to go way out, forty klicks to the border, with some of these pigeons. He had a specific area to go to, and if he saw a lot of bad guys, he'd put a red band on the bird. If he saw just a few bad guys, it was a yellow band. If there were no bad guys at all, he was supposed to put a green band on the pigeon.

Sure enough, the fated day arrived. We sent him off to trail-watch for us in the Plei Trap Valley, happy as a clam—just an old guy with a walking stick, a knife, and a bag with a few pigeons inside. All he wore was the usual Montagnard loin cloth—no weapons, nothing to suggest that he was anything but an old Jarai farmer. He looked so innocent that, if they caught him, he could just say, "I'm just an old farmer, checking out a new area to move the village to."

A week went by, with no carrier pigeon—and no Montagnard. Another week went by—nothing! We started to wonder, Did he get captured? Did something terrible happen? Then, about three weeks after he left, we got word. The old guy was back home in the village. The intel sergeant went running down to the guy's house.

"What did you see?" the sergeant had to know.

"Didn't see anything," replied the old man.

"Did you let the pigeon go?"

"No," the old man said.

"Well, what did you do with it?"

"It was number one chop-chop!"

Don't Feed the Animals

While I was with II Corps Mobile Strike Force we had a Montagnard killed by a tiger. It happened at night, in a RON position. A tiger jumped up hill, over a guard, moved two or three paces, and was then on top of one of the Montagnards who was asleep. It evidently attempted to smother the guy with his tongue, covering his mouth and nose. Of course the guy woke up. The tiger then instantly grabbed him by the throat and ripped his throat out. The tiger then grabbed the Montagnard by the leg and dragged him away into the woods, with an entire Montagnard company shooting at him in the dark. Of course they couldn't hit him. The rest of the night you could hear the tiger chewing on this guy. We recovered the body the next day, most of it, anyway. The lower leg and foot were missing, but the femur was picked clean as a whistle.

Medals

The subject of medals is a difficult one for civilians to understand and appreciate, so I will try to explain how soldiers think about the subject of awards and decorations.

They are not, as some people claim, meaningless "fruit salad"—at least, not for the people in this book. The colored ribbons on a soldier's dress uniform each have a kind of code; if you know the code, you get a pretty good idea of what a guy has done, just by reading the ribbons. They are arranged in a strict order of priority, from the top-left on down.

The Medal of Honor is the most precious and rare American decoration; as Jon Caviani emphatically insists, it is awarded, not "won." Seventeen Medals of Honor were awarded to SF soldiers for actions in the war. It would have been more but even this process is subject to the most petty brand of politics, and Green Berets are notoriously poor at the kind of game-playing that is sometimes involved in decorations. Otis Ashley Hedges III thinks his recommendation might have gotten farther had his team leader not beaten up the guy who later reviewed and disapproved his nomination. But John Caviani got one, and so did sixteen other SF operators—far more, man for man, than any other participating unit.

Other combat decorations are the Distinguished Service Cross, Silver Star, and Bronze Star with V (for valor) device. The Air Medal, with V-device, was sometimes awarded to Special Forces personnel for actions in flight. The Army Commendation Medal was sometimes awarded for heroism.

Many genuinely heroic actions by men from this community produced no decoration or award. There was a feeling within Special Forces at the time that the community was really above all that. As a result, the highest award on the dress uniforms of many of the men whose stories are in this book is a Bronze Star with V, a decoration handed out by some other units in almost wholesale fashion for very minor engagements.

—Hans Halberstadt

MIKE WITCOSKY

Mike Witcosky was a medic in Southeast Asia in 1971-72. It was toward the end of the game, and President Richard Nixon started pulling American ground combat units out shortly after Witcosky arrived and was assigned to 5th Special Forces Group. Since 5th Group had been one of the first in, it was one of the first out. For Mike, that meant being assigned to MACV and a program called Heavy Hook for a while, then to the 46th Special Forces Company and a little camp on the Thai/Laos border at a place called Lam Phong Dam.

Heavy Hook was one of the many covert operations that were forced on Special Forces during the war, most under the umbrella of the innocuous-sounding name of Studies and Observation Group. *But anybody who knew anything about SOG thought of it as the kinkiest, weirdest collection of operations and operators. Even today, many of the participants will keep the cover on their role in the game.*

Heavy Hook involved a lot of reconnaissance operations in Laos and Cambodia, in places where Americans were officially not present. Green Berets, along with a few other operators outside the official SF community, executed trail-mapping missions, prisoner snatches, and air crew recovery missions.

Big Medicine

I flew into the camp for my first assignment aboard an old C-7 Caribou. The team sergeant was waiting for me with a jeep. I threw my stuff in back and climbed aboard, and he drove me up to the dispensary. He stopped and said, "There are people hurt in there." That was my welcome to my first assignment as a Green Beret.

The old medic had left about a week before. Since then there had been a firefight, and there was a Thai soldier inside who'd caught a load of shrapnel. His knee was all laid open with a bunch of steel stuck in it. That was my very first case. I whipped out my orthopedic surgery textbook to get a refresher on the anatomy of the area I was going to work on. I started digging all the steel out of the wound, extending it and cleaning it out, flushing it, and then sewing it up. Then I held my breath! But it healed perfectly. It was amazing, my first major success.

People showed up at the camp nonstop, day in and day out. It could be war wounds or accidents. One of the village elders fell out of a tree and showed up with cerebral spinal fluid running out of both ears, basal skull fractures on both sides. They showed up in the middle of the night with this man, and I was supposed to take care of him.

About the third week I was in camp, a large group of people showed up with the most senior elder for the entire valley on a wooden stretcher. The old chief was extremely sick: very dehydrated, coughing, a temperature of one hundred and five degrees. He looked like he was about to "buy it." He had a very bad case of pneumonia.

I took him into the dispensary. Then I warned the people that the chief was very near death, that I was sure he was going to die, and that there wasn't much I could do—but that I would try. I got a sample of the junk he was coughing up and looked at it under the microscope. In it was the bacterium that causes bacterial pneumonia. Penicillin is the drug of choice for this stuff, and I thought, "Great, I know what the bug is!"

So I started an IV and administered some penicillin—and he turned the corner, big time! He made a dramatic recovery. We were able to feed him, and about five days later I got to send him home. After that I was "big medicine." The chief presented me with a medal, and they all made a big deal out of the event. It had a tremendous effect on the way I was treated in the whole valley. I wore that medal the whole time I was over there, and I guess it protected me, because I had nothing but good luck the whole time I was over there.

First Combat

My first combat operation was a recon, and I was assigned to a team headed by a guy named Leving. He had been a logger from Oregon, about six-foot-eight, and he carried an M60 around like it was a pistol. I was the new guy, and they were all career SF types. I felt like the weak link on the operation.

While we were out on that operation, I got sniped at. We were moving along a trail, thinking nobody's around, and a bullet went right past my ear, *boom.* I will never forget the sound of that bullet; I could feel it! And I just froze in my tracks. I didn't know what it was. Leving grabbed me, jerked me off my feet, and threw me to the ground. Then all the shooting started. Everybody opened up, even though it was just one sniper. It didn't last long, and by the time I got my face out of the dirt and looked around, it was all over.

Firefights and Rescues

There wasn't a strict routine to the missions we got in camp. During Operation Rolling Thunder, a lot of B-52s were being lost. The crews would bail out over Laos or Cambodia, and we'd go after them. Often the team would be split up into small groups. Two or three guys would hop on a Jolly Green Giant with the Air Force "PJs" [parachute jumpers—rescue specialists] to go out looking for these guys. We went after fighter pilots, too, but with disappointing results. But we managed to pick up a number of B-52 crews. Those missions were always a spur-of-the-moment deal—you just grabbed all your stuff and ran down to the tarmac, piled aboard, and took off. That was some of the most gratifying work I did over there.

A lot of the work that I did was long-range recon. We'd go in for about a week, usually, get inserted some distance from our AO, then travel overland to the objective. We did a lot of mapping of roads and investigating Pathet Lao training bases.

Once we got into a firefight with a group of Pathet Lao troops, and one of the guys on the team killed a Chinese major. He had a satchel full of papers and maps, so we dragged his body back, along with the papers—and the CIA guys just went nuts, they were so excited!

We had our share of firefights, but a successful mission really involved getting in, accomplishing our mission, and getting back out again—undetected. If the enemy figured out we were in their area about a half hour after we left, that was a successful mission. When we got into trouble, it was maybe half a dozen of us vs. maybe a regiment of them. We considered ourselves lucky if we just brushed the flank of an enemy unit instead of the point, if we saw them before they saw us. But we had a couple of lucky encounters where we bumped into enemy units and managed to get away.

The worst of these was the NVA, because they were well-disciplined troops. It only happened a couple of times, and we were lucky enough to see them before they saw us.

I found it interesting how easy it was for a small group of people to bed down for the night and, if they did it right, just disappear into the bushes. On some occasions we thought we were in the middle of nowhere and bedded down for the night, only to discover later that there was a major road nearby, with heavy traffic and lots of people coming by. Suddenly there would be trucks and people, conversation and activity. We had to wait, and wait, and wait until they left.

"Well, I Think They're Going to Shoot You."

I was initially assigned to Heavy Hook, and then, when Heavy Hook was phased out, I went to the 46th Special Forces Company. I was the junior medic on the team, but since the senior medic was also an engineer and spent all his time on engineering projects, I was effectively the only medic in the camp.

We trained all sorts of people: Thai Special Forces, border police, and lots of tribesmen brought in by the CIA. These were Lao and Cambodian troops flown in by the CIA. That operation was run by an interesting guy whose first name was Jack but who was known as Three Fingers because he had two fingers missing from one hand. He used to drop in to check up on his troops. At graduation time he would bring a couple of John Wayne war movies; we'd project the movies against the side of one of the buildings, and everybody would get drunk and whoop it up. Three Fingers financed just about everything that went on in our camp—all the food, a lot of the equipment.

The dispensary where I worked was right next to the main gate in this camp. One day I heard a lot of yelling and commotion and went out to investigate. There was a taxi at the gate—a very unusual event since the camp was quite secure, and most taxi drivers had more sense than to bring people there. The taxi driver paced back and forth nervously while his passenger was proned out on the ground. The Thai guard had one boot on the guy's head and the muzzle of his M16 in the guy's ear. The guard was extremely angry, and there was a lot of yelling.

The guy on the ground was obviously an American journalist; there were cameras everywhere. He was, as I recall, from *Time* magazine. He had been trying to chase down this CIA operative that we called Three Fingers all over Southeast Asia. He was trying to document what we were doing and had somehow discovered about our camp. He saw my face and said, "My God, an American! Help me! Help me!"

"This isn't my camp," I told him. "I'm a visitor here. It's their camp, and they can do with you whatever they want. What the hell did you come out here for? You made a big mistake!"

"What are they going to do with me?" he begged.

"Well, I think they're going to shoot you."

He was really scared and pleading for help. So I had a little conversation with the guard in Thai and told him that he really couldn't kill the reporter. He was, after all, an American, and it just wouldn't do. So then I told the reporter that I made a deal with the guard and he was going to let him go, but he had to leave immediately! And he threw his stuff in the cab and disappeared quickly from view.

Fishing, Green Beret Style

We decided, after the camp was set up, that we would start putting on "feeds" for the village. The first time we scraped together some money and bought a cow and had it butchered and then had a huge barbecue. The village people just loved that! We had great rapport with these people, partly as a result of things like this. So we decided the next time to have a fish fry.

The camp was on a lake, and we had a little aluminum skiff that leaked. One day a couple of us decided to go fishing. We dumped a box of hand grenades in the skiff and paddled out into the lake. Now, the village people were used to catching fish with hand nets, by beating the water—the result of which was normally a small catch of tiny little minnows.

So we paddled out in the middle of the lake and tossed a few grenades over the side. After a *thwomp,* all manner of fish started floating to the surface—huge fish, little alligators, turtles, all kinds of fish. We piled this stuff into the boat and paddled back to the shore.

A crowd of village kids had been attracted by the noise and had collected on the shoreline, watching us. When we started pulling these big fish out of the water, the kids just went nuts, they were so excited. We collected at least 200 pounds of fish, including some very large carp, and went back to the shore. The kids were beside themselves. They had never seen such big fish, apparently, and didn't know they existed. So we gave one big fish to each kid, and some of the fish were as big as the child. They all went running back home with their fish, yelling and screaming with delight.

We ended up eating some interesting things with these people—locusts, for instance. Once in a while huge locusts would fly around in the area, and the local people would catch them. Then, the locals would roll them in a banana leaf, cook them, and eat them. I tried that once and didn't find it particularly tasty. One thing I really did like, though, was ant larva, a real delicacy. They were very sweet; I was surprised.

Target Practice, NVA Style

The NVA and Pathet Lao would mortar the camp occasionally. They always seemed to aim for the team house. It seemed to be a never-ending desire on their part to put a mortar round on the roof of our team house. But whoever they were using for a mortar team sure didn't know their business, because they never did hit it. There were far more important targets within the camp for them to shoot at, but the team house had some special appeal for them. They got close a few times, but they never hit it. The team house and the helicopters seemed to both be a special invitation to the enemy mortar crews, but they didn't ever score on either target or do significant damage to anything in the camp. They dug some holes and threw some dust in the air, but that was about it.

When the camp was built, the trees inside the perimeter were left, while those outside were cleared for better fields of observation and fire. The camp must have been kind of pretty when it was built, but the enemy mortar rounds went off when they hit the tops of the trees, so now they were in pretty bad shape.

Always Something on the Stove

We had a Thai woman and her husband working for us in the camp. She did the cooking, and he ran the errands and did the shopping. She was a spectacular cook! They bought fruit and vegetables on the local economy, and we got our milk and meat through a barter system with an Air Force sergeant who worked in the officer's mess at the US base nearby. We got fresh milk and steaks from him—traded for various bits of NVA uniform items and weapons which he then turned around and sold to American Air Force personnel. All these steaks and supplies were sent out on an Air Force helicopter twice a week or so, and the pilots must have known where it was coming from, but nobody ever said anything about it.

There was always something waiting for you on the stove, no matter what time you got in. She'd sit you down and start jabbering, and then she'd bring all kinds of food! We really appreciated her—and she really enjoyed being appreciated.

The people around the camp were all Meo tribesmen, and I don't think they'd ever seen an American until the camp was built, about six months before I arrived. They were very, very primitive. A lot of the things we did just amazed them—the helicopters in particular were very exciting for them.

Body Count

Once a month an administrative helicopter would fly up to our camp with a pay officer from the finance company, along with other officers dropping in for visits or inspections. One month a new "candy-striper" second lieutenant appeared. After pay was dispersed, we all adjourned to the team house for a cold beer.

After a while, the team leader noticed that the lieutenant had disappeared. He sent me out to look for him with the guidance that I should make sure he didn't get into any trouble.

After some searching, I found him down behind the motor pool. He had gathered some of the security team and had them laying on the ground, around the wire, and on top of the bunkers, playing dead while he took photographs. I yelled at the guards to get back to their positions and told the now-indignant young officer that the commander wanted to talk to him.

We went back to the team room, and I explained to the commander what had been happening. The CO was so mad that he read the lieutenant the riot act—and sent him to wait in the helicopter [the most dangerous place in the camp, an obvious target] until it left with the guidance that he was never to set foot in that camp again. And he didn't.

"They *Paid*."

I never felt really bad about anything until an incident in the village outside the camp. I had been working with some of the young men in the village, teaching them some basic medical techniques for treating injuries and improving the health of the other people. The enemy came into the village one night and shot up a bunch of the people, including the ones I had been training, as an example. They came through the village, and anyone who showed any evidence of contact with the Americans was used as an example. There were a couple of people dead and a number who had been cut up. I felt bad that I had brought that on them.

But we burned their ass for that. The next morning, when we found out, we tracked the enemy down. They *paid*. We mobilized some of the foreign special forces that were in our camp, some of our best students, and one particular platoon that had been exemplary, and we tracked them down through the woods.

They moved about fifteen klicks through the woods before we caught up with them. They were loud and obvious and easy to follow. Undisciplined. We caught up with them, flanked them, and ambushed them. That was the end of that. There were about twenty of them. It was probably the best-executed ambush we had ever done; they made it easy for us. We had a lot of people, two M60s, one at each end of a well set-up ambush. It was extremely effective.

In thirty seconds the whole thing was over.

What I Remember Most

I enjoyed the time. I enjoyed the camaraderie. When I first went into the Army, I was worried about the war, worried about the kind of people I was going to be around. I didn't like the idea that I might be "greased" because somebody else screwed up. But in Special Forces everybody was really tight, dependent on each other, and you could always rely on these guys. If something was supposed to happen, a rendezvous, an extraction, it always happened! It made me feel extremely confident. I always felt like I was in good shape. I was around good people who knew what they were doing, even if I didn't know what I was doing, since I was so new at it.

And I felt very good about all the things we did. We did a lot of "civic action" work that improved the lives of the people around the camp. We helped the young people do things to avoid contracting TB; improved their water supply; and treated broken bones, infections, and cuts. I never felt very comfortable about the military operations where you're fighting and shooting people, killing people, although I was able to rationalize it.

It was a very emotional experience for me. When I start thinking about it now, it still has a weird effect. I don't mind, necessarily . . . I just get reflective.

The small group and the close-knit nature of the team had a lot to do with my ability to tolerate things like that. My team sergeant was a crusty old guy—a veteran of World War II and Korea before Vietnam. His decorations filled up all the available space on his dress greens. I went out and ran operations that would sound just about impossible. But I did them with people I was so close to, that I had so much confidence in—and thought nothing of them. They weren't that hard! If you planned it right, used your brain, you could find a way to get it done. I had so much confidence in my team that I never really worried. I really enjoyed my time in SF. When it was time to go, it was a very hard decision for me to get out of the Army.

I found SF people to always be very truthful. If somebody made a mistake, they took responsibility for it rather than trying to shift the blame. Of all my time in the military, I never encountered that high level of integrity or the level of intelligence and insight—except in SF. Everywhere else in the Army was completely different.

DON GREEN

Don Green served two tours in Vietnam as a Special Forces sergeant. He later completed OCS and was commissioned as an officer. He recently retired from the Army as a major; after serving for many years with 3d Battalion, 12th Special Forces Group.

Khe Sanh

I went to Khe Sanh in February of 1963 as the junior radio operator of an A-team. We were the second team assigned there, after the camp was opened. It had been an old French fort, the remains of a camp that had been overrun in, I think, 1954. Our camp was south of Highway 9, built around a three-thousand-foot runway that had been constructed just before our team arrived.

The camp was on the higher of two hilltops, and it was based on two surviving French buildings. Both were constructed of brick and stucco. The larger we used as our mess and kitchens, the smaller as our supply building. There were also two newer wooden buildings, one for our A-team, the other for the Vietnamese LLDB B team. On the other hill were barracks for our Strike Force.

Initially we were working for Combined Studies, a CIA program. Our supplies came by way of Air America [the CIA airline that flew throughout Southeast Asia during the 1950s and 1960s. It was intended to be a cover for the CIA's covert air operations, but everybody—except perhaps the American public—knew who was at the controls. It was about the least secret covert operation imaginable]. We were keeping busy until MAAG took us over. Then, for a while, we didn't seem to have a mission and had long periods when we didn't have anything to do. There was speculation about closing the camp and finding a new mission, all discussed while we were sitting around the compound in our shorts and shower shoes, barbecuing and drinking beer. It was more like being at a country club than at a combat outpost. But it was the first time in Asia for most of us. We were novices to the whole place and culture, and it was a good and interesting time.

Fire and Ice

One of the things I will never forget was our refrigerator. It was powered, somehow, by kerosene. As long as the thing was mostly empty, it worked well and was quite cold. But when we filled it up with fresh supplies that we got through the Navy commissary in Saigon, it didn't work very well, and the food would spoil. So it was feast or famine.

We always kept at least one American awake and on duty at all times. The "graveyard" watch-stander had the responsibility to refuel the kerosene tank on the refrigerator and to make breakfast, because the cook couldn't come in the gates until after eight in the morning. As a result, we invariably had either Cream of Wheat or pancakes for breakfast, since none of us were skilled enough to reliably produce anything more ambitious.

One night our senior demolitions sergeant, Smitty, decided to be a good guy and to fill the kerosene tank during his watch on the swing shift. In good "demo" specialist form, Smitty managed to set fire to the refrigerator. He ran out of the mess building to the supply room next door, where two of our guys were sleeping. He banged on the door, yelling, "Hey, Butch, what do you do if the refrigerator is on fire?"

Butch pried his eyelids open and regarded Sergeant Smith carefully. "Smitty . . . is the refrigerator on fire?"

"Yes!"

So they both ran back to the kitchen to see what could be done. Two ancient French fire extinguishers were found, but they were of complex French design, and the instructions were in French. So Butch and Smitty used the usual Special Forces approach to almost any problem, which is trial and error.

The fire extinguishers started gushing foam, but Butch and Smitty were unable to control the weapons. Instead of hitting the target, they ended up spraying the foam all over the kitchen floor and everything except the burning refrigerator. When the foam was all expended and the extinguishers were empty, Butch and Smitty resorted to using large cooking pans to try to collect the foam to redeploy it on the fire, but their tactical plan failed. The refrigerator was completely burned. It wasn't entirely useless, though. We carted its carcass out to the bazooka range and used it for target practice.

Fireworks

We had an 81-millimeter mortar right outside the supply room. If the camp got hit, we used it to fire illumination rounds. Butch was our weapons man and was in charge of the tube, and Charley Webb was his assistant gunner. Both were out on a night operation and were supposed to set off a smoke grenade when they were ready to come back inside the wire. But somebody didn't get the word, and the attack alert was sounded when they "popped smoke" outside the wire.

The backup mortar team was Smitty (the demo man who had set fire to the refrigerator) and Leo. They both ran out to the mortar pit and got busy, preparing to fire illumination rounds so we could see our targets. They were a bit out of practice with the weapon, unfortunately, and didn't notice that rain water had accumulated inside the tube. When they dropped the first round, it went off more like a roman candle than like a conventional mortar round, and the propellant caught fire rather than detonating as intended. Instead of firing conventionally, it squirted fire from the tube for a few moments, threatening to explode, before finally launching itself weakly into the air.

The round traveled only about a hundred feet, just barely clearing the Vietnamese B team house before burying itself nose down in the dirt right beside one of the perimeter guards, scaring the hell out of the poor guy. It didn't detonate but just burned dramatically while it flew through the air. It scared the guard so much that he took off, right into the wire, and dragged a fair amount of it behind him until he realized that it was a false alarm.

When the excitement died down, that guard had a lot to say to us. We couldn't really understand the words, but he was not pleased about the incident.

Interservice Rivalry at the DMZ

We conducted a company-sized operation north of Khe Sanh, up toward the DMZ [demilitarized zone]. I'd always pictured the DMZ as a kind of bleak, barbed-wire kind of place, with bunkers and people facing each other across a sort of no-man's-land. It wasn't like that at all in 1963.

Other than a little outpost at Quang Tri, a little outpost at the road bridge into North Vietnam, and a single company of ARVN north of our camp, there wasn't anything up there at all. We were the first ones to conduct company-sized operations in the area since the French had been defeated in 1954, nine years before.

Under the treaty, there was supposed to be a six-kilometer buffer zone on each side of the border where no troops were allowed. Well, what we found on that excursion in 1963 were elements of an NVA regiment in the southern portion of the buffer zone! We found one of their camps; it was deserted, but only because they heard us coming and they took off. We found North Vietnamese money, letters, stamps, and other materials that indicated the presence of a large NVA unit.

This information was reported through channels. The South Vietnamese army decided to conduct a major operation against the unit, using our camp and air strip as the air-head for the mission. Preparations were begun, but the whole thing was done in such a stupid fashion that it was obvious what was going to happen. The ARVN rangers were brought in, along with some US Marine Corps H-34 helicopters and US Army OV-1 Mohawks for air assets. Well, they started flying practice sorties into the area where the operation was going to be conducted, making it impossible for the NVA not to notice that something important was in the works. Even though I was a very young, very junior troop, I knew that they would either find nothing, or get their asses shot off.

The Marines sent out a platoon of guys who did double duty as guards for downed helicopters in the field and as military police when they were back in Da Nang. They bunked with us; and we fed these guys, provided their beer, and got to know them pretty well.

Luckily for all concerned, the weather closed in, and the whole operation was canceled. If it hadn't, the NVA would likely have chewed it up. But we became very good friends with these Marines. They were all really big guys, six-foot-plus.

Well, everything returned to normal, and a few weeks later I got to Da Nang and was in one of the bars, getting drunk. I staggered to the door and opened it, and there were two big Marines in shore patrol uniforms (white helmet liners with a stripe). I looked at them and figured they were going to arrest me and take me in. One looked at me and said, "Where do you want to go now, sergeant?"

"See that bar down the street?" I told them. "That's the place."

They were a couple of the guys we had housed for the operation, and they recognized me. They picked me up and carried me down there, opened the door to the bar, and left me. So much for interservice rivalry!

Terry and the Pirates

During my first tour, in 1963 and 1964, Vietnam was a very exotic place, sort of like the setting for Terry and the Pirates. There were all sorts of strange characters running around: former OSS [Office of Strategic Services, the forerunner of the CIA] guys from World War II, ex-French Foreign Legion soldiers flying Air America planes, and some oddball American types. I was quite young and impressionable at the time, and it was a wonderful adventure. As a radio operator, I was normally kept in camp to manage the message traffic, and it seemed at the time that the other guys were having all the fun. That's one of the reasons why, when I came back in 1969, I volunteered for SOG, to get out in the field.

Buon Mi Ga

Our team was sent from Khe Sanh to II Corps and the camp called Buon Mi Ga. We were running the Village Defense Program there that trained and armed peasants to defend their communities against small-scale VC attacks. They were issued bolt-action .30-06 Springfield rifles, which they carried with them in the fields.

We found a large cache of VC rice nearby and sent some of these Village Defense Program people out to try to salvage some of it. We had a number of them collecting this rice, when a conventional force American advisor showed up. He looked at these guys in black pajamas with old rifles and needed lots of reassurance that they were not, in fact, VC.

Studies and Observation Group

A lot of the guys in the recon platoon I was assigned to on my second tour turned out, like me, to have been radio operators earlier. Some had been with the Phoenix program, others with the Mike Force and other activities, and they were tired of being RTOs. We all wanted to get out and do things. Studies and Observation Group was entirely volunteer, and it didn't matter what your MOS [military occupational specialty] was; if you volunteered for SOG you were going to go to a forward base.

One of the things I liked about SOG was that, no matter what your rank was, you worked your way up from the bottom, based on experience and performance, to the position of "Zero-One," team leader. When I went over again in 1969, after some time in college and the reserves, I was an E-5 [buck sergeant] team leader, with a lieutenant and a captain working for me as my assistants. That wasn't unusual. Rank didn't matter; experience was what did matter. I was at C&C Central, FOB-2 in Kontum, and they gave us the opportunity to try new ideas and techniques. This wasn't like the "Lurp" companies that later became the Ranger companies, which were highly standardized, six-man teams with virtually no flexibility.

We carried just about whatever we wanted, and we ran patrols with anywhere from four to fifteen men on a team. As long as what you were doing worked, nobody would mess with you. You got a mission, and, as long as you could execute the mission reliably, that was all they cared about.

"Those Guys Were Trying to Kill Me!"

The team leader for RT [recon team] Colorado had gone on thirty-day leave, and rather than have the rest of the team sit around idle for a month, I got the team for a month to show what I could do as a potential team leader.

We went into an area just across the border from Ben Het. The mission was to look for what was called a "vis tram," an NVA battalion way station where the enemy troops moving down the Ho Chi Minh Trail could camp. These were spaced a day's march apart. They were set up like campgrounds for units of battalion size, about 450 men. Normally the NVA attached a security element to each of these sites to guard them and to maintain them.

The helicopters inserted us late in the afternoon, just before last light, at a landing zone that the intel shop figured was a bit north of the enemy way station. We got off the choppers, crossed a creek, went up a little embankment, peeked through the bushes—and there it was. The place looked like a manicured park!

The trail was immaculate, so clean that it looked like it had just been swept. Bushes had just been trimmed and were still fresh. Everything we saw suggested that we had scared off some of the NVA maintenance and security element. I knew we'd found something, but it was almost dark, so I moved the team up the hill, away from our insertion area.

Our SOP was to sit down at last light as if we were going to spend the night in that position, wait a while, then silently move a few hundred meters to a new position. If we were being watched, the enemy would likely not see the second move and would attack the first site after full dark, expecting us to be there. And that's just what happened. Not very long after we set up in the new position, grenades started going off where we had been. It was a probe, and of course they didn't get any response so they knew we'd moved. We stayed put and silent.

It was not silent down the hill. Somewhere down there were a lot of people, and the commotion sounded like they were having a company-size party. It could have been all sorts of units, but I wasn't about to go prowling around to find out. We had no night vision devices of any kind, and I did not like the idea of stumbling around in the dark. Instead, I tried to call in one of the big AC-130 Spectre gunships. I had the frequency, but I couldn't raise anybody. So we stayed awake until first light, listening to the noise down the hill.

As soon as we could see, we pulled in the Claymores and moved out. I took the team in a big circle, away from the spot where we'd been. We hadn't seen anybody yet, but it was obvious that there were people in the area. We noticed fresh footprints and other evidence that we were not alone, so I started looking for a place to stand and fight if we had to.

We came to an open, grassy place on a ridge line not too far away. The grass was about waist-high, and we crouched down in it, facing outward in a defensive perimeter. Nobody could see us, but we were pretty sure that we'd been followed, and here was a place to find out.

Neither of the other two Americans had CIBs [Combat Infantryman's Badges], so I jokingly told them, "If we don't encounter anybody today, we'll go back down the ridge and see if we can capture some poor old farmer!"

I shouldn't have worried. I looked over at the tail gunner just as he stood up, extended the stock on his CAR-15, and prepared to fire. Oh, shit! I thought. Then the shit hit the fan. He had spotted a squad of NVA maneuvering on our position and opened up. Then one of the other Americans started firing his captured RPD machine gun, and we all stood up and opened fire. We laid a lot of fire on them. Then I gave the traditional command under these circumstances: "Let's get the fuck out of here!"

Nobody argued with me. We broke contact and were soon extracting ourselves from what turned out to be two squads, one coming up the hill, the other trying to flank us from the ridge. Although they knew about where we were, they couldn't really see us, and their fire was going over our heads.

It was my first experience in combat at extremely close quarters, and I experienced all the classic symptoms—tunnel vision, suppressed hearing. I heard later that B-40 rockets were exploding near me, but I didn't notice. We couldn't actually see them; all we saw were their muzzle flashes from about twenty or thirty meters away in the dense foliage surrounding this grassy area. But we seemed to get quite a few of them, because their fire slacked off. We broke contact again and did a head count. One guy was missing; it was one of the Montagnards. He had been killed while trying to move up hill to the cover of a tree trunk.

I got on the radio and made contact with our "Covey," the little radio relay airplane, normally an O-2 or an OV-10. Luckily, it was the OV-10, because that plane has some armament available for ground attack—rockets and machine guns. The Covey was an Air Force aircraft with an Air Force pilot, but the back-seater was one of our recon company guys who had a lot of experience on the ground. That day the Covey rider was S/Sgt. John Plaster, who had spent a long time in recon, but he had been doing that for a year and was getting bored. He extended for another six months, but he wanted to try something different, and that's why they made him a Covey rider.

The Covey airplane was very essential to us in several ways. Our radios couldn't reach very far, and there was no way we could talk to anybody directly, unless they were quite close. So the aircraft relayed messages back and forth. It could also help us pinpoint our location. We could use a signal mirror to show him where we were, and he could use his navigation systems to give us a precise fix. He could also function as a forward air controller and coordinate air strikes to support us. And he could, in a pinch, use his marking rockets and four M60 machine guns to provide a little fire support himself. This was John's first mission as a Covey rider and my first mission as a team leader. Unfortunately. It was a big experience for both of us.

We moved to another ridge line, trying to get away. One of the team heard movement on the next ridge, and I reported this to the Covey aircraft. The pilot volunteered to lay down some suppressive fire. Well, my attention was focused on dealing with the NVA, but then I heard what sounded like a giant woodpecker going *rat-a-tat-tat* down our ridge line! The guy was firing up the wrong ridge line—our ridge line!

It was one of those dilemmas where you don't really know which way to jump. Either way might take you into the line of fire instead of out of it. So I just stood there, petrified, yelling to the RTO, "Tell him to cease fire, cease fire!" The pilot stopped just as one round landed right between my feet.

I thanked the pilot, then told him we needed to get extracted. We also needed directions to an extract LZ. But since this was John's first mission, and he was inexperienced at this, he gave me a heading that was about ninety degrees off the intended direction. We moved in that direction for several minutes before he caught his mistake and called us with a correction. About an hour later we made it to an opening in the jungle about the size of a football field. It was the result of what must have been an "Arc Light" B-52 strike, because it was a jumble of knocked-down trees from some sort of bombing.

Just as we got to the edge of the opening in the jungle, the slicks appeared overhead and the A-1E Skyraiders showed up for fire support. The timing was excellent. But during that hour, I was calling my friend John all sorts of names for sending me off in the wrong direction. I had my nine guys and called, "Cobra Lead, here's what I've got. What do you want me to do?"

There were three slicks, so he directed me to put three guys in each. Well, we had been running for hours, and I had almost lost them from panic;

they were really shook. When the first slick came in, he hovered in a good position above and beside a blown-down tree where it was fairly easy to climb aboard. So eight guys jumped on the chopper!

That left me alone on the ground with the radio I had taken from the RTO. So I told them to throw somebody off. They kicked off the smallest guy; he was a Yard, about four-foot-nine, an M79 gunner. The first chopper pulled out, and we waited for the second to come and get us. But this pilot hadn't been paying attention, and he went into the wrong part of the clearing. He couldn't see us, and we could see the door gunners trying to find us. I jumped up on a tree stump, pulled out my signal panel, and started trying to attract his attention—and the hell with the NVA. He finally noticed me. He came over and hovered above a tree stump, but in a very bad position, where I couldn't possibly get aboard.

"I can't get on the chopper," I told him on the radio. Then the little Montagnard jumped on like an Olympic high jumper! I don't know how he did it. The two door gunners and my Montagnard finally hauled me aboard. We took ground fire going out, but we made it, and I finally made it back to FOB-2 at Kontum.

S/Sgt. Emmett Dover, another radio operator, was waiting for me on the runway. "Don," he said, "what happened?"

"Those guys were trying to kill me!" I told him. I meant it as a kind of joke, but my legs went shaky on me, and I almost couldn't stand up.

"Happy Birthday Dear Do-on"

We were in the rain for eleven straight days. The technique involved hiding and staying put. We turned into prunes, and all of us came down with immersion foot. There's an old SF adage: Travel Light, Freeze at Night. Well, I listened to those old hands, and consequently I didn't have anything to keep warm. It was up in the mountains, in November, and it was chilly!

I was the team RTO. Every morning the Covey aircraft would fly over, and I'd send out a message, the gist of which was, "We are still here. We are okay." I was preparing the date/time codes for the message one day after we'd been out there for a week or more—and I realized that it was my birthday! I'd lost track of time, so that was a bit of a surprise. I was twenty-five!

Now, of course you didn't talk normally out there. You used hand signals or whispered to the man next to you. So I started tapping everybody on the shoulder, and I whispered to each, "Hey, today's my birthday!" Then they were all passing it around, in whispers: "Today's Green's birthday! Today's Green's birthday!" Then they all gathered round and started singing, in a soft whisper,

Happy birthday to you,
Happy birthday to you,
Happy birthday dear Do-on,
Happy birthday to you.

JACK ABRAHAM

Jack Abraham retired from the Army as a colonel and started a new career as a project manager for a large civilian firm.

Putt-Putt and Martha Raye

This happened at Boun Ea Yang. We had a little Montagnard we called "Putt-Putt." Putt-Putt was not "all there"; his elevator just didn't go all the way to the roof. Whatever he saw you do, he would duplicate. If you walked up to a tree and kicked it, Putt-Putt would do the same. The problem with that was that Putt-Putt was barefooted. He was funny as hell. If you took your finger and drew an imaginary line around your head, he would do the same thing.

When we lost the camp at Boun Eano and moved to Boun Ea Yang, we lived for a while in extremely primitive conditions. Our mess tent was no more than a regular tent with some mosquito netting hanging down the sides. There was no way you could control the flies. So it became a habit that you ate with one hand and waved the flies away with the other. It also became a habit, while shooing away these pests, to say, "Fucking flies!" Putt-Putt picked up this habit, and all you had to do was to move your hand, and he would say, "Fluckin' flies!" We thought this was mildly amusing, but not a big deal—until Martha Raye came to the camp.

We were very honored when she decided to visit us. I told the team sergeant, though, "Now, no matter what happens, Ferrell, you make sure that Putt-Putt is not around Martha Raye!"

"Yes, sir," he said. "No problem."

Martha Raye arrived, and we were sitting in the mess tent drinking hot Cokes or hot beers, I don't remember. Like the rest of us, "Maggie" was shooing the flies off with one hand. From out of a cluster of Montagnards looking on came Putt-Putt's voice: "Flucking flies!"

I thought Martha Raye was going to shit. She was about to die, laughing. She thought that was *so* funny! Of course I was profusely apologetic; I was very embarrassed. "I'm so sorry, Maggie—I don't know what to say . . ."

"He's right!" she said. "The fucking flies are terrible!"

I will never forget Putt-Putt!

Martha Raye

Martha Raye is one of Special Forces living legends. She served during World War II as a nurse, maintained a reserve affiliation, and was a lieutenant colonel in the reserves despite her entertainment career. She took a special interest in SF, visited many camps, was wounded during visits to two of them, and drank many of the troopers right under the table. They all fell in love with her, and she with them. They still consider her part of their community. Her house has always been open to any SF soldier. If you ask the SF community, Martha Raye had more "balls" than most of the rest of the men in the Army.

Martha Raye was a big deal with Special Forces. She was our gal! We were standing at the bar in the club at Ban Me Thuot, drinking with the "leg" colonel who was the district senior advisor. This colonel was trying to impress Maggie with his accomplishments. Maggie put me on the spot. She said to him, "Colonel, when you start soldiering like Captain Abraham here, then you'll be winning the war."

CLYDE SINCERE

Clyde Sincere retired from the Army as a colonel after twenty-two years of service, but he didn't get completely away from the profession of arms. He works today as a project manager for a company that provides training assistance under contract to the Department of Defense. He is highly active in the Special Forces Association and the Special Operations Association.

"Oops, Wrong Uniform!"

It was November of 1966. I was a "strap hanger" [just along for the ride—not part of the tactical unit] on a Mike Force operation commanded by Capt. Bob Jacobelly, 3d Company of the II Corps Mike Force.

We were moving along a trail when the point element came back to report that six NVA were moving down the trail toward us. We set up a hasty ambush. When the six NVA entered the kill zone, we opened fire. All of them were hit. Four seemed to be killed immediately, and two took off but left blood trails. We started searching the bodies.

While I was working on one of the NVA, I noticed out of the corner of my eye that one of the "dead" enemy soldiers started to get up, then lay down again. "Playing possum" is an old trick that can get you killed when the "dead" guy rolls a grenade at you. I called over to one of the guys: "Hey, he ain't dead!"

One of our guys (I won't mention his name) moved over to the NVA soldier and kicked him, to get him to react. But the guy was a good actor—he didn't move! So then our guy shot the NVA in the leg. He was still good! Then our guy took a machete and ran it right through the guy.

"I think you got him now," I told him. "But God will get you!"

We started to follow the blood trails, with Bob Jacobelly and me out in front of the troops. We spotted one of the NVA at the base of a tree. I ran up to the guy; he was covered with blood, from head to toe. He was just sitting there. He handed me something, but I was paying more attention to the blood.

Bob yelled, "Sir! Grenade!" The NVA had handed me a "potato masher" grenade. He'd pulled the string they used for a safety, but he hadn't hit it against his helmet or the ground to activate it—but I didn't know that at the time! All I knew at that moment was that I was about to accept a hand grenade offering from this guy. I was kneeling on the ground in front of the wounded NVA soldier . . . so I took off running, on my knees! I wore the fabric right off the knees of those pants, getting away. As soon as I was out of the way, all four hundred plus guys opened up on the man, and then there was nothing left of him.

Those six NVA were part of a larger unit, and we captured parts of six heavy machine guns from them. From the parts we were able to assemble three functional machine guns, one of which is still on display today at the Special Forces museum at Fort Bragg.

Those guns were really heavy to carry, but we brought them out. We speculated on how many lives of the US Army 4th Division we saved by the capture of those guns, because there was a joint operation in progress with the 4th, and their helicopters were extremely vulnerable to the 12.7-millimeter antiaircraft machine guns.

Although we wiped out that squad of NVA, we nearly were wiped out ourselves later, on the same operation. The NVA discovered that an

American unit was coming into their area of operations, and Charlie [slang for *Viet Cong,* from the phonetics *Victor Charlie*] left us alone. When we made contact with these enemy units, they didn't engage but pulled back and disappeared. Instead, they waited for the 4th Division. They hit Col. Bob Lee's battalion and killed nearly all his company commanders.

The NVA mauled the 4th Division, even though the 4th was well dug in, behind sand bags and in bunkers. The NVA sent two regiments against that one 4th Division battalion. They sent a single battalion after Capt. Bob Jacobelly's company of Mike Force strikers, once they had engaged Colonel Lee's battalion, and Bob was just about shot in half by a machine gun. He lived and spent the next year in a hospital.

I took two prisoners back to Pleiku, and I was still there when we got word that the Mike Force was under attack. I loaded a chopper up with ammunition and supplies, all bagged in sand bags, and we flew them out there to resupply the company. The crew chief, a guy named Leonard, was supposed to have been packing to go home. But because of the emergency, Leonard flew the mission. A supply lieutenant, a guy named Hess, had been in country three weeks. The lieutenant jumped up beside the door gunner.

When it was time to land, the pilot called up the unit on the ground. They popped smoke. The VC and NVA knew our SOP, and they often popped smoke, too, trying to lure the helicopter into an ambush. We tried to counter this by having the unit on the ground authenticate the color—in this case, yellow.

Well, the NVA popped smoke, and it was yellow, too. We didn't see the first smoke from the friendly unit. We had already passed them when we saw the yellow smoke that was supposed to mark our LZ.

As the pilot came in to a hover above the LZ, the NVA opened up on us and shot the chopper to pieces. Hess and Leonard were killed immediately; a heavy machine gun virtually took their heads off. The copilot was very severely wounded. The door gunner on the other side was also wounded. Major Cartright, the pilot, turned to me and said on the intercom, "Hey, Clyde, somebody's got to get off."

I was the only one who could still move, so I jumped out. As I jumped, Lieutenant Hess' weapon hit the ground beside me, an M16 with magazines taped together, "cowboy style."

I started running to the tree line, still thinking our guys were in there. Then the NVA came out. I thought, "Oops, wrong uniform!" I hit the ground and got off a few rounds. Then they threw a grenade that got me, and I had to stop. There was enough blood on me that they just came over, collected my weapon and my boots, and left me to die.

I lay there for a couple of hours before Frank Quinn, my sergeant major with the Mike Force (and who was also a "strap hanger" on the operation, but with one of the other companies), Sgt. Danny Panfil, and a couple of Montagnards came down and started looking around the area for me. They got me back to the lines.

Although I was covered with blood and looked terrible, I wasn't really hurt so bad that I couldn't function. The Mike Force had fought bravely and had lost their commander and had about fifty percent casualties. They were running low on ammunition. I took over, got on the radio and called Pleiku and said, "Hey, we need a resupply"

I forget the little redheaded major's name, but he was an asshole. He came out and—at fifteen hundred feet—he threw out the resupplies! You can imagine where it landed—in Cambodia! So Frank Quinn and some Montagnards and I ran across the dry lake bed to the Cambodian side. We picked up all the ammunition we could, then we ran back and distributed it to the troops.

During the battle, a little Montagnard M79 gunner ended up laying beside me in a shallow depression. He was shivering and crying from fright. I took the M79 from him and pointed it toward the enemy and pulled the trigger. It fired. The projectile hit a tree and bounced right back at us! I handed it back to the guy and said, "Here. It's yours; you know how to use this thing!" It scared the hell out of me—I didn't know that the projectile didn't arm for about twenty-five meters, and it hit the tree at about ten feet.

The battle lasted ten hours. Finally, they sent in a 4th Division relief force to help. When it was over, we policed up fifty-eight NVA bodies from our immediate perimeter. We were picking up the bodies to bury in a big pit the 4th Division engineers had blasted for us, when we came across a body that had been cut in half by the effects of a cluster bomb strike.

"I never knew what the inside of a human body looked like," I said to one of the sergeants with me; he just about turned green. It was just strange at the time to see a half of a man, from the waist up.

When it came time to go and we were loading bodies on the choppers, I discovered that, as I was loading Montagnard bodies on one side of the helicopter, the crew chief was pulling them off on the other. I "braced" the pilot with a weapon, threatening to kill him. I told him that if I ever caught any crews doing that again, I wouldn't be responsible for my own actions. I told him to tell the other chopper pilots the same thing.

I thought they would report me, but at that moment my mind snapped. They said that they were only there to pick up wounded. My thought was, *I've got to get the dead back home too.* You don't leave Montagnards lying on the battlefield if you can help it!

During the operation, NVA documents were captured that showed they knew who we were and where we were, all the time. They were just waiting for something bigger to come along. We didn't even carry entrenching tools. We slept in the open, and if the NVA had wanted to, they could have killed all of us easily, if they chose to. We took over fifty percent casualties as it was. That was the last time the II Corps Mike Force went out without entrenching tools. We learned our lesson from that.

Bob Jacobelly and Frank Quinn got the Silver Star for that, and everybody got the Purple Heart. I got a Distinguished Flying Cross for getting off the helicopter. We didn't usually get medals; we figured that this was part of our jobs. We often went on long operations with a lot of action, and nobody got anything except Purple Hearts.

They Fell for It Every Time!

Black Jack missions got their name from Colonel Francis Kelly's call sign, "Black Jack." The senior officers all had call signs; mine was "Thunderbolt." We trained to operate in a particular AO, for thirty days or more at a time. Every seven days we got a resupply. The way I did that was with A-1E Skyraiders and empty napalm containers.

I went to Nha Trang and worked out the system with Bob Barris, the assistant S-4 at that time. We sawed the ends off these napalm containers, added a cargo parachute, and filled them up with food and ammunition. Sixteen of these things would provide enough resupply for a whole Mike Force for a week.

A flight of four Skyraiders could deliver these to us out in the field. They dropped them from three hundred feet. The chute would open, and the container would just hit the ground! Then the guys would unbolt the ends, and inside would be sandbags filled with food and ammo, each one tagged for distribution, with color codes for the contents. It was an excellent way to bring in mortar ammunition, and almost anything else.

Each Skyraider carried four of these containers plus another four with real napalm in them. They flew cover for us while we policed up these containers, and that took quite a while.

One thing we always did—and it always worked—was to pile all these containers and parachutes up in the drop zone, then booby-trap them. We got them with this every time. You would have thought they would learn, but they fell for it every time!

"Somebody Stop Them!"

I was extremely proud of how well the Montagnards fought on the Cambodian border, and when I took the third Black Jack operation out for a thirty-day mobile guerrilla mission (Black Jack 23), I took them.

We were bombed on March 9, 1967, by the United States Air Force. I asked for a "combat proof/sky spot" to verify our position and coordinate with our air cover. The two pilots dived on me and bombed my unit. They thought we were enemy in the open. One of my American guys was killed, along with several Montagnards, and we had twenty-seven wounded. I was screaming on the radio, "Somebody stop them!" But we didn't have direct radio communications; they were on UHF and VHF, and we only had FM. A buddy of mine, Ralph Miller, was an FAC or Covey and came up on the radio to say hello to me. He was the one that got them to stop bombing us any further.

The troops were so shell-shocked afterward that they were useless as a unit from then on. I relieved everyone when we got home and reconstituted the unit. They had fought *so* hard on the first battle on the Cambodian border, only to be bombed on this one. It just ruined them. So we broke them up and put the individuals in other units.

There was a big investigation. It turned out the same two F-100 pilots, flying out of Phan Rang, had killed a substantial number of civilians at Lang Vei the day before in another indiscriminate bombing. Both were kicked out of the Air Force.

OpCon to the 1st Air Cav

Colonel Kelly put Black Jack 23 and me, as commander, under the operational control ("OpCon") of the 1st Air Cav, operating out of Bong Son at the time. We were supposed to work on the western side of the Cav's AO.

Maj. Gen. John Norton, the Cav commander, said, "Clyde, if you get in serious trouble, I'll send you a company to reinforce you. Two hours later, if you still need help, I'll send you a battalion. Two hours after that, a regiment. If that doesn't do it, I'll give you the whole division!"

Well, on a single day we got ambushed between twenty-five and thirty times. My poor combat recon platoon was taking the brunt of this, so as a considerate commander and to give them a break, I put them at the tail of the march and let them bring up the rear. The next time we got ambushed, we got hit from the rear, and they got nailed again. During all this time we didn't get so much as a squad from the 1st Air Cav!

We were on Hill 709 and surrounded. I was lying on the ground with Andy, in the middle of the perimeter, about four or five in the afternoon. Suddenly I heard a blood curdling scream; it was Andy. He said, "Sir, somebody's squeezing my balls!"

Everybody was looking at Andy. I said to him, "Andy, I'm the only one here, and I'm not that kind of guy."

He was passing a kidney stone, which is supposed to be as painful as anything. The troops were looking at me, and I said, "Hey, not me—I'm not touching him!" Anyway, we got a chopper in to evacuate him. They lowered a stokes litter on a cable, we put him in, and up he went.

I had called for help, and Major General Norton sent Capt. Vern Gillespie out to see what was going on. Vern was talking to me over the radio from the chopper, from about fifteen feet in the air, when Charlie opened up and shot that chopper right out of the sky. Well, Vern fell into my arms! The shock of the hits on the helicopter had knocked him out. Then the chopper crashed at the foot of the mountain. Within less than an hour, Major General Norton had two companies surrounding that chopper!

That was my cue to take my force and depart. We headed down the mountain, to where those two companies were. Gillespie was the only one in a regular American uniform. We put him in front to help identify us to the Cav, since the rest of us were in black pajamas. We got down in a dry creek bed and received some more fire. The casualties weren't bad (cuts and bruises from the flying gravel), but it sure shook up the troops again.

Aloha

As the commander at My Loc (which became FOB-3 following the closing of Khe Sanh on 30 June 1968), a field-grade officer, I wasn't allowed across the border into Laos, Cambodia, or North Vietnam on insertion missions. However, it was okay for me to go along on extractions following a "prairie fire," which usually meant that the team was compromised and in serious trouble!

On November 30, 1968, Maj. Sam Toomey came up from MACV SOG headquarters in Saigon and asked for a recon team that could be used for an Elder Son/Italian Green mission—substituting "fixed" mortar rounds and ammunition that would explode when fired—at a recently located enemy arms cache. Lt. Raymond Stack was the recon team leader, and Major Toomey and five enlisted men—Art Bader, Rich Fitts, Gary LaBohn, Mike Mein, and Klaus Scholz—went on the mission. I was in the chase ship and could only go as far as Khe Sanh, where I had to get off. They went on.

As I understand it, they never made it to the cache site. I don't know for sure, because nobody made it out alive. The team got picked up and were coming out when the chase ship picked up a transmission from somebody for helicopters to stay clear of a set of grid coordinates because a FAC had reported a heavy caliber antiaircraft weapon, a 37-millimeter, on the ground. The chase ship crew assumed that the lead chopper, carrying the team, copied the broadcast, but apparently they missed it. The lead ship got shot down at four thousand feet!

The gunship escorts reported that the chopper exploded on impact, and that there couldn't be survivors. Even so, there was a lot of pressure for us to go in there to retrieve the bodies. But 5th Group said emphatically, "Don't you dare! There will be two regiments of NVA surrounding that crash site, just waiting for you. Unless you've got something bigger than that, forget it!"

Well, I wasn't going to go in there with my little Hatchet force against two regiments. We'd just add to the body count, and we didn't.

We could hear the NVA on the radio, talking about all this. They reported that it was a helicopter full of Vietnamese. The explosion and fire and the fact that nobody was wearing American uniforms—the recon team was wearing tiger-stripe fatigues—made everybody unrecognizable. So we didn't make an issue of it at the time.

But, many years later, the bodies were recovered, and they were finally buried in Arlington Cemetery. Unknown to any of us, the media had secretly wired the chairs of the families at the graveside service. All the remains from the seven guys were put in one casket, and I had the privilege to put seven MIA bracelets (one for each man) on top of the casket to be buried with them. All seven names were on the same stone. I spoke to all the families, told them about the circumstances, and told them why I was sure that everybody on the chopper was dead.

One of the families, though, the LaBohn family, sued the government to have that name removed. They just couldn't accept the idea that their guy had died. Sam Toomey's father was a retired colonel, and his wife was Hawaiian. They brought a little ukulele, and at the end of the service they sang "Aloha," which can mean hello or good bye. It was very beautiful.

Going Native

I loved the Yards. I was very lucky. When I had an A-camp at An Loc, I had a little Hmong captain who had been made an officer by the French; he was my counterpart. I had a Vietnamese XO, but he was as worthless as tits on a boar hog. The majority of the LLDB in our camp were Montagnard. We had only two Vietnamese—the XO and a sergeant. The sergeant was brilliant! He worked like a horse. The Yards loved him, and he loved the Yards. He got along fabulously with the Hmong captain—but I had to watch the XO like a hawk.

I had one sergeant I had to send home because he was getting too "native." He was always taking the side of the Montagnards over that of the American NCOs—regardless of who was right or wrong. I had to take him aside many times and counsel him on his actions as they related to this matter.

I sent him home. When I got back myself, I picked up a copy of *National Geographic*, and sure enough, there he was, back at my old A camp, as the team sergeant.

When he finally went home, after fourteen years, he walked up to the door of his mother's house, and knocked. An old lady came to the door. "Get away," she said to this disreputable character.

"Hey, Mom, it's me!" That's what happens when you stay away from home for fourteen years.

Martha Raye

"Maggie" came to visit the Mike Force a couple of times. One evening she said, "How about some coffee in the morning?" In the morning we gave her a cup of coffee, and she said, "What the hell is this? I wanted vodka! I was just being nice!" So we got some vodka for her.

I gave Maggie an AK-47. Now, she wasn't authorized to take that AK home any more than the rest of us, so she took it apart and taped the pieces to her body. She walked off the plane with a crutch and a limp, and that's how she got it in the country.

When I gave her the AK, she noticed the sign I had over my door that said "Fuck Communism!" She loved it! She saw it and said, "Can I have that? I want to put it in my 'team house' back in Bel Air." (She kept a room in her home set up as a Special Forces refuge, her "team room." A Green Beret was always welcome to spend the night at Martha Raye's.)

So I said, "Sure!" We took it down, and I gave it to her, and she hung it up in her team house.

She called me one time and said, "Clyde, I had a woman reporter show up here, and I took her in the team house to show her how things were. She saw that sign. She said, 'Isn't that sign utterly disgusting!' I told her, 'Get your fucking ass out of my house!'" That's the way she talked.

Another time we invited Maggie out to our camp, and there was a big battle at Bong Son. She immediately left us and went to Bong Son to help out. She worked there until she was exhausted.

She loved the enlisted men. She said she liked taking the officers' money in poker games, and she loved being around "her men," the sergeants.

The Agency

If you get to know any Vietnam-era Green Beret and start swapping stories about the big war, sooner or later you will find yourself at the edge of an informational "black hole." You'll know this because your friend will say, "I had two official tours over there. . . ." or "I went over in 1969 as a 'person,'" or some other evasive answer. That's because your friend did a tour in the employ of the US Central Intelligence Agency, and was sworn to eternal secrecy about the experience.

The Agency used SF personnel for many worthwhile programs in Laos, Cambodia, Thailand, all at the same time that the US government was saying, in effect, "Nope, we certainly wouldn't do a thing like that!"

It is still going on, too; I recently asked after a friend who hadn't been visible for a few months. "Bill just retired," I was told. "He's flying the 'black flag' down in the Caribbean." It's nice to know the CIA still needs a few good men.

—*Hans Halberstadt*

CONRAD "BEN" BAKER, CISO

Ben Baker is one of those old, legendary "China hands." He lived in Asia for twenty-eight years. Much of that time was spent in the deep, dark world of covert operations. As deputy director of the US Army Counter Insurgency Support Office (CISO) from 1963 to 1974, he was responsible for keeping the camps supplied with all the essentials of uncivilized life. During that time, he made over fifty TDY trips to Vietnam, Thailand, and Laos, visiting over one hundred special ops locations. His many years (1947-1975) in the Far East, Corps of Engineers, logistics background, and those field trips served him well. He designed knives, rucksacks, air drop containers, and other items for the indigenous forces. Most important, he developed the indigenous patrol ration. Although he wasn't an official Green Beret, Ben was as hardcore and was as much of an operator as anybody in the theater.

Combat Support, SF Style

Especially early on, MACV was antagonistic to Special Forces, and didn't do us any good. If we hadn't had our own supply/support system through CISO, the guys in the field would have died on the vine. They wouldn't have gotten anything from the regular logistics system. Later, you could just steal anything you wanted out of Cam Ranh Bay, an operation that leaked like a sieve.

When the CIA was supporting the camps, the guys on operations got a sock full of rice and a can of sardines. That's about all they got to eat on a mission. When I got out there to Okinawa, the guys were using twelve-gauge shotguns, old M1 carbines, World War II-surplus foreign weapons without spare parts, and the old, heavy .45-caliber Grease Gun. We finally got them standardized on the M2 carbine (which is identical to the little M1, except that it will fire full-auto) and M16s, though they didn't use them for cross-border operations, where "sterile" uniforms and AK-47s were standard. That's the reason we manufactured magazines for the AK-47. We could capture AKs, and we could buy the ammunition (good ammo!) from the Russians, through Finland, but we couldn't get magazines, so we made them in Korea.

Operation Switchback

Operation Switchback transferred the CIDG program from the CIA to the US Army as of July 1, 1963. The support of paramilitary operations was called the Parasol-Switchback Program. The American CISO was the control organization based on Okinawa for offshore procurement, storage, equipment repair, and limited research and development of material in support of special operations in Southeast Asia.

Parasol-Switchback was staffed by an Army colonel and Army NCO and a few hand-picked Department of the Army civilians with top secret clearances. It enjoyed the highest logistical priority of any US forces, as authorized by AR 580-5(S). The CISO paid the salaries of one hundred nine Okinawan workers in the US Army Ryukyus Islands [USARYIS] depots, and leased nine LSTs [Landing Ship, Tank] for direct shipment from Naha Port to Nha Trang in the Republic of Vietnam. Project Code "PIR" earmarked our shipments.

I immediately realized that if you didn't see the in-country operation, you couldn't understand it. That was okay with higher headquarters, just as long as I carried a DD Form 489, Department of Defense noncombatant's Certificate of Identity, that identified me as a Supervisory Supply Officer with the equivalent grade of lieutenant colonel. Can you imagine going out to the boonies and getting captured with that ID, wearing a uniform with only my name, my Vietnamese jump wings, and a blue triangle patch with "U.S." on it, and armed with a 9-millimeter pistol? The bad guys would surely release me if I showed them my card! No way. (So I didn't carry the card.)

Walt Shumate

I was out at Buon Sar Pa, checking up on the camps to make sure they were getting what they really needed, when I met the legendary Walt Shumate for the first time. He approached me one day and looked me over with a jaundiced eye. "What do you need, sergeant?" I asked him. He gave me a long list of stuff.

I said to him, "Sergeant, you had better not tell me you need *ten* of something when you only need one. Because, if you do, you will rue the day you lie to CISO. If you tell me you need ten, you're gonna get ten. But don't tell me you need twenty in order to get ten!"

"Okay, yessir, yessir," Walt said, and reduced the quantities on his list. I got on the radio and called back to CISO Okinawa and ordered his stuff. About three or four days later, an airplane arrived from Nha Trang, loaded with everything he had ordered. After that, we became close friends. Walt Shumate was just about the only Special Forces sergeant who would even give me the time of day. I was a "leg" at the time, a "dirty, rotten, carpetbaggin' civilian leg!" Six months later I was given a short course, and I parachuted with the 5th Group into Thailand and Laos. Col. Mike Healy later appointed me an Honorary Life Member of the 5th Special Forces Group (Airborne). Walt and his wife, Helen, corresponded with me and my wife, Shirley, until he passed away on March 1, 1993. We sure miss Walt.

Ho Chi Shumate

Walt Shumate asked Shirley to take care of a small, furry, bug-eyed lemur he had brought back to Okinawa. He was making a quick trip to Vietnam; then he was reassigned to Ft. Bragg. Walt had named the lemur Ho Chi because "he moved slowly, only came out at night, and only ate bananas."

Anyway, Walt returned, picked up Ho Chi, and smuggled him on the plane home in his jacket. He was sitting in the rear by a fuse panel and fell asleep. Ho Chi decided to investigate the panel. The lights flickered, and all hell broke loose on the plane. Walt woke up and snatched a singed Ho Chi back, trying to look nonchalant, as crew members ran up and down the aisles.

Indigenous Ration

In 1964, people in higher headquarters told us it would take five years and five million dollars to come up with a special ration for the indigenous troops we supported, the Montagnards and the Nungs. Canned C-rations were heavy, expensive, and gave our Montagnards diarrhea.

Since we didn't have the time (or the money), I did the development myself. Within two months I had designed a rice-based ration weighing twenty-two ounces and available in five menus: beef, fish-squid, shrimpmushroom, mutton, and sausage. The total development cost was about two hundred dollars—and it came right out of my own personal pocket. It was called the Packet, Indigenous, Ration (PIR), and I developed it right in my own kitchen. Two packages per day provided a man twenty-six-hundred calories.

The Yards had all sorts of vitamin deficiency problems, so we included a vitamin pill with each ration; they didn't know what it was for, and since it didn't taste good, they were reluctant to eat it. So we just told them that it was good for their sex life and they'd have more male babies, and that was the end of that problem! Not stupid, they'd save them while they were on patrol and gobble down a handful just before returning home.

Special Forces starting using the PIR. About a year later, we had issued about a hundred thousand of them, when we received a letter from the US Army's Walter Reed Medical Center. The letter reported, "We are working on a ration for the Vietnamese indigenous personnel. We advise against the use of the PIR ration due to the potential for food poisoning."

During the next ten years, over forty million of the PIR rations were issued with an estimated savings of twenty million dollars over C-rations—and no one got diarrhea.

A Better Ditty Bag

I designed the rucksack used by the CIDG troops, and here's how it happened. The 5th Group needed five thousand rucksacks for their indigenous troops. The US rucksack was on a metal frame, loaded with gadgets, pockets, and straps. It took a master's degree to pack one of the damn things, and the pack cost a fortune. We told them that there had to be a better way. So 5th Group sent us a ditty-bag kind of thing that they had taken from a Viet Cong and suggested that we try to improve on it. That was all they really needed. We went one better and made a rucksack with shoulder straps, three outside pockets, and a back pocket for a pad or map. Manufactured in quantity on Okinawa, they cost two dollars and eighty cents each instead of thirty-five to forty dollars.

We issued three hundred and fifty thousand of the rucksacks and probably saved at least ten million dollars.

Martha Raye's Happy Hour

I was up at Pleiku one time, when thirty-plus wounded were flown in. Everyone not otherwise occupied pitched in to help. I was working at the beginning of the line, helping to pull surface shrapnel out of wounded Yards. Martha Raye was down at the other end of the line in surgery and worked there for about a day and a half straight. After it was all over, Martha went down to the sergeants' hooch to drink with them. She never wanted to have much to do with the officers; she preferred to socialize with the NCOs. Since I was a civilian, I was permitted to join the group. We sat down at a big table, and each of us had our own bottle. Let me tell you, she could hold more than any of us guys.

Pushing the Button

We received an urgent requisition at CISO for a thousand resistors peculiar to the Hallicrafters HT-1D radio. We investigated and discovered that somebody at NATICK Labs [the designer of the radio] had ordered the installation of a red, rubber-covered, destruct button on the HT-1D radio. When the destruct button was pushed, a resistor was shorted out, making the radio temporarily useless.

Our curious Montagnard troops could not resist pushing the red button on each of the one thousand new radios that had just been issued, just to see if the switch actually worked. We sent an urgent message to NATICK Labs requesting that the red button be eliminated. In the same message, we requested air shipment of a thousand resistors to replace those already destroyed.

NATICK replied: "It has been determined that subject switch is absolutely necessary to deny use of the HT-1D radio by the enemy when your personnel are subject to imminent capture. Installation of destruct switch will continue."

Message to NATICK: "Info to the Joint Chiefs of Staff, the Secretary of Defense, the Secretary of the Army and Electronics Command. We are gratified for your concern for our troops' welfare. However, they are much more concerned with eliminating the enemy and using subject radio to avoid capture. So far, our indigenous troops have field-tested all of your initial shipment of HT-1D radios and confirmed that the 'destruct' switch is of the highest quality. The test, however, has denied use of the radio to friendly forces, not to mention enemy forces. If we wish to deny use of this radio to the enemy we will (a) elongate the antenna, twirl it rapidly around our head, and smash it against the nearest rock or tree; (b) failing that, we will shoot it, burn it, or booby-trap it; and (c) failing even that, we will stomp it to death. Repeat—eliminate the damn button. Baker sends."

A reply was received from the Secretary of Defense to CISO and to NATICK Labs.

To CISO: "Your verbose message clearly understood."

To NATICK: "Eliminate the damn button."

And that's the truth; it really happened.

Jeep Caper

One day we "borrowed" around seventy-five new jeeps that had just arrived on Okinawa and loaded them out to Vietnam before USARYIS [US Army Ryukyus Islands] even knew they had arrived. We were in dire need of jeeps, so we stole them from the transportation officer on Okinawa, a chair-borne civilian who wasn't smart enough to walk a hundred yards down to the dock to see if his shipments had come in. Of course, CISO had men down there all the time! When we saw something we needed for the war, we took it! Then we'd go pay for it.

We got the seventy-five jeeps, so I went down to see this guy with a check for about three hundred thousand dollars. He almost cried. "You mean you got my jeeps? It took three years to get those jeeps!"

"I got your jeeps. Here's your money."

"I want my jeeps," he whined. "I don't want your money!"

"Okay," I said, and I took my check back and walked out. He groaned. I knew we had more jeeps coming in soon, but we needed those jeeps yesterday, so we just shipped them out. When our batch of jeeps showed up, old dumb-ass never noticed. The night after they were unloaded, about midnight, my guys drove seventy-five jeeps up to his office. We parked them, bumper to bumper, locked tight; and we put the last one against the office door with a forklift. He showed up the next morning, completely locked out of his own office. It took them hours and hours to move the jeeps; they needed a crane to get the last one away from the door. That's how we gave him back his jeeps.

The Case of the Detoured Datsun

Tony Abrescia, one of my CISO supply officers, was making his rounds down at the docks at Naha Port on Okinawa, when he found a huge container with our shipping code "AT6846" followed by a phony number, awaiting shipment to Nha Trang. On the container was stenciled "Security Shipment—Do Not Open. Call Sergeant 'Smith,' 5th SFG, on arrival."

Tony called me up, and I went down to the port and opened the container. Inside we found a brand-new blue Datsun sports car. Then we picked the lock on the trunk. Inside was a PX-sized supply of ladies' size-small bras, panties, and nylons, as well as lipstick and makeup.

"Close it up and ship it!" I told Tony, because I knew I would be in Nha Trang when the LST arrived with the container. Tony was aghast. But he did what he was told.

I went over to Nha Trang to meet the shipment. Now, CISO had made an arrangement with the South Vietnamese government that we would monitor all shipments and eliminate all contraband at our end to the fullest extent possible. In return, they agreed not to touch any PIR shipments. I walked into the office of Mr. Nguyen and told him, "Somehow a commercial container got loaded on our LST, an error that should have been corrected, and it needs to go to the commercial port of entry." I gave him the number on the box and told him not to make a habit of this, but that the container belonged in a commercial port, and his men should move it as soon as possible.

As late as 1974 Mr. Nguyen was still riding around Nha Trang in his blue Datsun.

Snoopy

Back on Okinawa I kept a pair of purebred AKC beagles that had an occasional litter. Realizing that the Logistic Support Center at Nha Trang was in dire need of a mascot, I gave Sgt. First Class Bill Coombs a pup. Named "Snoopy," she was probably the only dog in Vietnam to eat steak and live in a bomb-proof, air-conditioned dog house.

When Martha Raye was in town, Snoopy was in dog heaven. Seems that the one thing you couldn't get in Nha Trang was a beef bone, since meat was shipped in boneless. Martha would invariably bring Snoopy a huge beef bone and get a wet kiss in return.

Liz

The Tactical Operations Center was located in an old French villa in Saigon. In the garden was a large cage that was home to "Liz," a twelve-foot python. Numerous troops pulled Liz out and took photos of each other holding her, and Liz generally tolerated it. But then she started striking out and biting people. Liz was about to be terminated with prejudice when it was learned that the Vietnamese cook was stealing Liz's live duck ration. The cook was sent off to the Army for training, and Liz went back on her duck-a-week schedule.

The Barfly at Can Tho

We had a problem getting enough parts for the Lycoming airplane engines installed on 5th Group's airboats. While awaiting transportation to the airboat company at Cao Lanh, I went into the club at Det C4, Can Tho, for a drink. No sooner did my brandy arrive than their mascot, a small honey bear, jumped up on the stool next to mine.

The bartender said, "She likes brandy."

Too late. That bear bit my thumb, and I bled like a stuck pig for about an hour. How did I know the lady wanted her drink first.

Elephant and Driver (One, Each)

Working at CISO mainly involved close coordination and follow-up. We could get anything from anywhere: silenced weapons, veterinary medicines, explosives, boots from size 3 to size 15XXX, you name it. If we couldn't get an item, we made it—like AK-47 magazines by the thousands, and small-size uniforms for our diminutive CIDG troops.

There was a shortage of forklifts in early 1964, and 5th Group was getting desperate. Following is a requisition to CISO, dated March 10, 1964, from Maj. Raymond Kaufman, QMC, S-4 at 5th Group:

"Attention Mr. Baker:

"As a result of your office's inability to provide urgently needed forklifts to meet the immediate requirements of this command, and in view of the theater-wide shortage of subject vehicles, request you procure from local sources at least four (4) each male-type well-trained elephants. These animals must be capable of lifting 8,500 pounds, must be air-transportable, can withstand being painted yellow, and have a basic knowledge of Vietnamese and English. In addition, it is desired that 120 days spare elephant fuel and trainer pikes be provided with the major item. We realize that this is not exactly in keeping with US Army MHE Standardization Program Requirements; however, operational requirements warrant such extraordinary actions. Subject elephants, as they become uneconomically repairable, will be cannibalized to make elephant-hide courier pouches for the Group, and elephant-hide boots in sizes 5, 6, 7, and 8, which are also in critical short supply. Coordination has been made with the Indian military attaché in Delhi, who has agreed to provide elephant trainer/tech reps to this Group; subject individual's name is Gunga Din. Request immediate action on this OTR."

He got his forklifts.

Bony Cows

"From: CO, 5th SFGB, Plei Djerang, RVN, Lt. Col. Lamar

"To: XO, Detachment B-50, Nha Trang, RVN

"Subject: Funds and Cows

"We maintain an average of over 500 Montagnards at this location. I do not consider two cows (and the occasional hog thrown in) to be an excessive amount of chow in ANY sense of the word when you consider the following factors:

"1. When you remove the hide, hair, guts, and bones from one of these half-dead cows, you don't have but 100 pounds of meat left.

"2. These Montagnards all have one thing in common: a continuous hungry gut. They can and will eat the equivalent of two round-eyed GI's daily.

"3. In view of the above, and in order to keep them happy and ready to fight, we must make every attempt to keep said gut full of rice and bony cows. So keep the cows coming at a rapid pace, and we will kill the VC.

"Thank you for your kind attention."

He got his cows.

Crocodiles

"Requisition Order Form

"From: Plei Djerang, Engineer, Det A-214

"To: 5th SF Group (Airborne) S4

"1. Crocodile, 10-12 year old, minimum length 8 feet, 20 each.

"Crocodiles are needed to stock the local swamp as protective devices. Air land at Chu Dron. Greenwood."

"Action: Disapproved, for the following reasons:

"1. Not available from local or CONUS sources. CONUS only has alligators.

"2. Local sentry dog school commander refuses to train crocodiles to not eat tender Montagnard babies unless we supply him with fresh live VC to use as bait.

"3. Air Force won't fly the damn things anyhow."

Ears

Special Forces became notorious for stories about the taking of ears from dead VC and NVA, but the real story is more complicated than what appears to be the mutilation of enemy dead (a war crime). In fact, it was a Montagnard tradition, as Ben Baker describes.

I was out in the boonies at a camp close to Ban Don that nearly got over-run. One of the SF guys got wounded, so I went out and took over his machine gun. We shot the shit out of them on the wire. We repelled the enemy, they managed to get in the wire, but they didn't overrun us.

When it was over we had a big sacrifice for the dead Montagnards, in traditional tribal style. The Americans all got their bracelets—but me, I'm not supposed to be involved in that kind of stuff; I'm supposed to be a yellow-bellied carpetbagger!

When it was finally time to go on to other things, I got on a helicopter. They gave me an elephant scrotum bag to take with me, and I put it in my rucksack without looking inside. You get pretty tired after being up for three days and nights, pumped full of adrenaline, so I went to sleep in the chopper. When I woke up, I remembered the bag they'd given me, the one I had stuffed in my rucksack. I pulled it out, opened it up, and damn if it wasn't full of ears!

The witch doctor had cut the ears off the enemies so that their souls would wander forever, searching for the missing part, and couldn't be reincarnated! It wasn't a war-crime sort of thing; it was to keep the enemy from coming back again. And they really believed that kind of superstition.

Anyway, I started throwing the ears out of the helicopter, one at a time. I was sitting on the right side of the chopper, by the door in front of the door gunner. While I was shucking these things out into the air, the door gunner reached over and pounded on my shoulder. "What's that, man?" he yelled.

"It's an ear, man!" I yelled back. And I took one of the ears, put it between my teeth, and spit it out into the slipstream, right past his head. If he had not had a safety belt on, he would have sailed right out of there. He passed out and turned gray!

Here's a guy who shot people from the air, but when he saw a body part up close, he couldn't take it. When he landed at Pleiku, he was still slumped over. The copilot asked, "What happened to him? Did he get hit?"

"No, I think he's just a little sick," I said and walked away.

Avio Feola

Sgt. First Class Avio Feola worked for the S-4 of 5th Group and was in charge of supply distribution out of Saigon. One late afternoon in 1965, he was loading a truck convoy of supplies west of Bien Hoa, and one of his trucks, loaded with ammunition, turned over.

The Viet Cong owned that stretch of road at night, but Avio wasn't about to let them take his truck. When help arrived in the wee hours of the morning, they found Avio sitting on the top of his overturned truck with his gun and radio.

One of his rescuers asked, "What if Charlie blew up that ammo?"

Avio replied, "Well, in that case, they still wouldn't have gotten my truck!"

Advice from Kipling

In my twenty-eight years of service in the Far East, I have lived by this advice from Rudyard Kipling. I have carried this in my wallet since I was a buck sergeant in Shanghai, China:

It is not good for the Christian health,
To hustle the Asian brown;
For the Christian riles and the Asian smiles,
And he weareth the Christian down.
And the end of the fight is a tombstone white,
With the name of the late deceased;
And the epitaph drear, "A Fool Lies Here,
Who Tried to Hustle the East."

Now that's the way Ben Baker lived!

JON CAVIANI

Jon Caviani spent twenty-three months and eleven days as a POW in North Vietnam. He received the Medal of Honor on his return to the United States for his actions at Hickory on June 4 and 5, 1971. He stayed in the Army and served as sergeant major of the operational squadron of Delta (the US Army counterterrorist unit). He retired from the Army in 1990 and now lives on a ranch in California.

SF Veterinarian

When I first went to Vietnam, I had visions of going off to an A-team. But they noticed I was a medic, and a farm boy, and they told me, "You are now a veterinarian." And that's what I did for about six months. I don't know who was more terrified, the water buffalo or me! After a while it became like anything else: You just smacked them, shoved in the needle, and gave them their shot.

The war pretty much passed me by during that first six months. I liked it. I lived in the villages, did my medcaps during the day, and took my rifle out into the woods at night. The VC pretty much left me alone, and I treated VC water buffalo and NVA sympathizers along with the rest.

Where's the Beef?

One of my jobs was to take a high-quality bull around to the different camps for breeding, trying to improve the quality of the herd. We hauled this bull around from camp to camp; it had cost us about sixty-five thousand dollars. We flew the bull around in a C-123 and dropped him off at an A-camp; then two weeks later, we came back and picked him up and took him to another camp.

I dropped this bull at one camp (it might have been Gia Vuc) and then went back to my unit to work on my chicken and pig project. When two weeks had passed, it was time to go back and pick up the bull. I flew back to the camp—and I didn't see the bull anywhere. I asked the Yards, "Where's the bull?"

They said, "Well, we had this real big celebration. . . ."

Since the bull was the biggest and the baddest, they figured that if they sacrificed him they would have the most good luck possible, so they ate him! And I had to go back and tell the "old man" about it; I thought I was going to be a private! God, he was mad!

Ruff-Puff to the Rescue

Another sergeant and I had gone out of the camp at Ba To, across the river. We were talking to the Bru village chief when we noticed some beautiful urns up on the hillside. We asked the chief if we could take them, and he said, "Sure, take them."

So the two of us went up the side of this hill in our jeep. It was a gentle slope, with a nice view of the Ruff-Puff company down below. We got out of the vehicle, and like damn fools, we left our rifles in the jeep. We were checking these things out, and the other sergeant had one of the jars up on his shoulder, when a bullet went right through it! The jar shattered, and we hit the dirt. There was a little depression in the ground, and we dove into it. A few more rounds popped our direction; we knew we weren't going to make it back to the jeep!

We used our pistols to provide a little return fire, exchanging shots with whoever it was in the bushes. Then I heard a blood-curdling scream, and I looked around. There was a guy who must be fifty years old, with his old, old rifle, complete with bayonet, and this old guy was charging! While we were watching this interesting performance, we heard another scream, this time from *up* the hill! An NVA, complete with an AK, jumped out of the bushes, and he had his bayonet out, too! The two guys charged each other, the Ruff-Puff guy doing the high-step just the way the French used to teach.

The two of them converged, and the old guy did the most beautiful parry and horizontal butt stroke I ever saw in my life! He put the younger guy down on the ground! Naturally, we came running, and we tied the NVA guy up, patted the Ruff-Puff guy on the back, and loaded him and the NVA in the back of the jeep for the trip back down the hill. The Ruff-Puff guy was the hero of this one—we weren't taking any credit at all!

We got down to the village and then discovered something quite sad: the NVA was in reality the village chief's son! The village chief had banished him years before. The villagers insisted on taking the man, and they talked to him that night. He had left his unit to come home.

The next day the village chief sent somebody over to report, "The execution will be tomorrow."

We tried to talk them out of it, but they were adamant. If nothing else, we could have gotten some more information from the man, but they wouldn't stand for it. They really didn't like the North Vietnamese! The next day, the Bru who had soldiered for the NVA was executed—by his father.

"Jon, Use the Knife."

The most terrifying thing I ever did in my life was to kill a guy by throwing a knife at him. We had moved up to an area and encountered a sentry. We didn't have a silenced .22 pistol, and we had to take this guard out. Nobody felt comfortable moving across the road before we got to him. It was gravel, and the noise would have given us away for sure.

I had always practiced throwing my knives, and I carried one over my left shoulder, in my ruck. We were contemplating this situation when my partner—I forget who it was—turned to me and whispered, "Jon, use the knife."

I shook my head no.

He nodded his head yes!

Ordinarily I would just reach up, grab, and throw—but not this time! I carefully considered and calculated the throw. When I finally let go, my adrenaline must have been way up, because the knife went in up to the hilt. The sentry gurgled a little and collapsed. That was scary! I had this vision that the knife would fly right on by the guy, and then he would turn around and nail us. I didn't like that.

C&C North Recons

I started running with S/Sgt. Keith Kincaid. Keith, bless his heart, was the most unlucky son of a bitch I'd ever been around in my life! We'd go out, and within seconds of getting on the ground, it seemed like the whole world was there to greet us! We even tried inserting "dummy teams," and, no matter, the whole world would break loose on us! God!

I told him, "Keith, I don't know about this!"

We went in on one LZ on the other side of the fence where they were waiting for us. We had been unable to go in and do our own visual recon of the area before the mission, and the "zoomies" [US Air Force fighter planes] did it for us. We figured that the Air Force had swooped down to take a closer look at the spot—a sure way of giving away the plan!

My first mission with Keith was just like that. About twenty minutes after we got on the ground, Charlie showed up. Keith put his head up to look at something, and a round came by so close it just slammed Keith's head into the ground. A couple of grenades got thrown—and I still hadn't seen anything! I was looking, but I wasn't seeing anybody. A couple of my Montagnards got hurt by the grenades.

I got the Yards over beside me; one had been hit through the artery in his arm. I opened him up, put a hemostat on both sides, set up an IV with Ringer's lactate through his ankle, ace-bandaged him up, and went to work on the other guy. The second had taken some shrapnel between the scrotum and the anus. There wasn't a lot to do for him, but he wasn't in trouble, other than just beginning to go into shock.

Suddenly Keith decided to pull back. There I was, working on the Yards, and when I looked up, there he was—and he was pissed, because I hadn't fired a round, and because I was blocking his egress! I grabbed up the Yards, and the helicopters started coming in. I raced over, threw the first guy in the chopper, raced back, got the other guy on my back, raced back to the helicopter and tossed him on, then climbed on myself. Because we had the wounded, we went into the med-evac hospital at Quang Tri.

When I got back to my unit, one of the sergeant majors started talking to me as if I'd been a coward on the mission. I thought I'd been doing my job!

"How much ammo did you fire?" he said.

"None," I told him. "I didn't see anything to shoot at!" I really didn't like the feeling of that.

So we were going to go back into that area again, about a week and a half later. The G-model Huey had just come out, the one with the 40-millimeter grenade launcher on one side and the mini-gun on the other, but otherwise it looked just like a slick.

We had gone into isolation to prepare for the mission, then went up to LT-1, up around Quang Tri; then we went out on the mission. It was the same area where I'd gone on my first mission with Keith. I started by doing a map reconnaissance with the aerial photographs from the Air Force. I noticed all kinds of stuff that nobody had mentioned in the briefings; I spotted a goat trail that looked very promising. I told Keith, "We have got to go in here!"

On the way in, from the helicopters, we could see that the NVA was building an all-weather road, with timbers and drainage. It was not a good feeling—there were a lot of people on the ground!

Keith was the team leader, and he was in the lead ship. His ship landed and unloaded first. I was in the next ship. Even before we landed, I could see seventy to a hundred people in pith helmets and NVA uniforms running with weapons at port arms toward the LZ. The door gunner wasn't even firing on them! I grabbed his helmet from him and used the intercommunications system [ICS] to report the targets on the ground to the gunship. That G-model came in and opened up on the NVA formation along its long axis and worked them over with the mini-guns.

Our helicopter flared over the LZ, and it was time to go. We were at about ten feet, but the pilot wasn't going lower, so we had to jump. We all jumped out. At the same time, Keith was trying to call the whole thing off, but we were having commo problems and couldn't hear him.

Once on the ground, there wasn't a hell of a lot to be done, and the helicopters got the hell out of there. Keith's group had run into a platoon of enemy as soon as they landed, and his element got shot up pretty badly. He was trying to get the next ship to come in and get them out—we weren't going to be running any recons out of this LZ!

Fortunately, we all were loaded for bear, so we had a lot of ammunition. We set up a perimeter. I got the open area; Keith got the trees. I was getting all my people into position when a .51-caliber heavy machine gun opened up on us and plowed a furrow in the ground right next to me.

Every time that gun fired, you could see where the rounds were hitting, and it was obvious that his traverse was limited; the barrel must have been up against a tree. I could tell that he was going to have to move the whole gun if he was going to get any closer to us. I took one of my Yards, one with an M203 [which replaced the M79 grenade launcher; it serves the same function but is attached to an M16].

I told him, "You watch right up there, and if you see where he's shooting from, hit him with a grenade." Every once in a while my Yard would chunk a 40-millimeter up there.

There was sudden movement to my front. I had already put down my RPD [a Russian machine gun similar to the US M60, very popular with Special Forces and considered by many superior to the M60]. I reached for the shotgun that I always carried, a sawed-off shotgun loaded with 00 buckshot. We were firing at each other through the brush, twenty yards apart. Up jumped three or four NVA. I took them: *Boom! Boom! Boom! Boom!* The guys used to give me shit for carrying the shotgun, but nobody was giving me any shit about it this time.

Finally, we were able to get some helicopters to come in and get us. My guys and I got on our chopper, and off we went. As we were lifting off and climbing out, one NVA guy stood up below us, with his AK on "rock and roll" [full auto], firing straight at us! And he didn't hit us with *one* round! Next thing I knew, somebody shot the NVA in the head, and he went down.

We swung out, and I told the pilot, "We've got to cover the exfiltration of the other guys." As we maneuvered, I could see a large number of NVA racing toward the position of the other part of the team.

I was beating on the door gunner: "See that? Those are people down there, and they are headed for my team! Fire them up!" We all started firing. We shot the hell out of them! Keith's helicopter got in and collected him and his guys. We turned around and started to leave . . . *Blam*, the helicopter took a hit, and down we went.

Fortunately, we didn't lose anybody when we went down. We got on the ground. The pilot, the copilot, and the door gunners—they didn't like this development at all. We got out, and I told them, "Okay, you've got a thermite grenade—destroy the KY-6 (a scrambler used to help provide secure radio communications). Take the M60s out of the chopper and flip the bipod legs down. Let's go!" I told them.

We moved to an area where we could set up a defensive position and still see the helicopter. "Don't shoot until they fire at you!" I told them. "If they are running at you, let them come. If they see you, they'll shoot. You can take them then."

I got on the horn with Sgt. Donald Chaney, my Covey, and asked if there was an exfiltration LZ in the area.

He called back, "I've got a nice one at about a hundred and fifty meters from your position," and he gave me an azimuth to it.

"Okay," I told him. "Do you have another?"

"I have another LZ at a hundred meters," he said, and he gave me another azimuth.

"Okay, send the helicopters in to beat up the first LZ. Shoot the hell out of it! Then you have them race over to the other one to pick us up!"

So the helos started shooting the LZ up big time, with guns and rockets. And we could see Charlie just racing past us, over to catch us where they thought we were going to try to get out. The helicopters finished shooting, then started to land. Then they picked up, slid over to where we were, and got us. The crews had eyeballs as big as saucers! We all piled aboard, and we pulled pitch. The crews still had extremely stoic expressions, but by the time we passed 2,500 or 3,000 feet, you could see the faces start to crack into smiles.

We lucked out on that one and didn't lose anybody, and Keith didn't lose anybody out of his group. And that, basically, was what it was like to run recons in that area at that time. Occasionally you got to stay longer, to RON, and maybe spent two days and didn't see a damn thing!

The Yards

I was told that I was supposed to run with some Americans who despised the Yards, and they let the Yards know it. The result of that would have been that if that American got hit, I'd be the one who'd have to carry him out; the Yards certainly wouldn't. These guys called them all the derogatory names: "slant-eye," "gook." I did that once, and one of my Yards turned around to me and said, "Is that what I am?" I never did that again. I had Yards who died for me.

I had a deal with my Yards: "If you get shot, I won't leave you on the ground. I will come back and get you." And I did that! I was very, very close to them. I lived with them in the highlands when I was a vet.

Special Forces was successful in Vietnam because we understood the people, because we knew basic tactics. We were misunderstood by a lot of Americans who thought of us as "sneaky Petes." But we conducted conventional tactical operations; we knew basic first aid, basic engineering, and basic communications. Other units didn't. Even when we were closing down the camps and handing the operations over to the Vietnamese Rangers, I remember the Yards saying, "Can you take us out on one more operation?"

I remember ARVN troops sitting down on the helipad, saying, "We aren't going out on this operation until we get paid." I never had that problem with the Yards. The Yards knew that, if it was humanly possible, we would recover their bodies if they were killed on an operation. Most of us disliked the ARVN immensely.

The Vietnamese thought of the Montagnards as savages—the same as Americans did of the Indians during our western expansion, because we didn't want to understand them. The Indians weren't up to our standards.

That's the same way the Vietnamese looked at the Yards, and it was a real tragedy.

In other ways the Montagnards were similar to the American Indians. Many tribes didn't get along with each other. If you put Rhade, Steng, and Jarai all in one camp, you were just asking for a battle right in your own compound. We succeeded with these people by understanding them. The tribes were all different, and they had to be treated differently.

We were able to operate effectively because we were very sensitive about our security. We knew we were heavily infiltrated, and we learned to work around it. Even the Yards didn't know where we were going. I'd come back sometimes from isolation and planning a mission into Area Oscar, and they'd look at me and say, *"That* bad?" But they always had confidence in me, and I had equal confidence in them.

Sometimes, we'd be walking along and I would have a Yard on either side of me, one holding each hand. I didn't have a hand on my weapon; I put my life totally in their trust. They knew that. The hand-holding was brotherly, and I thought nothing of it, although other Americans would sometimes say, "Look at the fucking faggots!" But that was the Yard custom, and they were great! They made you feel a part of their community.

Recon Tools of the Trade

RPD—the Soviet-Designed Light Machine Gun

I normally carried a captured and modified machine gun the Russians called the RPD. I did not like the AK, and I'm glad Charlie had it. It was too powerful a rifle for the little VC and NVA, and they couldn't manage the recoil. After the first shot, everything else was going to be over your head! That was kind of a blessing. If they had had the M16, that would have been a different story.

I liked the RPD because it probably had the best buffer group of any automatic weapon anywhere. It fired 7.62x39-millimeter ammunition from a drum under the weapon. Unlike the M60 used by most American units, the RPD was balanced. Charlie recognized the sound of the RPD when it fired, and he usually stopped to think when he heard it: *Is that our guys?* If that slowed him down for just a second, you could get out of his ambush kill zone, get up to the side, and then flank the ambush.

We took off the bipod, cut the barrel off, and put a sling on it. Then you had a very good weapon. The only thing I didn't like about it was that it used twenty-five round, nondisintegrating link belts. In combat, you found yourself reaching down to retrieve those segments from the ground because they were hard to come by. It was a fantastic weapon, accurate, powerful, easy to use. I carried one, and some of the other guys were believers, too. But other weapons were also powerful, and one of our guys carried a little Swedish K.

M79

I also carried a sawed-off 40-millimeter M79 grenade launcher, with most of the stock cut off and the barrel chopped down to look just like a pistol. The range was unchanged, and it was really useful. We could shoot accurately with it to two hundred meters, normally with the HE [high-explosive] round.

Shotgun

I also carried a cut-down pump shotgun loaded with 00 buckshot. There is no question that a guy knew he'd been shot when you hit him with a load of buckshot, unlike the "dart" rounds that would go right through the guy but would leave him shooting at you because he didn't know he was dead yet!

The stock was cut off at the pistol grip, and a loop of "dummy cord" was tied to it. I carried the shotgun in my rucksack, muzzle down, with the grip sticking up over my left shoulder. I could pull it out without taking off the ruck.

Rucksack

We all mined our rucksacks. If we had to jettison them, we had a Claymore inside, primed and fused to a striker taped to the rucksack quick-release. If you had to drop your ruck in an emergency, it would drop and fire the fuse-lighter. [The fuse allowed time enough to get a safe distance away before the Claymore exploded. The hope was that the NVA or VC who were pursuing us would pause to pick up or search the ruck about the time the Claymore would detonate. At very least, the explosion would slow down the pursuing enemy force.]

Medal of Honor at Hickory

My commander said, "I've got a place I want you to command."

I didn't like the idea; I liked doing what I knew. He said, "You're gonna do it anyway." He sent me to the radio retransmission site called Hickory, across the river and northeast of Khe Sanh.

I went out there, and the place was a mess—concertina wire hanging down on the ground, old French mines poking out of the dirt. The first order of business was to get the defenses repaired. We got the Navy's Seabees to bring up a little bulldozer. We used that to get rid of the old mines and dig new fighting positions. We fixed the wire and made a lot of progress.

But we were also seeing a lot of enemy activity outside the wire. We reported it, and the intel community reported back, "Bullshit!" This was typical. We were seeing a thousand NVA guys a day, sending helicopters out to shoot them up; and the intel weenies still refused to believe me. They had been setting up a network of electronic sensors all across the northern part of the country, and these sensors weren't indicating the level of enemy activity that we were seeing. So our reports were dismissed. They said, "Our assets don't show anything out there."

I sent them a message in the clear in response: "Then you don't have any fucking assets out here!"

There was a hill overlooking our camp, Hill 1051. The 101st Airborne tried to land on top, but it didn't work. Some helicopters came in to get a couple of teams out, and one of the gunships made a straight run in from about three miles out. When he was about a mile out, I saw a single NVA kid stand up with a rocket-propelled grenade, put it on his shoulder, and take careful aim. The ground around this kid was getting all torn up from the fire from the gunship, but he just stood there, preparing to fire.

I grabbed for my rifle, because the kid was right at the range I like to snipe at, about a thousand meters. But before I could do anything, he put that RPG right through the cockpit, and the "bird" went right in. Then I had to call the gunship flight leader to report what had happened.

The buildup around us continued, and we were obviously in a bad tactical location.

The night of June 4 was rainy and miserable. I checked on the Yards and the perimeter defenses a couple of times. Under cover of the rain, the NVA had emplaced Chinese Claymore mines around the camp. Some of the Yards noticed these things. We put everybody in the camp on the wall.

There were some concrete half-culverts down the hill, by the helipad. Sergeant Hill and some of the Yards moved down there. I took over the .50-caliber machine gun. I had it set up with a special ammunition mix, four "ball" to one HEI [high-explosive incendiary] round that I'd gotten from the Air Force.

While I was setting up the position, I noticed one of these Chinese Claymore mines off to the side. I called "Claymore! Hit it!" I was whipping the gun around on it when the NVA fired it. Sergeant Hill caught a piece just above the knee.

We started firing about that time. Charlie came up out of his holes, and we had a merry little firefight going for a while. They were using some old RPG-2s that were so slow you could see them coming and roll out of the way. They kept shooting, trying to knock out my fifty. I finally put a few rounds on the guys who were firing on me. A couple of the HEs must have killed them, because there wasn't any more fire from their position.

A sniper started working from the southwest of my position. Every once in a while that son of a bitch would put one really close to me! The guy was close, not more than seventy-five or eighty meters away. I couldn't spot him, though, and I got really pissed off. I called one of the Yards over and told him, "Watch right over there."

About this time a young kid—a slovenly, overweight kid with glasses (Walton was his name)—came running over. He was a sensor reader, a technician. He said, "Sarge, I think you better come back and check on your people. Everybody is just standing around. They don't know what to do."

He was pointing out to me my duties as the commander; he was right, and I had been wrong. "I'll take over the fifty," he said.

"What do you know about a .50-caliber machine gun?" I asked him.

"Nothing. I thought that, since you are Special Forces, you could teach me in one or two minutes."

Just then another shot went past my head. The Montagnard came running over, and he pointed to a spot where the sniper was. I could see where the mat was moving over the guy's hole. I reached down and grabbed my rifle. I lined up on the spot and waited. Then his rifle started to come up out of the hole . . . and as soon as he came up and began to level on me, *Blam,* that was the end of that son of a bitch!

I moved back into the compound and made sure everybody knew what to do—which I should have done in the first place. Then I went back to work on those Claymores, because nobody would want to stick their head up over the berm as long as those things were out there.

I grabbed an M60, peeked over the edge, then hosed one as soon as I could spot it. I went down the line blowing these things, one at a time. I got to the last one, flipped the gun over the berm, and started to move; and they blew it on me. That took care of the Claymores.

Then Charlie started laying on indirect fire. Those sons of a bitch could shoot! They're probably the best damn mortar men in the world! They dropped over a hundred rounds on my camp, a space maybe sixty meters by a hundred meters, and not one of them was outside the berm. Those shots had to have been made at a range of over 1,500 meters—almost a mile.

They were firing a lot of rockets at us, but because of where the NVA were firing from, the rockets were mostly going over the top of the camp, chopping my antennas all to hell in the process. Then everything calmed down, and it got pretty quiet. So I started evacuating guys.

I decided it was time to destroy all the electronic equipment. So I went down to the vans to throw in the thermite grenades [which are magnesium-filled, incendiary grenades that burn with extreme heat. They were often used to melt critical equipment, including gun tubes]. I turned on the oxygen bottles (so much for several million dollars worth of government equipment). I came walking down the stairs to talk to my commo man just as a B-40 rocket came zooming in, right between the vans, and blew up about six feet away. It blew me on my ass.

"Man," I told the commo guy, "that was close!" The fins on the spinner ripped the back of my pants leg as it went by.

When I picked myself up and discovered that I hadn't picked up any shrapnel, I told the commo guy, Sergeant Jones, "We're going to have to evacuate the camp; I want to get you out of here. You have more experience on the ground, but you know too much about this equipment. We can't risk getting you captured. I don't know how long we can hold them off, or if we can hold them off."

Meanwhile, Walton—the fat, slovenly electronics technician—had been manning the .50-caliber and had knocked out about four machine guns! Then there was a big explosion down at that end of the camp. I went over there. A bunch of Yards had been wounded, and I started hauling them down to my Vietnamese medic.

I came around a corner, and there was Walton, dragging that big .50-caliber back to the camp. The NVA had finally managed to collapse the position, and Walton was trying to get it back where he could use it again. People were shooting at him; there were AK rounds whipping past him.

I knocked the gun on the ground and asked him, "What the hell do you think you're doing?"

I looked at him. His glasses had been frosted by a near miss that had hit a sand bag in front of him. "Sergeant," he said, "I think I'm blind."

I reached over and moved his glasses up. "Does that help any?"

"I can see again!"

"Have you got another pair of glasses?" I asked him.

"As a matter of fact, I do," he said. "Down in my bunker."

I told him to lie down there, at the berm, with the .50-caliber, and I raced down there to get them for him while people shot at me. I got the glasses, raced back, and put them on him.

"It's a miracle!" he cried. "I can *see!*"

About that time, I heard one of the other guys moaning; he had taken a piece of a rocket that had hit nearby.

"I'm going to take him down to the medic," I told Walton, "but you are going to have to cover me!"

I tossed him a CAR-15. "Do you know how it works?"

"Yeah," he said, "like an M16, only faster!"

"You're catching on, Walton!" I told him.

I loaded the guy up on my back and took off across the helipad. From behind me I could hear Walton firing; he was putting short bursts into the bushes on either side of our route. I turned around and there he was, zigzagging, returning fire from anybody nearby—not a bad performance, especially from somebody who isn't supposed to be a combatant and is about forty pounds overweight.

We raced for the other side of the camp. I deposited the wounded guy and Walton on a helicopter and told him to get the hell out of there. I had already written Walton up for the Medal of Honor for what he'd done with the fifty, and I gave the paper to my wounded team member to take back. When everybody seemed to be aboard, the helicopter took off . . . and there stood Walton.

"I fell out," he said.

I used a common military expression of respect and admiration. "You lying sack of shit!" I tossed him a weapon and grabbed my RPD. "Get over there and take that position," I told him, indicating a spot on the berm.

About 4:00 PM. some more helicopters were inbound, and I got the word: These were the last helicopters of the day. I got Walton, my commo man, some of the other guys, and some Yards, and I loaded them all on the choppers. I instructed one of the Yards to point his CAR-15 at Walton.

"Walton," I told him, "this guy has orders to shoot you if you try to get off this helicopter. Get your damn ass out of here!" A 37-millimeter opened up on them on the way out, but they made it.

My Covey appeared overhead about 5:00 P.M., along with a fast-mover. It was Chaney again. "Jon, I got an Air Force general up here for you. He's got eight two-hundred-and-fifty-pound 'drags' [bombs with drag brakes]."

"Have him put them just to the south of the camp, on the helipad," I told him.

Chaney called back; the general had declined. "Too close," he said.

"It doesn't make any difference now," I said. "Besides, that's where the bad guys are."

The general still refused the drop. "He'll stay on station until the helicopters come in to get you," Chaney called.

"You tell him there won't be any more helicopters!"

"Okay, I'll drop them," the general called.

I pulled all my people back and we got down. He came rolling in and unloaded on the target. It was close, and we were bouncing all over the ground, but none of my guys got hurt. It really did a job on Charlie.

I called Chaney, "Tell him thanks!"

When the last helicopter left, there was just Jones, me, and seventeen little people left. Later I discovered that a team from Operation Heavy Hook in Thailand was en route to us about then, and they made it to just eleven klicks to the west of us when they were ordered to turn around. They were in a "Jolly Green" [a version of the Sikorski H-53, a large US Air Force rescue helicopter]—they could have picked up the whole team. My award says we were left on the ground because of inclement weather; it was inclement inter-service politics.

We could only defend half the camp, so I shrank the perimeter. We fought them off, over and over again. A half-hour went by without them doing anything. I knew then that we were about the get knocked over. I told the Yards, "Get the fuck out of here!"

I set myself up on top of the ammo bunker. I figured that if I had to die,

I'd die in style, and that when it blew I would never know what hit me. I was up there when I noticed a couple of Yards who had pulled back. When I looked back, I saw huge numbers of people coming toward the camp. I started firing them up. I had an attack of sanity and started thinking, *Just what do you think you're doing up here?* I turned and started down, and took a round in the back that threw me asshole over tea kettle. I landed at the foot of the bunker, and my Yards came running back to get me. I told them to take off. They went over the wall.

One of the last things I did was to call in a Stinger airstrike on our position, told them there were about seventy-five hundred bad guys in the open.

I managed to run over to the bunker where Jones was. "Get out of here!" I told him. But when I turned around, there were people everywhere, so I dove into the bunker with him. While we were talking, two NVA came in, the first without a weapon, the guy behind with an AK. As far as I was concerned, the number two guy was the real threat. I stepped behind him and brought the knife arm around his head. Then I brought the point up under his jaw, up into the skull, turned his head away, and let him fall.

I was moving on the number one NVA when Jones unloaded about twenty rounds into him. Until then, Charlie didn't know we were around, but that gave us away. A little while later, Charlie threw a grenade in and wounded Jones pretty bad. He decided to surrender. When he got to the door, they shot him down.

I played dead. One guy poked me in the chest three or four times, but I didn't move. I had hemorrhaged real bad and had a lot of blood on me, so he assumed I was dead. They tried to cremate our bodies. The bunker was lined with tarpaper, and they lit it on fire. After a while I decided I wasn't going to burn to death. I got up and made a break for the door—and they'd walked off! As I was walking out the door, I got hit with a round on my helmet. It was the only time I'd worn a helmet in Vietnam. The hit knocked me out. When I came to, the soles of my boots were all melted, and my hands and arms were all burned.

I crawled into another bunker and was trying to dispose of all my stuff except my ID card. I was hiding behind some cardboard in a corner of the bunker when an NVA came in. I heard him, and I held the cardboard with one hand and my Gerber knife in the other. He came over and lifted up the cardboard. My adrenaline must have been up, because I put that knife all the way through his sternum, all the way into his spine. He got a shocked, glazed look on his face, and expelled a load of tremendously bad breath as he realized that he was dead and there wasn't a damn thing he could do about it. And then I couldn't get the damn knife out of him.

I crawled under the cot, exhausted. When I came to, two guys were sitting on the cot, and one of them had ahold of my foot. He was checking to see if my boots would fit him. I guess he figured they were too big, because he just dropped the foot, *clunk*. I had already disowned the leg—he could have done anything with it. But they got up and walked out.

This bunker didn't seem to be a good place to stay, so I crawled out and around the side. Two NVA came wandering along and stopped beside me. Finally they walked off, and then I crawled down to the side of the hill and started my escape and evasion.

I lasted for eleven and a half days before being captured, right outside of Fire Base Fuller. The guy who got me was a little old man, about sixty-five or seventy years old, with an ancient Russian rifle. He was shaking just like a leaf. I thought that if I even blinked wrong he was going to shoot me.

Medal of Honor Hassles

There are a lot of disadvantages to wearing a Medal of Honor if you want to stay in the Army. There is a lot of petty jealousy. When you get a promotion, it isn't because you're a good soldier; it's because you're a Medal of Honor recipient. There are commanders who don't like having a Medal of Honor in the unit because they feel it will bring undue attention to them.

Getting into Delta wasn't easy because of the Medal of Honor—particularly when I had the covert squadron. It was not easy at all. I had units turn me down, not because of a lack of expertise in operations (which was never questioned), but because they wanted to know, "How do you conceal a Medal of Honor recipient in the unit?"

Well, that was easy for me. I didn't go to the conventions. I didn't do speaking engagements. I stayed out of the public view. It wasn't a problem. When I dropped out of sight, or when anybody in these units disappears, you don't question where they are and what they're doing.

Post-Traumatic Stress Disorder

I don't agree with the people who dismiss "post-traumatic stress disorder" [PTSD] as coming from fakes and phonies. I did my thesis on PTSD and have done a lot of research on it. Most people know that about fifty-eight thousand guys got killed on the battlefield during the war. What people don't know is that over two hundred thousand have died in car wrecks, from alcoholism, from drug overdoses, and from suicide since then.

The reason, I think, is that a guy could be on the battlefield one day, and he could be home on the street the next day, twenty-four hours later. During World War II and before, it might have taken you a year to get home in the belly of a troop ship. During all this time you were communicating. You had a chance to say, I feel really shitty about what I did. Your buddies could talk you through the feelings over a gradual period of adjustment. When you went to Vietnam you went with a two-way ticket, by yourself. The guys who went off to World War II went for the duration, and they went as units.

I don't think you see the same problem with PTSD in Special Forces that you find with the straight infantry units, but we had much different standards and experiences. For example, in Special Forces, dope smoking wasn't a problem. We only had one dope smoker in my team, and he got a buddy of mine killed. If you saw somebody smoking dope, the guy was gone. We had enough things to worry about.

The average mission in C&C North was what we called the "seventy/thirty." You had a seventy percent chance of not coming back, a thirty percent chance that you would return. The attitude in my unit, though, was, "They ain't made the bullet that has my name on it. If they did, they shot it off during a training exercise." Our attitude was that you had a job to do and you did it. When you came back, you were treated well. We had cooks who took care of us, who made steak and lobster for us on Sundays, with wine on the table. We were treated well. But when you went into "isolation" and started working on a mission, it was a totally businesslike attitude. Then, you would never see a guy go to the club.

The one thing that really bothered me about our unit was that the guy that went in, ran his recon, "snooped and pooped," and got back out without a shot being fired—that guy came home with no awards! As a result, I knew guys who would go in, do the mission, and then—just before it was time for the helicopters to come get them—they would do something to really piss off Charlie just so they could have a firefight when they came out, so they would get an award!

The Airborne Mystique

The holy trinity of the US Army is called Airborne, Ranger, and Green Beret. Of the three, the Airborne (a.k.a. "paratroopers," an archaic term today) is by far the most inclusive; it is the gateway to the elite little enclaves in the Army. All SF soldiers must be Airborne qualified, but that isn't too much of a challenge. "Jump school" is a three-week program, open to virtually every man and woman in the Army, and about one in five of all soldiers wears jump wings. The current program, as one instructor recently said, is three weeks of low-impact aerobics. Students make five jumps during week three, with three "Hollywood" jumps (no combat equipment), one jump with rucksack and weapons container, and one "night" jump (seldom actually done after dark).

Anyone in the Army who isn't a super-duper-paratrooper is a "leg," normally pronounced "gawddam laay-g," and is an object of profound contempt, regardless of rank. This is more important than you might think; any officer who expects genuine personal respect from the troops in any of the combat arms better wear jump wings—at least.

Part of the SF battle plan involves jumping behind the lines, but there wasn't much of that during Vietnam or since. The Navy's SEALs tried it during the Grenada operation and got a few of their guys killed. On the other hand, the Army's Rangers jumped onto the airport at Point Salines from eight hundred feet, and although it was a tougher problem than anticipated, the drop worked as advertised. But as soon as those first Rangers got the runway cleaned up, everybody else air-landed.

But all SF units continue to train in airborne operations and all SF personnel must maintain current jump qualifications to remain on a team. That means at least one military static-line jump (twelve hundred fifty feet above ground level) per quarter, normally with rucksack and weapon.

—*Hans Halberstadt*

LARRY TRAPP

Larry Trapp retired from the Army in 1971. Since then he's maintained his friendships with many in the Special Forces and the special operations communities through the Special Operations Association and the Special Forces Association. He doesn't seem to have slowed down much: He currently manages a residential community, invests in real estate, and raises ostriches.

The Yards

When I first got over there, we were supposed to be teaching the Montagnards demolitions, map reading, radio procedure—to people who didn't read, spoke twelve languages, and had never seen trucks or airplanes or any modern things at all. All they really got to fight with, though, was a Grease Gun [a .45-caliber submachine gun left over from World War II] and a couple of grenades, if they were lucky. So I decided that we would teach them to shoot, and maybe a little squad tactics, and that's all they really needed.

After they were trained, an officer from another detachment showed up and asked, "Who here can give a class on the Grease Gun?" All of them put up their hands.

"No—I just want one," he said. "Who's the best? Step forward!"

They all stepped forward! They really were amazingly proficient, because that's all we had these guys do—take the weapons apart, put them back together, and shoot—and that's what they needed. If you took these guys somewhere far away to fight, they wouldn't do it, but bring them back to defend their villages and they'd fight like hell.

Walt Shumate Shaves His Mustache

Walt was a real cut-up, but he knew his weapons better than anybody else I've ever seen. Shumate and I were the same age, and we were both from Virginia, and we both liked to drink and fool around a lot, which occasionally created some resentment from other people on the team.

I remember one time, when Walt was on a team out of C&C Central at Kontum, we all went to a party at the liaison-services compound, and everybody was in civilian clothes. Shumate showed up, with his big handlebar mustache—not trimmed to regulation length.

The SOG commander, Colonel Sadler went up to him and asked "What are you doing with that mustache?"

Walt replied, "If you can't grow one, don't complain about it!" And Walt turned his back on the guy and continued his drinking. The colonel tapped him on the shoulder, annoyed, and Shumate turned to ask, "What the hell do you want?"

"I'm chief of SOG, Colonel Sadler!"

"Oh, is that right?" Shumate responded. "I've heard a lot about you— and it hasn't all been good!" He turned around again and went back to his drink, ignoring the colonel.

The next day, Walt sobered up, and we told him what he had done the night before. He shaved the whole mustache off—and went in and apologized to the colonel.

Defensive Driving, SF Style

Shumate, till the day he died, called me *Dai-uy*—it didn't matter if I was a major, a colonel, whatever, it was always *Dai-uy*. One day, while we were down in Saigon at the White Elephant, Walt came running up to me to report, "*Dai-uy*, I had an accident last night, but I got away clean!"

"You *what?* Tell me about it."

Well, it seems that he had been drinking with some of his Vietnamese army buddies, and somebody fell down and got hurt, so he had driven the guy down to the hospital at the air base. As he was leaving, the bumper of the jeep hit one of the Citroens owned by the Vietnamese doctors, and he kept going. The jeep wasn't Army property but one that had been leased, and the bumper was bent back in an incriminating way. "But I got away clean!" Walt insisted.

About that time the phone rang; it was the B-detachment commander, Major Garwood. "Somebody up there had an accident," he said.

"Really?" I said.

So the MPs were after us. I had just gotten a new jeep, and Shumate had my old gray one when he had the accident. My new jeep was yellow with a white metal top. The MPs showed up and asked me, "Were you in town last night?"

"Yeah," I told them.

"Were you driving a jeep?"

"Yes. There it is!" They looked at it and realized it wasn't the one, and went away.

But Shumate had told the Vietnamese that he was a weapons man on a Special Forces detachment, so the Vietnamese police, the American MPs, and the Vietnamese MPs all show up and they want to have a "lineup" of all the people on our team. Before they arrived, I sent Shumate off with the jeep and a bunch of spray paint, and I told him "Take that jeep and paint it and straighten that bumper!"

The police all show up. "We want to see your weapons man," one said.

I brought in Sgt. Fred Davis—a very big, very black man. The Vietnamese soldier Walt had been drinking with said, "No, that's not him!" so they all went away, but Garwood called back and said, "Somebody damaged that Vietnamese doctors' car, and I want it fixed!" So it cost Shumate a couple of thousand piasters, but he got it fixed.

Boys Will Be Boys

Shumate was in a bar, drinking with a Vietnamese army captain, when a young Vietnamese man came up, making insulting remarks and looking for a fight. They ended up outside, and Walt ended up beating the guy rather badly.

But the Vietnamese bystanders made a report to the local commander, leaving out some of the details about the behavior of the local young man. When it was time for our detachment to rotate back to Okinawa, Garwood called me up and said, "I have a hold on your whole detachment until you clear this thing up!"

Well, we were really ready to leave, so I went to see the father of the young man, explained what happened and apologized for Walt's behavior. "I'll guarantee you that Shumate will not be an E-5 sergeant when we get back to Okinawa," I told him. And I wasn't lying, because I knew he was on the promotion list to E-6.

"Boys will be boys," the father said. "My son has caused me so much trouble! He was kicked out of college in Saigon, which is why he lives with me here." We talked a bit more, and all the charges were dropped against Walt, and we all went back to Okinawa.

Baby Snatchers

My XO for a while was a guy named "Budge" Williams. When we went to Vietnam, his wife stayed on Okinawa where she was a school teacher. They were trying to adopt a Korean kid. Well, it came time to go to Korea to get the kid, and Mrs. Williams couldn't go because she was prohibited from travel on a military aircraft by herself, and her husband couldn't get out of Vietnam. She explained the problem to me, so I called in Bufford Lawson. I told him, "I want you to take leave and go to Korea; you won't get charged for the leave unless you killed or get in trouble. I want you to pick up this baby for the Williamses," and told him where the orphanage was, and I gave him all the details.

"You gotta be kidding!" he said.

"Just do it," I told him.

Mrs. Williams was still getting her mail at our C-detachment, and I ran into her the next day at the mailroom. "Hi, Mrs. Williams," I told her. "We ought to be hearing from Bufford Lawson pretty soon." "Oh, he's back," she said.

"No, he can't be," I told her, "he just left yesterday!"

"Yes, he's back—I've got the baby in the car!"

I found Lawson, drunk, at the NCO club. "What the hell did you do?" I asked him.

"You told me to get the kid, and that's what I did," he said.

"But how'd you do it so fast?"

Well, it turned out that he had the resident detachment at the embassy pick him up at the airport, run him out to the orphanage, collected the kid—then, without any orders or passport—got in line to get on the MAC flight to Okinawa. Once he got close to the check-in counter he started pinching the baby, which naturally started to bawl. They just waved him right on through! He spent about four hours on the ground, and was back early the next day!

After-Action Review

Despite what you often read, the armed forces of the United States did not lose the war in Southeast Asia. That war was the responsibility of the people of the Republic of South Vietnam, and they lost it fair and square. The American mission, starting in 1961, was to provide the ARVN with training and support for the campaign against the VC insurgents. That mission was successfully completed . . . by 1965, and it wasn't enough. It was—again, despite what you hear about it— a deeply moral and honorable mission . . . until about 1965.

The United States did lose two kinds of wars during the conflict, neither in Asia. The first was a moral dispute between the military community and the US government during the Johnson and Nixon administrations; the military lost that one when the Joint Chiefs allowed the armed forces to be used in a conflict without a clear objective, against an enemy who was allowed to control the battlefield. This was the first defeat.

The second defeat was also moral. That happened when the political institutions of the United States, including the news media, failed the military institution. It happened when Americans grew tired and frightened and confused about the war and our proper role in it. The American public, in essence, panicked and cut and run. That was the real defeat for the United States in Vietnam and Southeast Asia.

After 1968, many prominent Americans spoke out against the war—Jane Fonda was one, and Tom Hayden was another. They and many others promoted the cause of the North Vietnamese and accepted what the North Vietnamese government said at face value. Jane Fonda reported to the American people that the POWs were receiving excellent, humane care while many of them were being tortured and abused. The grim predictions of what would happen if South Vietnam were to fall were dismissed by the news media, by the peace activists, and ultimately by the American people.

All those grim predictions came true, without a squeak of apology from the people who said the "re-education" camps, the torture, the wholesale slaughter of the losers would never happen. The domino theory turned out to be true, and two million Cambodian innocents were slaughtered—and nobody in the US or Europe really noticed or complained. Hundreds of thousands of South Vietnamese went off to years of torture. Many thousands of others, particularly the Montagnards, were simply slaughtered.

Nobody really remembers all this except the people in the armed forces. As a result, the institution has been radically changed from the genuine "people's army" that existed in the early and middle 1960s. Today there is an invisible set of perimeter defenses around the Army, and within that, another inner perimeter around Special Forces, with invisible barbed wire and minefields. The real enemy has become, tragically, the American people who can't be trusted. That was the real lesson learned in Vietnam, and it isn't going to be soon forgotten. I don't think that the Army's Special Forces will be willing to get emotionally involved with an alien culture again in my lifetime; the risk of dishonor is too great. And that is really a loss.

The Special Forces did their best to free the oppressed in the cool, misty mountains of Vietnam from 1961 to 1973—just as JFK had intended. Although it didn't last, for the first time in their history the Rhade, Jarai, Bru, Sedang, and the other highland tribes were given a chance to free themselves, and they did it. The mutual trust, admiration and affection between the big Americans and the little Yards beat the VC at their own game; they won their war, together.

Even now, small bands of Montagnards continue to fight their way out of Vietnam, into the refugee camps. And twenty years after the last Americans left,

> Special Forces vets like Jim Morris make sure the Montagnards receive sanctuary in the United States. Many have settled in North Carolina, not far from Fort Bragg, and despite all that has happened, the relationship endures. What an odd, unique, wonderful thing to happen, how unlike the popular notion of the Green Berets. No wonder they are called the Special Forces.
>
> —*Hans Halberstadt*

Appendix

Resources and Associations

Special Forces Association, 5130 East Charleston Blvd., Suite 5-583F, Las Vegas, Nevada 89122. The Special Forces Association is the organization dedicated specifically to US Army Special Forces vets. For operators only.

Special Operations Association, 5130 East Charleston Blvd., Suite 5-583F, Las Vegas, Nevada 89122. The Special Operations Association is a fraternal organization that includes Special Forces, the Navy's SEALs, CIA, and other covert operators, and US Air Force special-ops personnel. Its membership is comprised of United States and allied forces participants in special operations in combat areas during World War II, Korea, Vietnam and South East Asia, and subsequent operations. Membership is restricted to members of special operations units during war and must have been exposed to hostile fire. The SOA is not a place for strap-hangers and wanna-bes.

RADIX, attention Steve Sherman, 2314 Cheshire Lane, Houston, Texas. Steve is the clearing house for information about specific individuals who were assigned to special operations forces in Southeast Asia and has developed an excellent database on people and units. Steve requests copies of orders to any Special Forces activity in the theater; contact him at (713) 683-9076. If you are looking for an old teammate or buddy, Steve's the place to start. Steve also reprinted the Green Beret magazines that were published by 5th Special Forces Group (1966–1970). This is one of the most lavishly illustrated combat journals from Southeast Asia, reprinted to a high standard of quality, that will be a treasured addition to any collection of Special Forces memorabilia. The reprint is available at the address/phone number shown above.

Montagnard Handicraft Company sells ornate bracelets; authentic Montagnard bracelets. Proceeds benefit the Montagnard community in the United States. Bracelets can be ordered by calling 407-872-1211, or writing: PO Box 568795, Orlando, FL 32856-8795.

Index